The Critical Phenomenology of Intergroup Life

The Critical Phenomenology of Intergroup Life

Race Relations in the Social World

Evandro Camara

LEXINGTON BOOKS
Lanham • Boulder • New York • London

Published by Lexington Books
An imprint of The Rowman & Littlefield Publishing Group, Inc.
4501 Forbes Boulevard, Suite 200, Lanham, Maryland 20706
www.rowman.com

6 Tinworth Street, London SE11 5AL, United Kingdom

British Library Cataloguing in Publication Information Available

Library of Congress Cataloging-in-Publication Data Available

Library of Congress Control Number: 2020944231

∞™ The paper used in this publication meets the minimum requirements of American National Standard for Information Sciences—Permanence of Paper for Printed Library Materials, ANSI/NISO Z39.48-1992.

To The Memory of Fabio Dasilva,
Scholar, mentor, friend

Contents

Acknowledgments

I wish to express my indebtedness to Virginia de Oliveira-Alves, for our fruitful discussions that greatly helped me in clarifying and reorienting some critical parts of the argument, thus strengthening and improving the text. Any remaining errors or inconsistencies, *supervacuum dictu*, are my responsibility. Thanks are also due to Courtney Morales and Shelby Russell at Lexington Books, for their assistance, flexibility, and patience with the preparation of the manuscript.

Introduction

The Idea of a Post-Racial World

Why pursue the investigation of race and race relations in the modern world? If we consider the case of the United States going as far back as the very early 1970s, with the official demise of the Jim Crow system having occurred in the U.S. South, and more broadly in the nation as a whole, there was already talk of the passage to a post-racial America. It is, in fact, reasonable and instructive that special attention be directed here to U.S. society, given, on the one hand, its international prominence, and, on the other hand, its unique historical background and circumstances of race relations, as compared to other American multiethnic and multiracial societies. With the systematic disintegration of de jure race-based segregation in the United States half a century ago, it was felt that this change also signified the end of the effect of race on social relations and of a racial consciousness among the general population. In 1971 this shift in public thinking, articulated by many members of the academic world as well as the general public, was reflected in an article that ran in the October 5, 1971, issue of the *New York Times*. It was titled *Compact Set Up for Post-Racial South*, referring to a newly established board in North Carolina aiming to deal with problems of the rapid changes taking place in the Southern regions, "in a post-racial period of growth and expansion." That was not the case, as the ensuing decades have shown. The fact is that race continues to significantly affect U.S. social life, in both tangible and nontangible ways, as we enter the third decade of the twenty-first century. This means that the progressive, ever-widening structural inclusion of African-Americans and other racial minorities into the institutional mainstream of U.S. society, set in motion after the end of the Jim Crow period, did not necessarily translate into their full-scale (i.e., structural, cultural, biological, psychological) incorporation into national life. In relation to this, it also failed to stamp out the consciousness of race in the public imaginary and its function as a structuring and sustaining force of social practices and arrangements.

From the standpoint of race relations, the emergence and expansion of the postmodern movement in the arts and humanities starting in the 1980s may be said to have, at least implicitly, operated based on the premise of an incipient post-racial phase in race relations in the United States, and in that sense, it may be said to have ignored the prevailing racial realities of the post–Jim Crow period, which endure right down to the present time. The postmodern emphasis on relativism, on the rejection of grand or totalizing narratives, of traditional dualisms, and so forth, all represented a departure from the recognition of the basic racial division of U.S. society and a turn to the idea that the society-at-large had entered a post-racial era.

Consistently with that, postmodern interpretations of race and race relations stressed the need for the scholarship to go beyond the "simplistic, narrow visions of race, identity and racism" (Gillborn, 1995: 3), on account of the ever-growing complexity and differentiation of intergroup life, in pluralist societies everywhere, in recent decades. The primary concern of postmodern scholarship in this regard was the *de-centering* of the racial subject, in contradistinction to the traditional modernist treatment of racially based inequality and oppression. Attached to the postmodern shift, and perfectly consistent with its broader thrust, is the idea of the need to address the "plasticity" of individual or group status. We may consider, in this respect, the idea of *plastic ethnicity* (Gillborn, 1995) or *plastic sexuality* (Giddens, 1992). The postmodernist and poststructuralist revision of the earlier (i.e., modernist) conceptions and identities of groups betrayed its relativizing effect, in dictating that "nothing has an essence; everything is structured in the mobile play of signifiers" (Giddens, 1992: 113).

The reality in virtually every multiethnic and multiracial national setting, however, to this day, is the unabated operation of race, racism, and race-based inequality. This is regularly manifested in various contexts of dominant-minority interaction, such as in the official enforcement of social control, in sports, in the workplace, in political life, and so forth, as well as in connection with global events, such as the diaspora of political refugees. In multiethnic societies everywhere, even in those which, once rather homogeneous from an ethnic and racial standpoint, have become increasingly heterogeneous in recent times (mainly due to politically driven migratory movements), the consciousness of race and its normative effect on social behavior and official policy are expressed. As recently as a few years ago, Glaude (2016: 54–55) wrote, regarding the specific case of U.S. society, that "race still enslaves the American soul" and relates an incident from the 1970s, the period immediately following the end of Jim Crow and the removal of legally upheld discrimination, which clearly shows how race, notwithstanding the dismantling of the formal framework of racial oppression, had never truly left U.S. social life, and the racial divisions and antagonisms that had openly and officially structured social relations during the Jim Crow period were "always just beneath the surface of our supposed racial progress." This has been the case even in reference to situations that, at first glance, "seem to have little to do with race." Historically, this represents the continuing operation of the binary pattern of racial organization in U.S. society, which has been carried out on the basis of a rigidly white/ nonwhite dualism. This binary division, as is known, strongly determined the patterns of racial stratification and oppression in the wider society during the Jim Crow era, in terms of providing a framework for the thoroughgoing physical, social, cultural, and psychological white/nonwhite separatism of that time.

A particular aspect of U.S. history is germane in this regard. Modern slavery, which, unlike ancient slavery, came to operate strictly on the basis of race, is known to have ended well over a century ago in the United States, but the fact that the freed Africans in U.S. society were seen as an aberration, and faced the greatest obstacles to their assimilation into national life, meant that the society-at-large did not know what to do with these human beings. Their liberation would have meant, in principle, that they were now eligible for full-scale social inclusion as citizens (which, in the main, is how things turned out in other slavery settings in the Americas), and yet this was denied them because of their racial otherness. Construed in binary terms, this difference did then, as it does now in modified form and degree, continue to have a deep and pervasive impact on U.S. social life. In a nonconcrete sense, nonwhiteness has historically operated as the fundamental representation of otherness. This has resulted, among other things, in the racialization—one might say, racial reconstruction—of social statuses that are not, strictly speaking, indicative to race—such as, for instance, being ethnic equating with being racially nonwhite; being non-Western equating with being racially nonwhite; nationality status equating with racial status, and so on. This has become a rather distinct feature of the current U.S. model of interracial life. With respect to the persisting tensions and antagonisms, when not direct violent confrontations, that have characterized interracial life in the United States in recent times, a writer (cited in Rothman, 2018: 51) remarks on how people continue "to focus on our racial divide and the consequences of slavery." Glaude (2018: 42–45) similarly remarks, in the theoretical context of the *ideal culture/real culture* gap, that the persistence of racism in American social life is expressed not just by racial extremists but, by and large, by ordinary folks, the suburban white masses, the "so-called *silent majority*." In connection with this, Staudigl (2012) has written about racism as operating by means of its *embeddedness* in the social organization itself, in institutional practices and arrangements, as *negative sociality*, with implications of the functional necessity for the normal operation of the social system as a whole.

The operation of race and its related aspects, in social action and thought, in societies everywhere around the world, is one of the most salient elements of the legacy of colonialism that has endured to this day. Writing in the third quarter of the twentieth century, Fanon (1967: 8) places into relief the continuing relevance of race in the modern world when he speaks of inter-group relations in world societies as hinging on the adversarial relationship between two camps: "the white and the black." Acknowledging the persisting influence of race in international affairs, he urged the de-racialization of the colonized and formerly colonized populations so as to bring to an end the ill effects of colonialism on the lives of non-European populations everywhere.

Biologists and geneticists have, over the last century, systematically debunked the notion of race as such and shown it to be scientifically worth-less as a biological concept, but its importance as a social and political concept has never abated, despite all the shifting material circumstances in the community of nations over this period. Social, cultural, political events around the world continue to be driven by forces that are specifically and ultimately racial in nature. Regardless of its irrelevance and indefensibility at the level of science, race continues to reign at the level of social life. In the end, we are forced to recognize with Goldberg (cited in Staudigl, 2012: 36) that everything everywhere, in some way or degree, is connected with race, that "all is race." The present study addresses this persisting situation, aim-ing to further clarify, by focusing on aspects of intersubjectivity, the process through which the lives of members of minority racial groups are adversely affected by the racialization of social life.

Chapter 1

The Problem of Race in the Modern World

Social distinctions based on all types of criteria have been a central feature of the structural organization of societies everywhere, through the centuries. They serve to sort people out into different categories within the total population and to establish a framework through which the people making up the resulting categories will be afforded differential access to the society's resources and advantages, to the centers of social wealth, power, and prestige. Thus, these social distinctions are not inconsequential; rather, they are the indispensable mechanism of social inequality.

Social distinctions stem from cultural definitions and prescriptions, enforced in every society, regarding how social things are to be organized, which amounts to the process of social rationalization, in the Weberian sense. Social distinctions based on gender roles and associated functions as the basis of gender inequality are the oldest and most fundamental of distinctions established in human history. The strictly economic interpretation of this aspect has it that gender inequality was set in motion several millennia ago when humans began to produce food through agriculture, and men, by virtue of their generally larger size and greater strength, in combination with women's common (and, at that time, restricting) experience of pregnancy, appropriated the fruits of production, to the exclusion of women. Women thus became the minority group in this economic, then political, and, more broadly, social, process. The present analysis centers on social distinctions based on race, which operate essentially in the same way as gender, inasmuch as the category of race began to fulfill a heuristic and normative function at a certain point in time in Western history, as the "white" populations of the world began to rule over the "nonwhite" ones, in a plurality of geographical settings. The idea of race and its formal inclusion into the bureaucratic administration of societies originated in the early phase of what is commonly

5

known as the Age of Discovery, the great age of maritime explorations and empire-building, which extended over several centuries. The large-scale exploration of the seas, which started in earnest in the late 1400s, also led early on, if indirectly, to a historical event that is immediately relevant to this study, namely, the emergence and growth of the African slave trade. The Age of Discovery amounted to a systematic, and eventually highly competitive, process of naval voyages and subsequent conquest and colonization of newly discovered lands, by a handful of Western European societies: first Portugal, then Spain, in the fifteenth century, and both were joined in these expansionist ventures by France, the Netherlands, and England, in the following century. Wars would break out from time to time involving these overseas empires, over control of colonial territories and trade (Chirot, 1986: ch. 3). As early as the first quarter of the 1400s, the Portuguese, under the leadership of King Henry the Navigator (1394–1460), proceeded to wrest control of the trade in the commodities from the East, most notably spices, away from the Muslims and the Venetians.

For a number of important health-related and culinary reasons, spices (especially pepper) during the late Middle Ages and beyond were literally worth their weight in gold. They were mainly obtained in Southeast Asia—in India and in the Molucca Islands of the Malay Archipelago (present-day Indonesia). Along with other luxury goods from the East, such as silk, spices formed the main driving force behind the first great wave of Western European imperialism. The spice trade had first been dominated by Northern Italian cities—specifically, Venice, Genoa, and Florence—cities that had become economic juggernauts during the Middle Ages. However, as the 1400s rolled on, the balance of power tipped progressively in favor of Portugal and Spain, as these nations sought to dismantle the Moorish and Italian control of trade with the East. The Portuguese in particular, and their voyages of discovery and colonization, which were aided strongly by innovations in maritime technology, were at the forefront of the great commercial revival of the period and continued to hold that status through the fifteenth century, thus having been the earliest sea-born empire erected on the commercial profits of the spice trade.

A central aspect and practically inevitable ramification of these naval voyages, which followed traditional trade routes around the African continent, was the exploration of the African coast by Portugal and Spain. This developed, first of all, out of Portugal's increasingly influential involvement in the trade with the East, and secondly, as a ramification of the Iberian campaigns against the Moors in North Africa. King Henry's growing interest in the exploration of the African continent led to a number of expeditions that he dispatched, from 1914 onward, down the western coast of Africa (Cooke, Kramer, Rowland-Entwistle, 2002: 93). Portuguese and Spanish mariners and slave traders would make frequent incursions into inland areas, where they would either simply capture Africans, or, by working their way into the centuries-old internal slave trade between tribal kingdoms, purchase captives from tribal chiefs and kings. The latter, according to Davidson (1966: 205), "saw no reason for not selling them to Europeans." These captives were initially taken to cities in the Iberian Peninsula, where they worked as domestic slaves and did most of the manual labor in the urban setting. The first cargo of enslaved Africans arrived in Lisbon in 1444. By the early sixteenth century the Atlantic Slave Trade was set in motion by means of the 1518 Spanish royal decree authorizing the transport of African slaves to the New World. By the early 1500s, the Portuguese were already taking African slaves to Brazil, the crown jewel of the Luso-American empire (McKay et al., 2011: 374–375, 448–453, 465–472). Over time, the practice of slavery led progressively, in the minds of Europeans, to the association between physical appearance and servile status, an association that crystallized with the full-scale installation of African slavery in the Americas.

Gossett (1969: 16) makes the claim that ways of thinking and social practices and, more specifically, social distinctions, based on the physical or racial makeup of groups, were in operation as far back as some five millennia ago. Still, it is generally understood that the dissemination of the idea of race in its modern and more theoretical version was spurred on by the great social transformation brought about by the Age of Discovery. From the latter's earliest phase, the European colonizing nations were exposed, ever more frequently and on an ever-larger scale, to human phenotypical diversity around the world, which heightened their sensitivity to group-based physical distinctions, and paved the way for the emergence of race as a frame of reference for distinguishing between human groups and, more broadly, for the idea of differentiated humanity. The human species was then conceived of as a cluster of distinct and separate biological segments, with their respective biological or "racial" endowments, which in turn determined the nature and degree of the cognitive, moral, and cultural makeup of each segment.

Race increasingly became the mark of the conquered populations and a fundamental criterion of social differentiation and organization. As the Europeans increased their dominance over non-European populations, over time a process of the racialization of the peoples of the world developed, that is, a comprehensive attempt toward systematic human classification on the basis of elaborate racial taxonomies. These taxonomies were steadily formalized over time and uniformly constructed to reflect the hierarchized value of the different racial categories. The idea of the essential or natural superiority of some of the categories, and inferiority of others, spread steadily and came to be taken as a given. Ultimately, this ideological conception of the "races of mankind" and their interrelations had the effect of not only shaping, but also justifying, colonial policy and practice.[1]

It is generally held among modern scholars that, in the present time, the social and political integration of societies or, alternatively, societal divisions, on the basis of either ethnicity or race, constitute a retrogression dating back to the nineteenth century, when social evolutionist doctrines held sway in societies of the Western world. Yet, it is still the case that social stratification remains shaped fundamentally by racial status in some multiethnic societies, with people being mainly described and sorted out, whether formally or informally, on the basis of their racial background, notwithstanding the expanding legal protection of individual rights in recent decades, independently of racial origin, gender status, religious affiliation, sexual orientation, and so forth.

In this regard, as indicated above, it may be stated that the problem of race continues to plague social life in societies around the world, although this situation takes place with greater intensity in certain types of societies, and in certain parts of the world. In the context of the American continent, one particular social system—the United States—is constantly reminded, to this day, of its unresolved racial problems, by the repeated flare-ups of tension and antagonism between the dominant and non-dominant halves of the population. This is a legacy of the Jim Crow period of legally sanctioned and mandated physical and social segregation of these two segments of the society, and of the society's particular ethnic developmental history. In other multiethnic and multiracial American societies, such as those which were, for quite some time, conventionally regarded as being relatively free of racial strife, and even as models of racial democracy (see, e.g., Freyre, 1933, for the case of Brazil), more recent scholarship (i.e., since the 1960s) has shown that, in actuality, racial disparities and race-based prejudice and discrimination in those societies, while *not identical in nature and degree* to the same problem in the United States, have been a clear factor in race and class relations. The underlying reasons for this positive portrayal of those national cases were that race-based economic and social disparities were largely swept, up until a half-century ago or so, under the ideology of racial democracy, against the background of a pre-modern social order dating back to the late nineteenth century, and marked by rigid class divisions and paternalism toward the lower classes, in relation to which *skin color* (not racial ancestry) was the primary criterion of social inclusion. The surge of industrialization and modernization of the last several decades has significantly democratized the social order in many of these multiethnic societies of the American hemisphere, and, consequently, facilitated the rise of national awareness of *race-based* (and not simply class-based) inequality, and the need for the society to address this problem at both the official and unofficial levels.

During the nineteenth century and the first part of the twentieth a number of factors—in particular, the end of modern slavery, colonialism, immigration, and decolonization—greatly intensified the consciousness of, and concern with, race proper, and the resulting impact on the affairs of modern societies, especially those of the European and American continents. A case in point is the spreading questioning and critical scrutiny of long-standing traditions and celebrations that clearly have a racial component, but were until recent times quite simply taken for granted. Salient examples may be taken from the surging societal reaction against the *Zwarte Piet* festival, traditionally celebrated in the Netherlands, and the comic-book character *Memín Pinguín*, which has enjoyed wide popularity since the early 1940s in a number of Spanish-speaking societies in the Americas.

The foregoing considerations should have demonstrated the enduring presence of race-based inequality in the modern world, and the need for continuing research in this area. We may now consider the factors listed above to which this situation may be attributed. We will look at the end of modern slavery first.

THE END OF SLAVERY

By the latter part of the 1800s, the spread of industrialization, together with the shifting circumstances of the international market, led to a series of ramifications, which accelerated the demise of the slavery system and way of life in the Americas, by pushing it to the point of obsolescence and, eventually, untenability. Some of these ramifications had directly to do with the increasing bureaucratization and democratization of the workplace, entailing the decline of primary, and the rise of secondary, relations between the working and the ownership classes. This meant that workers were increasingly recognized and treated as equal or interchangeable units of the production process, their worth in the industrial workplace and in the wider society being determined by their achieved, not ascribed, status.

With slavery having ended in every American society and throughout the Caribbean region by the turn of the century, the former slavery societies now faced the task of absorbing the mass of newly liberated Africans and their descendants into the mainstream of national life, which is to say, the task of granting them full-scale citizenship. This process would be fraught, in unequal measure depending on the society in question, with considerable difficulty, for a number of interrelated reasons.

In the post-slavery period, whatever the outcome might have been regarding the confluence of these two fundamental elements—that is, the mass of liberated Africans, on the one hand, and the prevailing network of structural and ideological conditions in the (former slavery) society in question; and on the other hand, it determined the emergence, in varying degrees, of a generalized consciousness of race in that society.[2]

Admittedly, former American slavery societies *as a group* would have experienced a resurgence of race consciousness, prompted by the task of integrating the freed Africans into national life. That is to say, the required adjustments and accommodations to be made in the class system, linked to the granting of citizenship to the liberated black population (and, therefore, their access to the economic, political, and educational resources of the society), would have given rise to a generalized concern with the question of whether or not the assumed inborn incapacity of the Africans to function as free citizens would limit, and ultimately defeat, their social incorporation. In other words, the question of whether this mass of African freedmen and freedwomen were indeed assimilable into the national stream; and more importantly yet, as in the case of certain American societies (e.g., the United States), the official effort to fully assimilate the former slave population should even be undertaken by the host society.[3] That said, in societal contexts in the Americas where the dominant "white" and "nonwhite" segments of the population, respectively, were kept strictly apart, both physical and socially, by formal and informal means, on the basis of racial ascription (e.g., the United States during the Jim Crow period), the awareness of race would have been not only most pronounced and widespread but also a constant aspect of social life. In such settings, the rigid segregation of the two racial parts of the population was enforced and maintained, notwithstanding the fact that slavery had ended, a phenomenon that shows clearly that the eradication of slave status did not automatically or necessarily translate into unhindered access to civil freedoms and rights for the former slaves, in *all* former slavery societies.

In the final analysis, it all came down to the question of race and racial background. In certain Anglo-American (vs. Ibero-American) settings, such as the United States, the difficulties surrounding the assimilative experience of the former slaves would prove formidable, remaining this way until fairly recent times. (The reference here is to the insurmountable barriers imposed on the daily lives of racial minorities throughout the Jim Crow period in the United States, which lasted until the late 1960s.) That said, the abolition of slavery as such, *throughout* the New World areas where slavery had predominated, made the question of race a critical factor in social relations, and in reference to full inclusion in social and institutional life. In more recent decades there has been a concerted effort in industrialized societies to address the numerous practices of social injustice perpetrated against minority social groups—women, racial minorities, the homosexual population, and so forth—which had persisted over the years. In this respect, the legacy of the Jim Crow period has tenaciously endured in some fundamental ways, albeit without the legal backing, and racial tensions and antagonisms in U.S. society have not been resolved satisfactorily in the post–Jim Crow era, which has resulted in frequent violent confrontations involving the hegemonic racial segment of the population (the "whites") vs. the minority racial groups (the "nonwhites"). A case in point is the violent unrest triggered over the fatal shooting of an African-American man in Ferguson, Missouri, by a white police officer, in August of 2014. The acquittal of this officer led to about a year of clashes between police forces and (mainly) African-American protesters in Ferguson, and, over the next few years similar incidents of conflict involving these two groups broke out in several major cities in the United States (St. Louis, Boston, Chicago, New York City, etc.). All of this has revived, across the larger society, the general realization of the persisting influence of race on U.S. social life. It must be mentioned that most industrialized multiethnic societies around the world—especially Iberian-American and Anglo-American ones, as well as those in the European and Australian continents—have witnessed in recent decades the rise of a concerted official effort to not only acknowledge and eradicate arrangements and practices of long-standing that have historically victimized certain groups in the national population, but also to express publicly the official recognition of past injustice and to bring reparation in some form to the injured groups. The rise of international concern with the protection of human rights and reparation for past injustice has reached the Asian and African continents as well, although perhaps to a lesser extent since, as a rule, the cultural history of those parts of the world has been essentially marked by an emphasis on the individual's duties to society, rather than on the idea of individual rights. This expectedly results in deeply entrenched social hierarchies and disparities of living standards, which are basically taken for granted and considered to be necessary.[4]

COLONIALISM

Colonialism is the most direct manifestation of global power relationships, in the specific sense of the operation of global inequality, whereby some powerful societies gain control of less powerful ones through military intervention and hold under political, economic, and cultural domination. During the Age of Discovery Portugal was the first nation to establish its supremacy as a colonizing power. As that period of maritime exploration and conquest of new territories rolled on, England began to emerge as the world's supreme colonial empire. By the nineteenth century, it was the world's most technologically and scientifically advanced society, as a result of having been the cradle of the Industrial Revolution a century before, and of its spreading industrial operations around the world, which sustained and reinforced the mighty British Empire. The latter reached its culminating point during that period. Concomitantly, England was also among the most socially and politically progressive nations in the world, as a result of a mature political system and the pursuit of democratic practices, such as the protection of civil liberties of the general population. Among industrialized nations of the time, England stood out for having averted the type of domestic political turmoil that characterized political life in some nations of continental Europe during the nineteenth century, such as France and Russia (Evans, 2011; Vijay, 2016: 4). The rise of liberal democracy within British society notwithstanding, the unabated growth of British colonialism meant the continuing brutal oppression of the colonies, throughout the 1800s. At the end of the nineteenth century, at the height of British overseas expansionism, the well-known British statesman Lord George Nathaniel Curzon, the Viceroy of India from 1898 to 1905, remarked that Great Britain ruled at that time over the greatest empire the world had ever known (Evans, 2011). At the outbreak of the First World War, a staggering 412 million people lived under British imperial rule—ten times as many people as the population of England itself (Maddison, 2001: 97; see also Taagepera, 1997: 502)—meaning that England was able, in this way, to impose political, economic, and cultural domination over a sizable percentage of the world's population. Colonialism is the aspect of greatest relevance here, for the purposes of the present analysis, since it was that which unceasingly fanned the fires of racial prejudice in English society, framing the national consciousness of race in the context of the natural superiority of the English people over all the colonized peoples. These ideas about race remained strong in governmental and scholarly circles, as well as in the public mind, well into the twentieth century. Reflecting the larger context of Western European ethnocentrism and racism, the British version drew strong support from the social Darwinist and eugenic doctrines of Herbert Spencer, Robert Knox, James Hunt, Karl Pearson, Thomas Carlyle, Charles Wentworth Dilke, and others (Horsman, 1981: ch. 4; Snyder, 1962: 108–114).[5]

France was not very far behind the British in its colonialist campaigns and achievements, having built an empire that, at its zenith, was also one of the largest in human history. At the height of its power, in the two decades following the First World War (the period known as the Second French Colonial Empire), its total territory, comprising metropolitan France and all of its overseas domains, had reached some "11 million kilometers of land and over 100 million inhabitants" (Aldrich, 1996: 1). The two phases of the French Colonial Empire are the First Colonial Empire, extending from the sixteenth century to the first quarter of the nineteenth century, and the Second Colonial Empire, from 1830 to the middle of the twentieth century. The first phase is characterized by the establishment of French colonial rule over much of eastern North America (*albeit*, in several instances, for reasons of weather or disease, or conflict with other European colonial powers, short-lived settlements[6]), a number of Caribbean islands, and some parts of South America. One of the more successful cases of French colonization in North

America which got under way during this period was that of Louisiana, in the late 1600s.

The Second Colonial Empire revolved around the French occupation and control of lands in Asia and Africa. France exerted its colonial rule over what are today central and northern Vietnam, Cambodia, and parts of China and in Africa, over much of the North, West, and Central regions of the continent. The French conquest and formal government over these lands in Africa in the late nineteenth to early twentieth centuries—along with the efforts undertaken by England, Germany, Portugal, Belgium, the Netherlands, and Italy, as they too vied for the control of African territory—formed the historical phenomenon that came to be known as *the Scramble for Africa* (see Shillington, 1989: ch. 21).

As in every other Western European empire of the period, racialist doctrines in France provided the major basis of support and legitimation for colonialism. The ideas of prominent nineteenth-century French statesman Jules Ferry, who supposedly did more than anyone else to revitalize the French Empire in its second phase (according to Power, 1966: 1), are a case in point. Ferry was twice prime minister of France in the 1880s, and his views are recalled here in reference to his staunch defense of French colonial expansion, on the basis of the principle of racial superiority. "The superior races," he declared, in addressing the French Chamber of Deputies in 1884, "have a right because they have a duty . . . [to bring civilization to] the inferior races . . . [to fulfill] this superior civilizing duty . . . [a duty that was] often misconstrued in previous centuries" (Ferry, 1897: 210–211).

Germany was also an influential member of the select group of Western European colonial powers in the late nineteenth century involved in the *Scramble for Africa*, judging from the 1884 conference assembled at Berlin in November of 1884, chaired by German chancellor Otto von Bismarck, and attended by all the major colonial powers, to regulate their imperialist activities in the African continent. In connection with that, racialist ideology continued to enjoy wide currency in Germany well into the twentieth century, being, of course, a driving force behind the policies of the Weimar Republic and the Third Reich. In 1933, Franz von Pappen, a chancellor of the German Reich, made a strong case, markedly driven by racist ideology, for the (African) colonies that Germany had lost after the First World War to be returned to Germany. He stated that Europe should remain "the intellectual guardian" of African peoples, "not yet ripe to govern or to manage themselves," and therefore the colonial powers should continue to bring to them "the blessings of civilization" (cited in Snyder, 1962: 453).

U.S. political expansionism started in earnest in the 1840s with the Mexican War, through which a very large amount of territory was annexed to the continental United States (a case of imperialist conquest which has not always been accorded proper historical recognition in the United States because of the payment involved for the territory gained; however, this was a payment made "under duress"; Burkey, 1978: 167). At that century's half-way mark, we are informed (Horsman, 1981: 1) that "American expansion was viewed less as a victory for the principles of free democratic republicanism than as evidence of the innate superiority of the American Anglo-Saxon branch of the Caucasian race." Toward the end of the nineteenth-century international colonialism was reaching its apex, and the United States was also figuring prominently in this trend by moving forward with the occupation and control of the Hawaiian Islands, Puerto Rico, and the Philippines (Chirot, 1986: 76–81).

Colonialism, as regards its operation as a model of dominant/minority relations between ethnic populations in the global context—and—more to the point of the present analysis, between "the races of the world"—signified a global arrangement that hinged fundamentally on race—that is, on the whiteness/nonwhiteness dualism. Religion and reconstructed science functioned as its primary sources of ideological legitimation. Toward that end, biological science was transformed into what came to be known as scientific racism. Religion, and specifically Christianity in its Protestant and Catholic strands, was also heavily relied upon for reassuring the colonial empires that their predatory actions were sanctioned by Divine Providence and therefore rested on the impregnable ground.

From the standpoint of science, the dominant ideological force, in the latter part of the nineteenth and early part of the twentieth centuries, protecting the interests of colonial empires by legitimizing their actions on biological grounds was social Darwinism—a loosely crafted and theoretically inadequate transposition of Darwin's ideas on the evolution of plants and animals, to the social world. This ideological orientation was brought to bear on the principle that colonialism had furnished irrefutable evidence of a racial hierarchization of humankind, insofar as it showed that the colonial powers—the "white" nations—were naturally suited to rule over the less fit human populations around the world and to annex these non-European lands into their sphere of political, economic, and cultural influence. As Hoffstadter stated it, social Darwinism was but one facet of the larger trend of ultra-nationalism sweeping across the colonial powers of Western Europe and North America over the course of the nineteenth century; this trend was promoted not only by race but by religion as well. Nevertheless, as regards the effect of race as a foundational legitimating ideology, social Darwinism stood out for its effectiveness as an instrument "in the service of the imperial urge" (1970: 172). A common theme at the time that added to this ideological *armamentarium* was the notion of the *White Man's Burden,* introduced by poet Rudyard Kipling in his 1899 poem of the same name (*in* Snyder, 1962: 87–88). Coincidentally, this paean to imperialism was published at the same time of the U.S. successful military engagement in the Spanish–American War, through which Spain's overseas empire in the Caribbean (Cuba, Puerto Rico) and in the Pacific (Guam, the Philippine Islands) came under U.S. jurisdiction. Thus, it is clear how this racial ideology offered strong support for U.S. political expansionism. It amounted to an explicit exhortation for the colonial powers to "take up the white man's burden." Like all the other aspects of racial ideology in the late nineteenth century, Kipling's poem further reinforced the awareness of race in the public imaginary and discourse. The newly annexed lands and the subjugated populations of these lands—"the new caught, sullen people," as Kipling put it—were clearly depicted as members of an inferior stock of humankind—they were "half-devil and half-child," an incongruous, and, from a modern perspective, abominable combination, which richly reveals the element of racial inferiority assigned to the colonized peoples, and the idea that race was omnipresent in imperialist ideology.

Territorial expansionism again comes into play in conjunction with *Manifest Destiny,* a variant on the white man's burden ideology. This was especially applicable to U.S. history, and the systematic incursions into Native American lands in the latter part of the 1800s—what came to be referred to, in the rather positive terms of an opening up and settling of virgin territory, as the *Westward Movement*—and the inevitable, violent conflict that ensued between the forces of the majority group and the tribal nations. Resistance on the part of the latter to the invasion of their lands typically met with genocidal campaigns against the "rebellious savages" on the part of military forces. *Manifest Destiny* is an expression that immediately suggests the idea of a sacred mission bequeathed by Divine Providence to a chosen group; that is, members of this group see themselves as having been destined by God to go out and bring the less-favored, generally non-Christian, populations of the world, under the morally uplifting, civilizing light of (mainly, Protestant) Christianity.

As a philosophy viewed as a mandate from Heaven, manifest destiny had a broader appeal as ideological legitimation of imperialism not only within the boundaries of the United States, but also internationally, insofar as it was also relied upon by the colonial powers of Western Europe, the neo-European nations of Oceania (Australia and New Zealand), or in any part of the globe where "the white man" had the upper hand. In the United States, in addition to justifying the conquest of Indian territory and subjugation of the tribal societies involved, the idea of manifest destiny informed U.S. foreign policy as well, during the entire nineteenth century and the early part of the twentieth century. In the early phase of U.S. colonialism, it had an impact on U.S. relations with Mexico, culminating in the Mexican–American War of 1846–1848 (in this regard, see, e.g., Romo, 1996: 86–87). In the late phase, it was brought to bear on U.S. imperialist actions overseas, such as, for example, in connection with the U.S. takeover of the Philippines, from 1899 to 1902.[7]

Furthermore, the idea of race, and of the innate superiority of the *white race* which affords it the right to reign over all others, is never absent from the legitimating ideology. At least implicitly, in his well-known *The Strenuous Life: Essays and Addresses* Theodore Roosevelt emphasizes the common theme, at that time, that particular groups within humankind—most specifically, the United States—had been endowed by Divine Providence with superior qualities, and the right to rule over the less-favored ones in the world. As he puts it: "In the West Indies and the Philippines alike we are confronted by most difficult problems. It is cowardly to shrink from solving them in a proper way; for solved they must be, if not by us, by some *stronger and manful race*" (2009: 8; orig.1900; emphasis mine).

In closing this section, we should stress again that the central theme that informed, in one way or degree or another, all the different strands of legitimation ideology buttressing the colonialist efforts of the United States and (Western) European societies at the end of the nineteenth century and beginning of the twentieth, was the idea of biological or racial differentiation within humankind, together with the fact that the racially superior groups on the earth had been divinely ordained to rule over the less endowed groups. There was, therefore, a sense of mission that pervaded the ideology of colonization as a whole, and was clearly understood and taken up by the colonizing nations. This is richly demonstrated in official statements by legislators (as well as prominent individuals in general, outside the political sphere). We could even go further and argue that there was even a sense of divine election built into such legitimating ideologies as manifest destiny, the white man's burden, and so on—and this played even more prominently in the case of the U.S. expansionist experience of the late 1800s to early 1900s.[8] Implicitly or explicitly, this notion is patently conveyed in the official statements and declarations of the time, concerning the U.S. participation in empire-building action during that time. That most ardent of expansionists, Senator Albert Beveridge of the U.S. Senate (cited in Weinberg, 1935: 308), speaks to this issue eloquently and unequivocally, throwing into relief all the major premises of the ideologies of expansionism in general:

> Mr. President, this question is deeper than any question of party politics; deeper than any question of the isolated policy of our country even; deeper even than any question of constitutional power. It is elemental. *It is racial.* (emphasis mine) God has not been preparing the English-speaking and Teutonic peoples for a thousand years for nothing but vain and idle self-contemplation and self-admiration. No! He has made us the master organizers of the world to establish system where chaos reigns. He has given us the spirit of progress to overwhelm

the forces of reaction throughout the earth. He has made us adept in government that we may administer government among savage and senile peoples. Were it not for such a force as this the world would relapse into barbarism and night. And of all of our race He has marked the American people as His chosen nation to finally lead in the regeneration of the world.

It seems clear as well, from a declaration such as the one above, that Western European or U.S. tutelage over the (racially) inferior peoples of the world was being proposed not just as a temporary measure designed to help these naturally deficient populations as they embarked on the path to self-rule (e.g., in connection with the annexation of Cuba or Puerto Rico by the United States after the Spanish–American War), but rather, as noted by Weinberg (1935: 308–309), as a new and permanent situation, insofar as the conquered populations were normally judged to be innately unfit for self-government—a situation that parallels the end of New World slavery in the nineteenth century when the forces of traditionalism in the former slavery societies questioned the former slaves' ability to live in freedom, to be productive citizens, to exercise their newly gained citizenship rights rationally.

We have focused here on the phenomenon of colonialism as carried out by the *nations of the West*, that is to say, the nations of Europe and the Americas, with the intent of establishing the connection between colonialism and the consciousness of race. The sensitivity to the aspect of race grew in intensity in proportion to the expansion of European colonialism, and it rested on the whiteness/nonwhiteness dualism, specifically the whiteness of the European and neo-European colonizers vs. the nonwhiteness of the non-European populations. By the late nineteenth and early twentieth centuries, the activities of European and U.S. overseas colonialism were carried out in the largest measure, as judged by the size of the colonial populations, by England, France, the Netherlands, Germany, the United States, Portugal, Belgium, and the Soviet Union. In the case of the United States, colonial control of overseas territory persisted until the outbreak of the Second World War.

As a unified historical force, political expansionism consistently accentuated the consciousness of race in all the societies under consideration, as has been indicated. Colonialism brought together national groups—that is, the colonizer and the colonized—who were, more often than not, widely dissimilar in their phenotypical makeup. This by itself would have brought about the realization, in both the colonizing powers and the subjugated populations, of the physical differences between them (and, naturally, of the cultural differences as well). But it was the endeavor on the part of the colonizers to establish moral justification for their imperialist policies and actions—whether in reference to biology, religion, or economics—that the concern with race was kept alive at the formal and informal levels.

It was not until the middle of the 1940s when the Allied armies vanquished the forces of the Axis, and the Second World War ended, and people around the world began to hear about and be properly shocked and repulsed over the unspeakable atrocities committed by the Nazi regime against the Jewish population, that public trust around the world in the doctrines of racial superiority began to wane. In the decades following the end of the war, the scientific community has, as a rule, steadily rejected not only the traditional idea of race itself, as being devoid of scientific credibility, but also racialist or biologically driven explanations of the cultural differences of human groups. In spite of that, some events and circumstances—for example, the post–Second World War decolonization phenomenon (which gained momentum after 1960), the surge of immigration by people from the former colonies to their respective "mother countries," the influx of political refugees from non-European lands to Western European and American ones, the persisting legacy of the Jim Crow period in U.S. society, and of *apartheid* in South Africa—have led to a new heightening of the general awareness of race in the former colonial powers' host or receiving societies. In recent years, some disturbingly racist tendencies and trends have progressively found their way into public policy, and begun to affect institutional arrangements and intergroup relations.

IMMIGRATION

Another major factor driving the intensification of the consciousness of race and racial diversity during the time frame considered here was immigration, which reached a peak in the American continent and in Oceania in the latter part of the nineteenth century, and continued on a large scale up to the early 1920s (see, e.g., Burkey, 1978: 195–204). Societies in the Americas and elsewhere that were geographically large and had several large urban centers, and were, by all indications, entering the initial phase of large-scale industrialization and urbanization, thus offering employment opportunities both in the urban and agricultural sectors, attracted the greatest numbers of immigrants from various parts of the globe.[9] Especially noteworthy examples in this respect were the United States, Brazil, Canada, Argentina, Mexico, and, in Oceania, the island/continent of Australia. The major waves of voluntary immigration into the Americas came from various parts of Europe—mainly Germany, Italy, Portugal, Spain, Poland, Greece—and Asia, primarily from China, Japan, Korea, and the Philippines. In the United States, a few other settling groups have formed a smaller part of the national whole, such as the Scandinavians (most of whom hail from Sweden but also include flows from Denmark and Norway). Altogether some 2.15 million Scandinavian immigrants, as a rule, people of a farming background, settled in the United States from 1820 to 1920, mostly in the Upper Midwestern states—Minnesota, Wisconsin, North Dakota. A small percentage of the Swedes were urbanites, to begin with, and settled in major Midwestern cities, like Chicago, which became by 1900 "the second largest Swedish city in the world" (Daniels, 1990: 164–183); and the French, who actually settled the Louisiana territory—the latter in its initial phase of colonization comprising parts of present-day Mississippi, Alabama, and Texas—and held it as French-ruled territory until 1803 (taking into account a hiatus period of 40 years, during which the whole territory of Louisiana came under Spanish rule through the 1762 Treaty of Fontainebleau; Howard, 1902: 28). Bands of French *Huguenots* had also pioneered the European colonizing presence in the continental United States by seeking to establish small colonies (Fort Caroline) in Florida as early as 1564, and a century later, in *New Netherland* (present-day New York) and South Carolina (the Charleston area). French settlements in Canada, of course, shaped the historical evolution of that society, and French-Canadians presently account for about 22 percent of the total population—close to a third of the total population, if Canadians of French descent, but non-French-speaking, are also included (Burt, 1942: 6). In Mexico, too, French imperialism was in effect, *albeit* briefly, in terms of the installation of a French-protected imperial regime, with Maximilian I (a native of Austria) as Mexican emperor. His reign lasted only three years (1864–1867).

The Western and West-Central regions of Africa contributed another twelve million people, approximately, over the course of some four centuries, through involuntary migration (New World slavery). In addition to the more prevalent migratory waves from Western European and Asian settings, some American countries, because of their particular historical development, received contingents from other locations as well. The United States, for example, has received a considerable influx of people from Mexico, Cuba, and Puerto Rico, over the last century. Brazil experienced significant arrivals of people from Russia, Ukraine, and Lebanon, in addition to the more familiar sources of immigration into that country. In Australia there were two major waves of assisted migration before the Gold Rushes that started in 1851, in the state of Victoria. This event acted as a powerful stimulant to British migration to that country throughout the 1850s. In the following decade the influx of English migrants continued on a large scale. Therefore, the English were not only the first European settling group in that country, from the earliest beginnings—the establishment of a British penal colony in the late 1700s but also remained the principal European immigrant group in the following century. By the middle of the nineteenth century Australia began to become remarkably diverse, in both the ethnic-cultural and physical senses, through the importation of Chinese, East Indian, and Japanese laborers. In reference to this aspect, racial considerations came to play a critical role in intergroup relations in that society, becoming the basis for strong official as well as popular opposition, when not violent xenophobia, toward the presence of the nonwhites (Cannon, 1971: 114–115, 167, 247–253).

Following the Second World War, England witnessed the arrival of a growing wave of West Indian migration, from island societies that had once been under English colonial rule, such as Jamaica, Barbados, Trinidad-Tobago, and former colonies. These migrants made what has been designated as the *Windrush Generation*.

As indicated, the impact of European and neo-European colonialism during the nineteenth century[10] served to heighten the general awareness of the question of race in all of these places mentioned, specifically in connection with the considerable cultural and physical variation between the colonizing and colonized societies. Therefore, certain migrant groups in these host societies were invariably targeted for discriminatory treatment (such as various forms of restrictions and exclusions) on the basis of their socially assigned racial status.

In the United States, the greater influx of immigrants throughout the late 1800s and the early years of the twentieth century, up to the First Great War, set in motion a dual pattern of reception and assimilation of the newcomers, whereby those groups that were officially codified as white were pushed to undergo the process of Americanization in earnest—that is, to become fully assimilated, along the lines of the melting-pot model of assimilation; whereas those immigrants classified as nonwhite met a different fate, in the sense that they were generally barred from complete inclusion into the mainstream (i.e., involving structural, cultural, biological, and psychological assimilation). This dual pattern of assimilation, if anything, served to accentuate racial hierarchies and differential treatment of the various classes of immigrants with reference to *race*. An essay from just after the First World War (Hill, 1919) highlights the intense efforts undertaken by various agencies and organizations in the United States at that time, to bring to fruition the "Americanization" (i.e., the full-scale assimilation) of the foreign-born, many of whom sought, in fact, through their own clubs and organization, to foster solidarity in their own immigrant communities and to preserve their native language, customs, and traditions, which stands for an opposition to the idea of their becoming fully Americanized. A number of different foreign groups are mentioned in this historical analysis, but the members of all these groups were people whom the wider society would classify racially as white, suggesting that the official endeavors to Americanize the foreign-born were not being channeled toward the alien groups classified formally and informally as nonwhite (e.g., the Asian groups). The exception to this general pattern had to do with language and also some technical training (Hill, 1919: 635), which was furnished for migrants classified as nonwhite so that they could function effectively as industrial workers.

The multiplicity of these incoming groups was marked by great phenotypical diversity, which, expectedly, over time, became a central feature of the national population. This applied in general, that is, to the population of the United States and all the other American societies and elsewhere receiving these newcomers from various parts of the globe. In many, if not most, of these societies, these diverse types blended effectively into the great national stew. In others, the general tendency was for the nonwhite ethnics to be systematically confined to what is known in the pertinent literature as the *ethnic enclaves* (e.g., the Chinatowns of the major U.S. metropolises).[11] There, they would spend most of their lives, with varying degrees of access to and participation in the institutional life of the wider society, while being, however, mostly limited to the ethnic enclave for participation in interpersonal life (i.e., friendships, marriage, etc.). This means that these people were incompletely assimilated, not only at the structural but also at the cultural, biological, and consequently, psychological levels. The historically prevalent compartmentalization of these nonwhite groups into the ethnic enclaves caused them to continue to cultivate their ancestral customs, to speak their language, to rely on the *foreign press*, thus evolving into subcultural status and a subcultural identity over time, within the larger national community, and to develop a subcultural lifestyle that set these groups off quite distinctly from the way of life of the host society as such.

In the United States, the growing impact of immigration, and the cultural and physical diversity that it brought to the society, correlated with deep and widespread concern on the part of the majority (white) population with the extent to which this would come to threaten the very fabric of U.S. social life. In ever greater measure, racial considerations were taken into account in this regard (on this aspect see, e.g., Scott-Childress, 1999: 47), this having a strongly normative effect on the society's management of the incoming groups. The latter were systematically subjected to official classification schemes and quotas based on prevailing understandings about race, the particular racial category each immigrant population belonged to, and so forth. In this respect, the spread of scientific racism fueled the steadily developing opposition to open immigration in the United States. Racialist doctrines were relied upon to assess the cultural virtues or deficiencies of the different alien groups entering the society, on the basis of the biological inheritance of each group. Zimmerman (1992: 28) informs us that in Australia, Canada, and the United States, immigration policies were considerably oriented by the belief in the cultural and biological superiority of particular European groups and that in the early years of the twentieth century many people, regardless of how well educated, considerate, and favorably disposed toward others they might have been, still adhered to the notion that Europeans, especially Western Europeans, had an innate, or biologically transmitted, superiority over non-Europeans.

The writings of U.S. sociologist Edward A. Ross on this issue richly illustrate this aspect. In his 1914 work *The Old World in the New*—an elaborate cataloging of the traits and dispositions of various incoming European ethnic groups, which he put together on the basis of each group's genetic or "racial" history—Ross railed against the emerging process of biological fusion between "Anglo-Saxon America" and certain European immigrant groups that he considered to be at a lower standing in the evolutionary scale of humankind. He asserted unambiguously that "the blood now being injected into the veins of our people is 'sub-common' [which is to say, subhuman]" (1914: 285). In assessing the capabilities and potential for national assimilation of these European migrants, he further remarks that "to the practiced eye, the physiognomy of certain groups unmistakably proclaims inferiority of type" (1914: 286). The basic distinction was that "the Northerners seem to surpass the southern European in *innate* ethical endowment" (1914: 295; emphasis mine). From the same period and in the same vein, one may cite the writings of Kenneth Roberts, who stated in reference to the potential of the immigration experience for increasing the level of ethnic diversity in U.S. society, that "if a few million members of the Alpine, Mediterranean, and Semitic races are poured among us the result must inevitably be a hybrid race of people as worthless and futile as the good-for-nothing mongrels of Central America and Southeastern Europe" (in Lerner, 1987: 91). Writing in the 1920s, a time when U.S. society had already experienced a massive inflow of immigrant groups from various regions of the world, racial propagandist *extraordinaire* Theodore Lothrop Stoddard warned of the catastrophic results of unchecked immigration, the danger of having the "white races . . . being inundated by the 'inferior' races" (*in* Gossett, p. 391).

Internal migration, too, would have had a similar effect on the level of race consciousness within a given multiethnic society. The United States is a prime example of this, in reference to the structural changes brought about by the *Great Migration to the North*, a demographic reorganization of U.S. society involving the very large segment of the African-American population that fled the violently oppressive conditions of Jim Crow in the Southern states, and flocked to the industrial cities of the North. Close to 1.5 million migrants left the South from 1940 to 1970 (Marger, 1991: 232), a large percentage of them settling in Chicago. In typical fashion of demographic shifts, and all the more so because of the race factor, the influx of African-American migrants into the cities of the industrial North affected the dynamics of urban life in general—but more to the point here, the relations between the various immigrant ethnic groups (the *white ethnics*) and the African-American newcomers from the South, in terms of their overall participation, competition, and antagonisms in the workplace. Those circumstances underscored the impact of "the race question" on U.S. local and national life during the Jim Crow period, as remarked upon by a distinguished African-American veteran of the First World War and chairman of the NAACP (cited in Sandburg, 2013: 79).

DECOLONIZATION

The great expansion of Western European and American imperialism in the first part of the twentieth century also triggered economic, political, and otherwise social ramifications or problems that accelerated its own demise, that is, the movement toward decolonization. These precipitating factors stemmed mainly from the very international network of capitalist processes and relationships involving the colonies and their colonial "mother countries," which colonialism had set in motion in the first place. One of the chief sources of threat to the continuing stability of colonial rule was the steady growth of indigenous nationalism. A critical indication of the incipient trend of decolonization came early in the twentieth century, as England, which had, up to that time, held absolute sway on the world stage on the basis of its imperialist enterprises, witnessed the waning of British colonial hegemony in the first quarter of the twentieth century. This massive, multifaceted reorganization, within the global network of colonialism, of the relationship between the colonies and their respective colonial masters, proceeded apace as the century rolled on. The culminating moment in the historical process of decolonization came in 1960 when the General Assembly of the United Nations voted the *Declaration on the Granting of Independence to Colonial Countries and Peoples.* By the end of the 1970s, the entirety of European colonial rule in mainland Africa had come to an end, and all of the former European colonies started their existence as politically sovereign states. More broadly, by that time, European and U.S. invasion and colonization of foreign lands on a global scale had essentially run its course, and the continuing imposition of political rule over those lands was no longer viable.

In a manner that roughly parallels the dissolution of modern slavery in the Americas, the struggles and armed conflict accompanying the decolonization process from its inception to its end in the second half of the twentieth century, in the various parts of the world that had been under European colonial rule, would have had the effect of rekindling the awareness of race as a normative principle, and its function as a pivotal element of social organization. For the European colonial powers, their practical concerns, having to do with the loss of territory, hence, of power and wealth, were solidly couched in racial ideology for theoretical support and reassurance. However much the imperial powers, in the decades following the end of the Second World War, might have pragmatically conceded that colonialism had outlived its usefulness, and proceeded to take measures toward a reorganization of their political relationship with their respective colonies, their fundamental conception of the colonized peoples would not have necessarily changed accordingly—that is, it is reasonable to suppose that deep in the minds of the colonizers lay the conviction that the efforts of the colonies to throw off the yoke of colonial rule were quite simply a violation of the laws of nature. It clashed with the indisputable fact of their innate racial inferiority, hence, incapacity for rational self-government, and obvious need for political tutelage by the civilized white nations.

Still, more importantly, the imperial powers feared that their colonial charges, now free from the supervision and control of their rulers, left to their own designs, would revert to the barbarism of yore, to the cultivation of their degraded cultural ways within their own borders, but also engage in the dissemination of these cultural ways around the world, through immigration. Immigration would represent, once again, as it had a half-century earlier, a threat to the *white races* and to white supremacy, and, therefore, a source of serious concern. As the movement of decolonization proceeded apace, people from the former colonized lands would flock to their respective "mother-countries" (or *core societies*; Chirot, 1986: 92), as immigrants, bringing disastrous results to the latter. Those fears were not unfounded. For some six decades, people from the former colonies have indeed migrated to the societies that once held them as colonial subjects, a legacy of the imperial past of those societies. Writing in reference to the French colonial empire, Aldrich (1996: 315) points to how, in the post–Second World War period, with the decolonization process well under way, "a stream of migrants" from its ex-colonies in the Caribbean, (North) Africa, and Southeast Asia steadily poured into France. In England, the influx came mainly from South Asia.

In this way, these fresh currents of migration in the period following the Second World War gave new impetus to the historical pattern of earlier times—a century earlier—specifically, the intense xenophobia observed in the societies of the Americas, Australia, and New Zealand, when immigration into those societies was at an all-time high. As noted above, the racial apologists at the time issued a blistering attack on the official open-door policy toward the multitudes of racial undesirables, who would come in and mingle their inferior "blood" and ways of life with those of the whites, thus producing the much-dreaded outcome of "racial degeneration" (Gossett, 1930: 389).

In the light of these considerations, the decades-long process of decolonization had definite and immediate implications for the discussion of race and for the operation of social life in all the societies of the Western world that were, at one time, more actively and directly involved with colonial empire-building. In structural terms, it gave rise to fresh waves of migration from the colonies, which profoundly impacted on the demographic constitution of their former colonizing nations, causing the national population of the latter to become increasingly diverse ethnically, racially, and culturally, a trend that has continued unabated.

The consciousness of race in all these host societies was significantly reinvigorated, in the sense that familiar racist interpretations of intergroup relations originating in the nineteenth century enjoyed wide currency again, to the effect that the specter of "blood mixture," with all of its attending insidious effects, came back to haunt the defenders of racial purity. These notions, however incongruous, unpalatable, and anachronistic they may seem at the present time to the majority of people in the industrialized world, still crop up with regularity, particularly when a new substantial influx of migrants into European or American societies takes place (e.g., the case of political refugees, such as the mass exodus of people from Syria, starting in 2011, trying to escape the horrors of that society's civil war).

Decolonization, it is thus argued here, triggered an ideological reaction in the imperial powers that sought to address a radical transformation on two levels, the economic and the political, to which serious adjustments and accommodations would have to be made. The decolonizing process immediately implied their loss of territory and resources, together with their loss of political control over non-European groups. The ideology of race would no longer be invoked at the official level, as had often been the case a century earlier, in colonial empires everywhere, when politicians (e.g., Jules Ferry, in France; William McKinley, in the United States; to take two salient examples) would have made a strong case for the expansion of European or U.S. imperialism because the mandates of Nature and Divine Providence dictated that it be so. (In the year 1900 President McKinley declared the occupation of the Philippine Islands and colonial control over the Philippine people to be a "high and sacred" duty imposed upon the U.S. government; in Snyder, 1962: 398.)

SCIENTIFIC RACISM AND THE CONSCIOUSNESS OF RACE

The extraordinary power of race and racial status in shaping the course of international relations, and the nature of intergroup relations within those societies most heavily engaged in political expansionism over the course of approximately two centuries, starting in the 1700s, owes primarily to the *essentialization* of racial condition, that is, the conception of race as a condition expressive of the very existence of individuals. An idea that emerged and matured over the centuries making up the age of maritime discoveries and conquest of new lands, and that had as a starting point the physical (i.e., visual) apprehension, by the colonial powers, of the phenotypical variation displayed by the colonized peoples, graduating to the larger belief in a differentiated humanity, crystallized in the belief that the physical traits of the colonized populations (skin color, facial features, the texture of hair, etc.) represented their *essential difference*. This conception of the racial condition of the colonized groups, and human groups in general, had ontological implications, insofar as racial status was understood as expressing a particular category of being. As such, it was considered to be fixed, in a metaphysical sense (Camara, 2003). Moreover, the racial condition becomes the context where physical appearance and ways of living are indissolubly merged. It comes to be what people *fundamentally are*, their master status overriding every other social status. To this day, the basic tenets of racist ideology remain grounded in this particular conception and classification of people, *albeit* without the corresponding infrastructure (i.e., legal supports, social arrangements and practices) of times past.

This ideological framework swept through the educated circles of Europe as early as the 1700s, and not even the greatest luminaries of the Enlightenment period, whether in the sciences or philosophy, remained immune to its effects (Eze, 1997). As Ward and Lott point out (2002:xi), from the Renaissance period onward, "various ideas regarding the inferiority of non-Europeans, often based on European accounts of non-Europeans, both in colonial accounts in the Americas and travel journals from abroad, emerged alongside a growing scientific interest in the subject." By the latter part of the 1800s, the period when Western European and U.S. political imperialism reached a culminating point, this conception of race as the immutable social condition and identity of individuals reached full maturity. It was the backbone of the larger philosophy that came to be recognized as social evolutionism, which held sway in both the European and American continents. Social evolutionism was couched in the larger philosophical doctrine of positivistic organicism, ranging from the pioneering work of Comte to that of Durkheim, Toennies, and Spencer. Certain strands of social evolutionism specifically stressed a biologistic interpretation of societal evolution, such as that found in the work of writers like Albert Schaeffle (1831–1903) in Germany; Arthur de Gobineau (1816–1882), Alfred Fouillé (1838–1912), and René Worms (1869–1926) in France; Herbert Spencer (1820–1903), Robert Knox (1791–1862), James Hunt (1833–1869), and Karl Pearson (1857–1936) in England; and William Graham Sumner (1840–1910) in the United States. The thought of virtually all of these thinkers was influenced, in one way or degree or another, by the theory of evolution of Charles Darwin (Martindale, 1981), forming the basis for what came to be known as social Darwinism.

In the early decades of the next century, specifically from about 1905 to 1930 (Kenaga, 1999: 233), the eugenics movement, a logical outgrowth of social Darwinism, stirred up the consciousness of race in the Western world and enjoyed enormous popularity and respectability, particularly in England and the United States. It was first rooted in the ideas of British statistician Francis Galton who coined the term *eugenics* in 1883 and sought to apply Darwin's theories of natural selection to the study of human society. In this regard, eugenics displayed the general tendency of racialist doctrines of the day, as evidenced in its indiscriminate application of evolutionist notions of natural selection to the social world, its concern with human anatomy as the basis for the elaboration of anthropological typologies that supported racial classification and hierarchies, such as those linked to craniometric studies. In the words of Galton himself, in a 1904 address to the Sociological Society at the School of Economics of the University of London): "Eugenics is the science which deals with all influences that improve the inborn qualities of a race [and] those that develop them to the utmost advantage" (1904: 1). In a 1907 work (*Inquiries into Human Faculty and Its Development*) he defined it as "the study of the agencies under social control that may improve or impair the racial qualities of future generations, either physically or mentally" (in Dowbiggin, 1997:vii). The racial implications for why there are cultural differences not only across individual members of each ethnic population, but across entire ethnic populations as well, seem abundantly clear. Additionally, the proposal of eugenics carried a special inducement to the literate public and the masses alike in the sense that, built into its ideological core, was a specific and sweeping agenda for social engineering, more precisely, for the implementation of sterilization programs for those classified as biologically defective.[12] The ultimate goal of eugenics was said by its defenders, people like Charles Davenport, Harry Laughlin, and Madison Grant, among others, in the United States, to be the betterment of the "human race." Nature could not be left to its own designs, for that would lead inevitably to the deterioration of the human stock. Instead, it ought to be directly manipulated by systematic human action, so that human traits thought to be undesirable could be weeded out through selective breeding, and a better, stronger, fitter human "race" could be produced. From this standpoint, the idea of U.S. society being the "great melting pot" was considered by eugenicists to be an abomination, as it meant the progressive weakening and degradation of the superior race. By the 1920s, eugenics theories had massively infiltrated U.S. popular culture and imaginary, and also had a strong impact on policymaking. By that time, the period following the First World War, U.S. society had been flooded over the previous decades by massive waves of newcomers from various parts of the globe, eugenics advocates became especially active in warning against the perils stemming from continuing unchecked

immigration.[13] This led to increasingly restrictive immigration policies targeting a whole array of groups deemed to be racially inferior—including
immigrants from Southern and Eastern Europe, Asians, Arabs, and Jews—
which culminated in the signing of the Immigration (Johnson-Reed) Act of
1924, by President Coolidge.

A parallel may be drawn between the strong general appeal of the eugenics movement and that which was accorded to Spencerian evolutionism. The
latter was wholeheartedly embraced by the *robber barons* of the *fin-de-siècle*
United States because it legitimized the rise of the industrialists to financial
success and rule over the economic and social life, by defending the idea of
their superior racial endowment and *fitness*. This is what had enabled them to
succeed in the social world. Put differently, their material success was por-
trayed quite simply as the working out of natural law.[14] In like fashion, the
eugenics movement was also enthusiastically received in the United States
and other politically expansionist societies of the time because it justified
colonialist policy and practice in reference to the superior racial endowment
of the colonizers. By the 1920s eugenics clubs and societies had sprung up
throughout the United States.

The rise of eugenics was accompanied by a greatly intensified consciousness of race in the late 1800s and the first few decades of the 1900s. When
it reached American shores, it exerted a strong influence, in varying degrees,
across the multiethnic societies of the American continent, most notably in
those with a history of political expansionism and large-scale immigration,
such as the United States, but also, to a lesser extent, in those which had not
been directly engaged in empire-building activity on a large scale, but had
nevertheless considerable ethnic diversity, stemming from immigration, the
indigenous groups, and also, in the case of former slavery societies (e.g., the
United States, Brazil, Colombia, Mexico), the liberated African-American
population. At the threshold of the twentieth century, the task that lay ahead,
for all American societies, was the assimilation of the newcomers, and ethnic
integration at the national level.

The fast-spreading influence of the eugenics movement during that time
reached Central and South American settings, as indicated above, shaping the
implementation of official policies and programs, and thus having a significant impact on the lives of racial minorities in these places. As in every other
societal context where it operated, the eugenics movement in Ibero-American
contexts reenergized the official and public debate and awareness of race.

This discussion has thrown into relief the fact that particular historical
circumstances of the last century and a half in Europe and the neo-European
world have led, at various times, to a reawakening of race consciousness
in these places. This phenomenon reached an apex in the latter part of the
nineteenth century, as indicated, primarily as a reaction to a revitalization of

imperialist activity, the great surge of immigration, the end of slavery in the Americas, and, half a century later, the gradual process of decolonization.

The remarks of the distinguished English statesman James Bryce are pertinent at this point. In 1915 he delivered the Creighton Lecture at the University of London, entitled *Race Sentiment as a Factor in History*, in which he draws attention to the extraordinary importance being assigned to race in the international stage, not only in official circles, among statesmen and intellectuals, but also and, more generally, among the general public. He pointed out how race had become a normative principle of international relations, often driving nations to "keen rivalry" among themselves, and to their own sense of superiority over others. "The world," he said, "is full of the rival pretensions and jarring claims of races" (1915: 26) and predicted that racial consciousness and pride were likely to become even "more pronounced" as the twentieth century wore on (1935: 35).

Those were prescient words. The consciousness of race would remain intense through the twentieth century, being reinforced by such events as the race-based genocidal campaigns against the Jewish population by the Nazi regime in the 1930s through the Second World War; the decolonization process, which accelerated after the Second World War and lasted several decades thereafter; and finally, the continuing currents of migration, the most recent being the large-scale migration of Syrians to various countries of Europe, the Middle East, the Americas, and (to a much lesser extent) Asia. Evidence of this racially inspired reaction against the newcomers may be seen in the sentiments being vigorously expressed in some of the European host societies against the admission of the Syrian political refugees.[15]

U.S. society constitutes a special case among societies of the Americas, inasmuch as for the better part of the twentieth-century American social life rested on the operation of a rigid legal framework of racial division and discrimination, the Jim Crow system, through which racial status determined every aspect of collective life, at both the formal and informal levels. Jim Crow was dismantled and terminated in the late 1960s, but unresolved issues of race continue to plague daily life in U.S. society, as evidenced by the rather frequent eruptions of racial tension and conflict, as in the *race wars* of recent years, involving the bitter clashes between segments of the African-American community and the police forces. That race-based antagonisms remain unresolved in the present-day United States may also be seen, inter alia, in the several instances of racially motivated turmoil on U.S. campuses in the post–Jim Crow era; in the prevalence of racial discourse in formal and informal contexts; in the persistence of social practices oriented by racial considerations (e.g., separatist tendencies, a legacy of the Jim Crow period, in academia, in the entertainment world, in the sphere of culture[16]); in connection with the latter, the criteria for employment in institutional settings being driven by "cultural diversity" (read: *racial* balance); in the continuation of the *politics of difference*, through which the compartmentalization of society's groups and individuals is guided by their "cultural" (again, meaning *racial*) background, and so forth.

Keeping in mind the major political trends and events of the late nineteenth and early twentieth centuries, and the special situation of the United States in the sphere of race relations, it is hardly surprising that W.E.B. Dubois would have stated in 1903, with great acuity and foresight, that the major problem of the twentieth century would be the problem of the "color line." More than a century later, and with direct reference to life in the United States, the cogency and accuracy of his prediction, as one analyst remarked, "is beyond dispute" (Wilkins, 1996: 3). As the second decade of the twenty-first century ends, the fundamental problem of race in U.S. social life—and more broadly, in other world ethnically pluralist societies—has yet to be resolved satisfactorily.

The writings of leaders of the *Négritude* movement (most notably those of poet Aimé Césaire), of philosopher Frantz Fanon, of political ethicist Mahatma Gandhi, and similar writers, have fueled national liberationist movements in various parts of the world where the population struggles to free itself from colonial domination, and/or to deal with the latter's aftereffects or legacy. The ideas of these writers have strengthened the resolve and efforts of oppressed peoples not only against colonial rule, but also, as the decolonization period rolls on, against the circumstances and forces (the racism built into the normal workings of institutional life, de facto discrimination, etc.) that continue to impair the ability of former colonies to achieve social, political, and economic self-sufficiency. The works of the West Indian writers, in particular, threw into sharp relief the central role of race in the process of colonization, while that process was still in effect, and how the shaping impact of race remained significant during the postcolonial period. As a result, the *consciousness* of race has persisted after the end of colonialism in many world societies, in connection with the migration of large numbers of former colonials, starting in the mid-1900s, to their respective "mother countries." With regard to the Caribbean migrants to Britain, they came in large numbers, from the late 1940s to about 1970, and came to be known as *The Windrush Generation*. They migrated to that country in order to meet the severe labor shortages afflicting the British economy in the wake of the Second World War. These migrants had to face all kinds of obstacles to their assimilation into the national way of life of the host society *because of their racial status*.

To revisit and draw together the earlier considerations which set the stage for this work, in both the Introduction and this chapter, it is against the backdrop of the persisting tensions characterizing the relations between dominant and minority ethnic-racial groups in ethnically and racially pluralist societies over the last quarter-century, and the unceasing concern with race in these societies as a result; and, in this connection, the ongoing scholarly efforts to elucidate the manifestations and effects of race, that I have undertaken this project. To mention but one, though all-important, trend of current times, which is the spread of reactionary politics on a global scale, it is generally recognized that this has occurred hand in hand with the recrudescence of racial prejudice. This in turn provides a solid basis of justification for continuing with scholarly efforts to deal with this problem.

NOTES

1. Horsman (1981: ch. 4) discusses how "racial Anglo-Saxonism" and racial status were invoked as nineteenth-century England as the main framework of explanation for British preeminence among the nations of the world. In the United States as well, the idea of U.S. exceptionalism, as promoted by racial superiority, was already in the early 1800s widespread and established in public discourse. Popular wisdom held that the Caucasians were innately superior, and that they were responsible for the development of civilization in the world, while at the same time the inferior races were thought to be destined to be overwhelmed or even to disappear. These notions circulated widely in the academic and popular press of the time, and by the latter part of the 1800s had reached the status of incontrovertible truth in the textbooks of American schools.

2. From the earliest periods of the operation of slavery in the different American (including Caribbean) societies, the signs pointing to what would eventually become established as the dominant pattern of assimilation of the African-Americans in the different New World slavery societies became clearly apparent. For instance, they could be seen in the degree to which the physical freedom and mobility of the slaves on the plantation enabled them to maintain continuity, in some degree and form, with their ancestral customs (through dances, celebrations, religious practices, etc.).

3. Social integration in American societies of more than a century ago hinged largely on the society's approach to the assimilation minority ethnic groups. In Iberian-American or Anglo-(or otherwise European-) American contexts, the march of industry and science through the nineteenth century, especially in the latter part of that century, developed in conjunction with a spreading concern with race. In the case of Iberian-American societies, the shifting social, economic, and political circumstances had specifically to do with the departure from Imperial regimes and the preindustrial social order (such as, for instance, in the case of Brazil) toward republican government and modernization. The awareness of race in that society (and others in the Americas), therefore, was bound up with major internal changes and the larger concern to define and establish the national identity. Araujo (2016: 87), for example, points out how the end of Brazilian slavery occurred concomitantly with the passage from imperial government to republican government (the abolition of slavery took place in 1888, and the proclamation of the Republic in 1889), and how those events

"were facts of extreme importance for the racial themes addressed by the intellectuals involved in the building of the new nation."

Thus, the infiltration of external ideological currents, more directly, the racialist theories of the Spencerian variety at the end of the century, tied in with the intent of the dominant classes in Brazil to maximize the European social and cultural heritage in the emerging national character (see, in reference to this aspect, the discussion of Silvio Romero's evolutionist position in Souza, 2004).This point is also underscored in Domingues and Sá (2001: 65), when they assert that the rising preoccupation with the question of race among intellectuals in Brazil during the last decades of the nineteenth century was entwined with the national effort "to insert the country in the contemporary march of 'civilization.'" The work of such eminent scholars of the period as Raymundo Nina Rodrigues (1977) or Oliveira Vianna (see discussion of the latter's racialist views in Buonicore, 2017), which was couched in a social evolutionism of Darwinian extraction, would then be considered from this perspective. Writing in the same vein, Freyre (1990: 345–383) provides ample evidence of the pervasive sensitivity to "the color question" in post-slavery Brazil (i.e., after 1888), particularly with reference to the aspect of intermarriage, inasmuch as the freed slaves were now occupying citizenship status and were, therefore, theoretically able to marry any person. This issue was one of great import in the minds of the elites of the country and it was, in the main, significantly informed by *color* prejudice (Nogueira, 1955). It was also part of the larger process of assimilation of the multiple immigrant groups entering the society in large numbers at that time.

A similar situation characterized other Ibero-American societies as well. Zimmermann (1992) and Montserrat (2001) indicate how the introduction of social Darwinist theories in Argentina during the same period not only spurred on the consciousness of race, but fell in more generally with the national emphasis on social reform and the idea of progress. Regarding the case of Mexico, Suárez y Lopez-Guazo reminds us (2001: 143), the ideology of racial improvement there was similarly tied to concerns with national development and progress, and "was legitimized and strengthened upon scientific grounds in genetics and evolutionism" (see also Stern, 2011).

In any event, it should be clear that in *all* of these cases of societies considered here, whether they be Anglo-American or Iberian-American, the preoccupation with race as part of the process of national definition and affirmation could not possibly have been extricated from the concrete operation of race-based social stratification. Thus, social Darwinism and any other variety of evolutionist doctrine ultimately served as a basis for the protection of the interests of the ruling classes, which meant the justification of the concentration of power and wealth in the hands of the majority racial part of the population. Social elites in American societies were (and are still) made up primarily of direct descendants of the European settlers—or, in any case, of people who were closer genetically and phenotypically to the settler. Said differently, the interest in the aspect of race in all these societies was fueled by the effort to preserve and strengthen the supremacy of the European-American element. It formed part of the broader movement toward the Europeanization of these societies and the devaluation of the non-European parts of the national population.

4. Data for Asia point consistently to the overpowering and far-reaching influence of Confucianism and Buddhism in Eastern Asian countries as a group. Littleton (1996: 54) informs us that the cultural and philosophical impact of Buddhism "has for centuries reverberated throughout South and Southeast Asia." This is immediately relevant to the present discussion. Confucian philosophy is predicated on "a strict hierarchy of values and well-defined code of social morality," preaching the person's adjustment (rather than questioning) to social conditions as they present themselves. This obviously served the interests of power structures and strengthened the existing order by sanctioning "all forms of repression" (de Bary, 1981:xii). This is the fundamental social organicism built into the Confucian philosophy of social order and stability. Hackett (1979: 30–33) adds that the "unconditional principle of righteousness" in Confucianism rests on the collective virtue and happiness achieved through the exercise of social duty, individuals working to achieve "universal human well-being," not on the satisfaction of personal, "self-seeking desires." Buddhism, for its part, with its emphasis on pure, transcending, undifferentiated consciousness constituting the basis of reality (Hackett, 1979: 100), ultimately favors the hierarchies of social life and the maintenance of the status quo.

As for the societies of the African continent, their background is strikingly dissimilar to that of their counterparts in Asia. However, some particular aspects of their history also have a bearing on the general question of protection of individual rights, or the rights of minority social groups. Modern African nation-states are a recent (i.e., twentieth-century) phenomenon, inasmuch as they have sprung from tribal systems, hence, from highly collectivistic social systems, where conformity to group rules and values were historically accepted as a given. Thus, in the main, it may be reasonable to say that the collective conscience in African social systems is still influenced by the collectivism of earlier times. From the standpoint of economic development, many of the African societies have not completely broken free from the crippling legacy of Western European colonialism. Therefore, industrialization, urbanization, and modernization of the social structure have yet to be fully achieved and can hardly be counted on to be a key factor in the official effort toward reparation of social wrongs perpetrated against minority groups or individuals.

5. For Knox and many of his like-minded peers in the England of the mid-1800s, race was the ultimate consideration, the foundation of ethics as well as practical action. "Race is everything," he said—"literature, science, art – in a word, civilization, depends on it" (1850: 7). The historian Carlyle, writing from the same period, asserts forcefully, with reference to the British presence in the British West Indian island societies, that were it not for the elevating effect of English colonization over the native inhabitants of those islands (i.e., the Native Americans of the Antilles, the Caribs, together with the black population), the latter would have sunk irretrievably into barbarism and degradation, for it was in their very nature to lead such an existence. "For countless ages," he states, "till the European white man first saw them . . . [the West Indian islands] had produced mere jungle, savagery, poison-reptiles and swamp-malaria . . . [while the nurturing and profitable cultivation of such crops as] . . . cinnamon, sugar, coffee, pepper black and gray [lay] all asleep, waiting the white enchanter would say to them: Awake!" (cited in Snyder, 1962: 111).

6. The fact that the pattern of the early French settlements in North America was of short duration applies to the South American context as well. An example may be seen in the 1555 campaign by Admiral Nicholas Durand de Villegagnon, which incorporated a contingent of French Huguenots and led to the establishment of a colony in the Rio de Janeiro and Guanabara Bay area in southern Brazil. It lasted only five years, after which the French were expelled by the Portuguese troops. That unsuccessful campaign notwithstanding, the French continued to pursue their exploration of Brazil's Atlantic coast into the next (the seventeenth) century, with the intent of establishing additional settlements, and those efforts resulted in the founding of the colony of São Luís (*Saint Louis*), presently the capital city of the state of Maranhão, in northern Brazil. That enterprise too was of short duration, as they could hold control of it for only three years (1612–1615), before being, again, driven out by the Portuguese (Poppino, 1973: 64–65; *Almanaque Abril* 1986: 140, 162–163).

7. In reference to U.S. political activity in the nineteenth century, Merk (1966) reworks the concept of *Manifest Destiny* by seeking to extricate it from the idea of rapacious imperialism, and casting it in the more positive frame of a noble civilizing mission, which embodied the virtues of the U.S. national character. Be that as it may, he concedes, in general terms, that this was the U.S. brand of supporting ideology for the country's colonialist activity in the late nineteenth and early twentieth centuries (1966: Preface).

8. A vigorous strain of religious Puritanism, as derived mainly from Calvinist theology, and oriented at the broader or supra-religious level by the cardinal Calvinist notion of predestination, appears to have persisted in the ethos of American society— that is, to have become ingrained in what Parsons (1966: 510) called the "ultimate values and value-attitudes" of the people, and Aron (1970: 267) has called "a way of conceiving the world orients action in the world." This would refer specifically to the religious idea of election/non-election conditioning the modern framework of social legitimation—and—inclusion vs. non-legitimation-and-exclusion. With reference to the idea of "election" as transposed to national uniqueness and destiny. Hudson (1965: 210) remarks that animating the fundamentalist Protestantism that welded together the "diverse people of the colonies . . . was the consciousness of being summoned to a God-given mission" (see also Brumm, 1970; Camara, 2013).

9. In a landmark study on German immigration in Brazil, Willems (1980: 44) mentions the numerous *federal colonies* set up by the Brazilian Imperial Government in the nineteenth century, whereby foreign settlers in the Southern regions of the country were provided, upon arrival, with all the resources deemed necessary to start a new life productively: 173 acres of land, agricultural equipment and seeds, and a subsidy.

10. In the societies of the Americas (save for the case of the United States, where imperialist activity took the same form and reached nearly the same heights in the late nineteenth and early twentieth centuries as it did among the Western European colonial powers), and also, for example, in Australia and New Zealand, colonialist activity primarily took the form of *internal colonialism*. This means the inequalitarian type of model of ethnic pluralism, whereby the subjugation of the non-dominant groups operates *within the society itself*, as may be seen in the experience of the

Native American tribal groups in the Americas, the Aborigines in Australia, the Maori in New Zealand—or, as has been argued (e.g., Marger, 1991: 140–141), Americans of African descent in the United States.

11. This concept needs to be differentiated as pertains to its operation in U.S. society. Several immigrant groups in the urban setting, whether they were officially classified as white (e.g., the Greeks) or nonwhite (e.g., the Chinese), experienced the life of separation from the majority population by living their lives primarily in the ethnic enclave. Generally speaking, this was especially true for the *first* generation of these groups, meaning that by the second generation they began to blend effectively into the national population and the sociocultural mainstream. In other words, they were assimilated at all levels of the assimilative process (i.e., at the structural, cultural, biological, and psychological levels). More germane here, however, is the fact that for the migrants classified officially and unofficially as nonwhite, the ethnic enclave functioned more as a *racial* enclave. This means that, while the *ethnic* enclave normally became a *temporary* arrangement, or temporary refuge for the first generation of white immigrants, lasting only as long as fresh waves of migrants from the same place of origin kept arriving, it remained a *permanent* home base— cultural, economic, interpersonal, and so on—for members of the nonwhite groups, within the larger society of which they were now members. This naturally favored, in the majority of cases, the development of a subcultural lifestyle for the group, which will set it apart from the national patterns of conduct and thought. Throughout the larger part of the twentieth century, when the Jim Crow system was in effect, the United States enforced, by law and by custom, a dichotomous pattern of assimilation of incoming groups determined by racial status, specifically, by racial bipolarity (i.e., white/nonwhite). This means that, as far as the residents of the *ethnic* enclave were concerned, for all the comfort and security—cultural, psychological—they derived from their membership in the enclave, the duration of their stay in it was determined largely by *culture*—which is to say, social integration for them depended largely on the degree in which they were assimilated culturally, in terms of the acquisition of the host society's language, patterns of conduct and thought, and so on, and these hurdles were normally overcome by the second, certainly third, generation. Racial sameness with the society's majority population afforded these people the freedom to even maintain some degree of continuity with their ancestral culture (preserving some customs, foods, etc.), without having this detract in any way from their progressive inclusion into national life. For the nonwhite migrants, however, the assimilative experience was distinctly different, primarily because it was determined by racial status, a condition which has been historically *essentialized*, or fixed permanently. Thus, it is a condition of *being* and, therefore, cannot be changed. For the larger part of the twentieth century, when Jim Crow racial segregation was rigidly enforced, this meant that these nonwhite migrants would have no option but to remain within the confines of the racial enclave *indefinitely*. In the post–Jim Crow era, this dual pattern of assimilation has weakened considerably in U.S. society, although the integration of nonwhite groups into the society-as-a-whole at the cultural and biological levels of assimilation has yet to be fully achieved.

12. For a general discussion of eugenics, nativism, and racialist thought in the late nineteenth through the first quarter of the twentieth centuries, the following sources are noteworthy: Gossett, 1969: ch. 7; Scott-Childress, 1999: 221–246. Another writer (Dowbiggin, 1997: ch. 3) discusses eugenics initiatives in Canada in the first two decades of the twentieth century, devoting special attention to the work of eugenics crusaders C.K. Clarke and Helen MacMurchy, and their active pursuit of sterilization programs targeting the "feeble-minded."

13. Examples of the heightening of xenophobia in U.S. society, at the informal and formal levels, in connection with eugenics, are found in, for example, Ross (1914), and Grant (1916).

14. Spencerian Darwinism appears to have been strikingly congenial with the historically prevalent radical individualism of U.S. society and therefore especially suited to the laissez-faire economic climate of the United States in the closing decades of the 1800s. Specifically, it showed great promise as a basis of legitimation for the severe class-based inequality that U.S. capitalism promoted during that period. Hence, Spencer's towering influence upon the captains of industry, as well as leaders in the letters, economics, politics, and science—in short, the larger literate public. The laudatory statement, addressed to Spencer, by scientific writer and lecturer Edward Livingston Youmans is representative: "I believe there is great work to be done here [in the United States] for civilization. What we want are ideas—large, organizing ideas—and I believe there is no other man whose thoughts are so valuable for our needs as yours are." In the same vein, the industrialist J.D. Rockefeller, echoing the central tenets and the language of Spencerian evolutionism, justified the predatory nature of capitalist competition by saying, "The growth of a large business is merely a *survival of the fittest* . . . the working out of a law of Nature and a law of God" (in Hofstadter, 1960: 31, 45).

15. Recent reports attest to the intensification of race consciousness (and race-based hostility) in a number of Western European societies that have experienced a heavy inflow of non-European political refugees (e.g., Fallows, 2018; Parry, 2015; Zucchino, 2016).

16. The operation of race as an ontological condition of individuals, *and determinant of group culture*, has been increasingly witnessed in the U.S. popular press, in the charges of cultural appropriation. These charges normally issue from minority racial communities within the larger society against what is perceived as inappropriate appropriations of minority cultural patterns by the dominant group. This phenomenon immediately negates the existence of culture as a dynamic, constantly evolving entity, constantly absorbing and modifying aspects of other cultures through cultural diffusion, syncretizing them with already existing patterns, and stabilizing them into the society's general culture. The idea of cultural appropriation in this context, therefore, reflects and upholds intrasocietal cultural separatism based on race (as in "white" appropriation of "black" culture). Ultimately, the transformation of race into an ontological category reinforces the idea of the *essential otherness* of the minority racial communities, their need to remain biologically as well as culturally distinct from one another, and, therefore, the impossibility of the full-scale integration of the society's cultural system.

Chapter 2

The Study of Racial and Ethnic Relations

The early sociological writings on race and ethnicity date back to the late nineteenth century and the early period of sociology as a scientific discipline in the United States. This was a trend that coincided with the great influx of immigration in U.S. society in the late 1800s to early 1900s. It is exemplified by the voluminous literature on race and ethnic relations produced during that time. Later in the century (after the Second World War), the steady expansion of the decolonization movement threw back into sharp relief the question of race and ethnic relations throughout the former colonizing nations, which themselves began to experience a reversal of the demographic movement, in the sense of beginning to receive increasing streams of migrants from their former colonies.[1]

It should be useful at this point to consider the scholarly literature on race and ethnic relations since the late nineteenth century in terms of two broad phases or periods which I will refer to, *grosso modo*, as the modern and postmodern periods. The modern period could be said to have encompassed the larger part of the twentieth century, starting in the early decades of that century up to the 1980s. By the 1980s the winds of change began to be felt in various spheres of intellectual activity, and postmodernism arose as a many-faceted social and philosophical movement that swept across the arts, humanities, literature, the social sciences, and architecture. The arrival of the postmodern period in race and ethnic research meant a significant turning point insofar as it signaled a reworking of the boundaries that defined the minority group, the *loci* of power, the question of equality and social inclusion, and the proper approach for dealing with intergroup inequality in the society-at-large. Before all that happened, however, much of the scholarly research on race relations that had been produced during the modern period had become the canonical material on this subject. This is represented by the work of such eminent writers as Small, Park, Thomas, Dubois, Gilman, Dollard, Myrdal, Frazier, and, in the latter part of this period, that of Parsons, Handlin, Hughes and Hughes, Simpson and Yinger, Wagley and Harris, Coles, Gordon, Van den Berghe, Rex, and Banton.

Postmodern scholarship moved away from the traditional universalist orientation of modernism, which favored the *grand narratives* (Lyotard, 1984), the quest for universal truths, the focus on centralized or unitary power, and its corollary monolithic dualisms (e.g., fiction vs. reality). This signified the breakdown of traditional boundaries and all-inclusive categories. Thus, in consonance with this shift, the postmodern discourse of race and ethnicity shunned, for instance, the idea of cultural integration as a *desideratum* for multiethnic societies. It favored, instead, a *particularist* conception of group culture, which prioritized the validity and importance of preserving each of the many cultural groups and strains constituting national life, and, more importantly, emphasizing the preservation and validation of *difference,* rather than uniformity. Out of this change sprang what has become known as the *politics of difference* (or *politics of identity*) which quickly became the normative standard at both the level of policy and cultural life in pluralist societies, and its impact is still felt to this day, although, from a formal standpoint, the postmodern movement has run its course. By the early 2000s writers were writing about the end of postmodernism and declaring that the world was once again "rearranging itself" (Gibbons, 2017).

Just as the fragmentation and eventual dissolution of the Jim Crow system in the United States in the mid-to-late 1960s, together with the acceleration of the global process of decolonization during the same period, had made that particular decade an exceptionally fertile time for race and ethnic studies, the same effect was manifested during the postmodern era through the expanding representation of minority ethnic populations and the vigorous application of the politics of difference. The latter exerted a powerful impact on race-and-ethnicity scholarship by redefining the vocabulary, the nature of the oppressed subject (the *decentering of the Subject*), and the way the hegemonic/non-hegemonic opposition, and the very idea of social domination itself, were now to be addressed.

THE STRUCTURAL VS. CULTURAL
DETERMINATION OF REALITY

The material dimension of social life, despite its great importance in revealing the concrete conditions of social oppression, does not address the operation of this problem at a deeper level, where it is driven and maintained by nonmaterial factors, specifically factors of subjectivity. This is the reason that many writers in the humanities and social sciences who wish to provide a more incisive account of the exercise of power over society's disadvantaged groups have, over the years, shown a growing resistance to elaborating their critiques in the language of Marxist economic reductionism. The latter, it is argued, fails to address the specific circumstances of oppression based on race, gender, sexual orientation, and other criteria. In this regard, scholars have generally agreed that the most fruitful approach for understanding social inequality, whether in general terms, or in the specific context of race relations, is to treat it as the product of the intertwining operation of material and nonmaterial factors. This point is thrown into bold relief in Alfredo Bosi's *Dialética da Colonização*, as shown in the following passage:

> Colonization is a process at once material and symbolic: the economic practices of its agents are tied to their ways of surviving, to their [collective] memory, to their modes of self-representation and representation of others, in short, to their aspirations and hopes. Stated differently: There is no colonial condition without the interrelation of [the structures of] work, beliefs, ideologies, and cultures. (1992: 377; my translation)

The importance of cultural forces in social evolution is acknowledged even in traditional materialist interpretations of history. At the very least, there appears to be a sensitivity to the complexity and difficulty of determining the exact nature of causal relations in the unfolding of history, as in the case of the interaction between economic ("structural") and non-economic ("superstructural") variables. Marx himself uses language in the Preface to his *Critique of Political Economy* that is somewhat qualifying, in terms of "the mode of production in material life [determining] the *general* character . . . [of culture]," and "the entire immense superstructure [being] *more or less* rapidly transformed" by change in the economic foundation of society (cited in Williams, 1958: 266). This awareness of the role of nonmaterial forces in social life, while maintaining the emphasis on the principle of socio-structural development being the "master process" of history, is shown in a comment by Engels in a 1890 correspondence to Joseph Bloch:

> According to the materialist conception of history, the determining element in history is *ultimately* the production and reproduction in real life. More than this neither Marx nor I have ever asserted. If therefore somebody twists this into the statement that the economic element is the *only* determining one, he transforms it into a meaningless, abstract and absurd phrase. The economic situation is the basis, but the various elements of the superstructure-political forms of the class struggle and its consequences . . . and then even the reflexes of all these actual struggles in the brains of the combatants: political, legal, and philosophical theories, religious ideas and their further development into systems of dogma - also exercise their influence upon the course of the historical struggles and in many

cases preponderate in determining their *form* . . . There is an interaction of all these elements, in which, amid all the endless host of accidents (i.e., of things and events whose inner connection is so remote or so impossible to prove that we regard it as absent and can neglect it) the economic element finally asserts itself as necessary. (in Marx, 1972: 294–296)

Thus, while orthodox Marxism normally draws attention to the historical background of the oppression to which minority social groups have been subjected, and to how this oppression is rooted specifically in *economic* oppression, more broadly construed Marxist treatments of the issue, as, for example, in the case of race and gender inequality (e.g., Collins, 1993), shift the focus to the complex interplay of class with race and gender, and are therefore closer to Marx's idea that people's lives in society are bound up with "an ensemble of social relations" (Marx, 1994: 100).

The present analysis is supportive of assertions to the effect that cultural and material conditions interact in a flexible, dynamic, and relational manner (see, e.g., Williams, 1958, in this regard), and not in terms of unilateral determinism, as stated in the more orthodox readings of historical materialism. At the same time, this study emphasizes the special character of cultural forces, and their effect in shaping social organization. Although originating in the material structure of society, systems of ideas may eventually not only insulate themselves against the impact of material forces, but also follow independent lines of development, and that in turn acts back on and shapes the material structure that generated them, thus giving rise to new social formations. These new social formations represent a preservation of traditional patterns of social life in modified form, insofar as these patterns continue to operate notwithstanding the material changes that may have taken place. A case in point is the fact that the racial prejudice that sustained the Jim Crow system in the United States, or the Apartheid system in South Africa, did not automatically disappear once the new conditions of life—the physical and institutional changes involved, such as the enactment and enforcement of anti-discrimination laws and the elimination of segregationist arrangements and practices—were put in place following the destruction of these systems of legally supported racial segregation. This problem—that is, the persistence of racial prejudice, tensions, and antagonisms—endures right down to the present time, and therefore it is imperative that the effort be made to identify the forces that keep it alive. These forces are to be found in the general sphere of culture, specifically in the operation of intersubjectivity.

I would like to enlarge upon this question here with reference to the concrete circumstances of minority-group assimilation. When a given multiethnic society defines and directs its efforts to the assimilation of minority social groups in purely *formal* terms, that is, purely in terms of the progressive inclusion of minority-group members into the economic, political, administrative, and educational spheres, without giving any consideration to their social and cultural life, this tends to leave minority-group life open to a whole range of problems. These problems can be very serious, to the point of intruding on, and impeding, their formal assimilation and integration in national life. This point is of great importance, in terms of drawing attention to factors that are normally overlooked, but which, it is argued here, can shed a more penetrating light on the process of social inclusion or exclusion. In this sense, these factors are better indicators of whether and/or how much individuals have internalized the society's core standards, beliefs, and values, and rely on them to guide their action. These factors are *cultural* in nature, expressive of the group's pattern of living, and they specifically have to do with social meaning and intersubjectivity. They also impact powerfully on the life situation of the members of the social system and thus become particularly relevant for minority-group persons regarding their well-being and happiness as members of the larger national community. For example, it is often the case that when members of socially disenfranchised groups engage in behaviors that violate the *mores* of the society, such as, for instance, by engaging in the destruction or theft of public property, this behavior is invariably interpreted by analysts as the inevitable consequence of *economic* marginalization. It is the case, of course, that economic exclusion is a motivational force of the greatest importance, but in isolation it fails to account fully for the problem. Additionally, it obscures the fact that *cultural* factors, expressed in terms of the psychosocial impact brought about upon the individuals involved, by the structures and circumstances of social and economic marginalization—namely, what the national community means to them, how they see themselves in the wider society, and the degree to which they fail to identify with the national way of life and its collective representations—can provide an alternative and at least equally compelling explanation. Fundamentally, this comes down to what things *mean* to persons, to what they see as truly important or unimportant, which will then define for them which courses of action to pursue or to avoid. These deliberations by individuals are, of course, predetermined or conditioned by life in the group. This points to the importance of these ideas for the problem of cultural divisions or, alternatively, cultural integration, in the wider society.

POSTMODERNISM AND CLASSICAL MARXISM

The tenets of orthodox Marxist theory, as is known, remind us that social reality is most powerfully and directly conditioned by the operation of the society's mode of economic production, irrespective of how the society is institutionally organized, and of the specific historical epoch under consideration. This perspective holds that individuals, whether at the personal or collective level, are fundamentally driven in their behavior and ways of thinking by the quest for access to and control of material resources. This deep-seated trait of human nature exerts a decisive impact on intergroup relations, ultimately constituting the basis for intergroup alliances and/or antagonisms. Thus, from this perspective, the nature of race and ethnic relations in any society must be seen as a reflection of the operation of material or economic forces, specifically of the society's economic system. From this angle, racial oppression and inequality are epiphenomenal or secondary to the larger oppression of the working mass by the owners of the means of production. In multiethnic societies with an industrial-capitalist economy, this means that the operation of the capitalist class system is the ultimate determinant of the relations between groups in these societies. The primary interest and focus of the analysis thus become economic class conflict and exploitation. Class, in this context, overrides all other considerations, and class-based inequality prevails over all other forms of group-based inequality. The materialist solution to racial inequality would, by implication, be achieved through the dismantling of the capitalist class formations and work relations, in other words, through an emancipatory socialist economic program.

From the beginning, postmodern theorists of race and gender oppression have leveled criticism on the Marxist position for its class reductionism, which results in an oversimplification of the problems of interethnic/interracial relations. During the 1980s and 1990s, this criticism was expressed concomitantly with the rise of identity politics, and the argument that minority groups like, for example, women and racial minorities, should not be lumped together indiscriminately as the problems of a large, undifferentiated economically oppressed community. Rather, the disadvantaged situation of "people of color," or other oppressed social collectivities, stood on its own. Furthermore, the consideration of the oppression of racial or gender minorities ought to take intra-group distinctions into account. That is to say, each broad minority category had to be related to in terms of its internal differentiation so that the particular grievances of each subgroup within it could be properly addressed.

It is true that race-and-ethnicity researchers during both the modern and postmodern periods were all centrally concerned with the question of power and power inequality between the society's majority and minority racial segments. Thus, the political thrust was always there, even if some writers might not be directly aligned with the postmodern research model or the classical Marxist position. Thus, for instance, Omi and Winant embark on a historical analysis of race formations by looking at how race intersects with "the evolution of hegemony" (1994: 56). Mills (1998) looks at the connection between race and social power by addressing the ontological and epistemological foundations of race relations, involving questions of identity, worldviews, and so on. In any event, race-and-ethnicity theorists of that period and beyond have largely adhered to certain key tenets of postmodern philosophy, such as the recognition, and therefore preservation, of minority intra-group distinctions, the naturalization of minority-group *difference* by means of its *a priori* acknowledgment and support, in conjunction with the rejection of integrationist ideals.

The dominance of the postmodern spirit has come and gone, as indicated above, but some of its key premises still persist, much like the iconic grin of the Cheshire cat, which is visible and whose impact is still felt, even after the disappearance of the cat's body. Thus, from this angle, to think and write about race in integrationist terms—this was the primary thrust of the discourse of emancipation driving Civil Rights efforts in the latter phase of the Jim Crow period in the United States—or even to fail to account for the possible divisions within each oppressed collectivity—that is, to treat these minority segments in undifferentiated terms—is still very much regarded in current times as a countercultural, less than completely valid, approach. The fragmentation of major ethnic and racial categories has proceeded unremittingly over the past few decades, and these divisions have in turn become reified through the society's bureaucratic system (and appropriated by the capitalist market for its own purposes), and that in turn has found its way into race-and-ethnicity scholarship.[2]

It should be profitable to take a closer look, at this point, at the work of two prominent scholars of race relations of the modern period, Pierre Van den Berghe and John Rex, and to identify some of their convergences and disjunctions. These scholars, although coming from different perspectives, have made an enormous contribution to the race-and-ethnicity literature of the past half-century and to our understanding of race relations. Van den Berghe's research has a strong comparative focus—he compares and contrasts the ethnic-racial situation in the United States, Mexico, Brazil, and South Africa—from the standpoint of sociobiology, in the specific sense of cultures appropriating biological traits of groups for purposes other than the presumed original evolutionarily intended purpose. For example, the genetic aspect of skin pigmentation being appropriated by the larger society in order to sustain and justify a particular social agenda, namely, that of enforcing the social domination over certain groups on the basis of phenotypical traits (1995: 365). Contrary to the earlier formulations by Freyre (e.g., 1933, 1951, 1990), Tannenbaum (1946), Pierson (1942/1967), and others, Van den Berghe contends, with other revisionist scholars, that qualitative differences across the ethnic-developmental backgrounds of the societies studied are not as significant as the fact that "important similarities of structure and historical evolution underlie the rather wide cultural differences between these countries" (1978: 37), and, therefore, racial prejudice and discrimination in countries like Brazil or Mexico have stood and operated historically as an independent pattern, as opposed to being epiphenomenal to the larger, general pattern of class stratification of the society. In a 1995 article in which he explores the application of sociobiology to the study of race and ethnicity, Van Den Berghe early on rejects the idea that his proposal for investigating "the interaction of genotypes and environments" calls for a prescription for a "rigid biological determinism" but, rather, invites the reader to consider the "linkages between biology and behavior . . . [the relationship between] genes and environment acting in concert."

Against Van den Berghe's culturalist and biologistic slant in the elucidation of race relation stands the work of South African–born British sociologist John Rex. His formative years in South Africa, and in particular his professional involvement with the South African Bantu Affairs Administration, expectedly instilled in him a keen academic interest in, and concern with, the question of race. He approached the latter, generally, from the standpoint of the classical Marxist emphasis on conflict, but in a stricter sense, from a neo-Marxist reconstruction of the idea of class formation and function. Rex departs from what he calls the "simple" (i.e., classical) model of Marxian social analysis (1983:xvi) by particularizing the discussion of class formation and development in terms of the geographically and historically specific structural circumstances shaping the interaction between dominant and minority classes in postcolonial societies.

Van den Berghe and Rex are in general agreement to the effect that *structural* factors exert a greater determining power over the racial dynamics of ethnically plural societies, but Rex devotes special attention to the interplay between the material and nonmaterial forces in the constitution of social life. As he puts it, his interest is in "the relationship between . . . mental elements, social action and interaction, and the social structure" (1983: 137). In fact, he even states that his studies of racism have been elaborated precisely with a view to "the role of ideas in everyday life" (1983: 139). Be that as it may, despite their interpretive divergences, Van den Berghe and Rex share overall, as have their peers over the decades, a greater concern with the determining power of structural forces, over normative or cultural ones, in the constitution of social reality and, by implication, of intergroup relations.

Overall, the foregoing discussion should suggest the emphasis placed by race-and-ethnicity theorists of the modern period on the stronger impact of structural, rather than cultural, factors, on the operation of racism and race-based inequality. A group of authors from the early modern period (cited in Rex, 1983) includes those who treat ethnic-racial inequality and minority status in reference to the class/caste scheme (e.g., Warner, 1936); as a particular version of the classical Marxist economic class antagonism (e.g., Cox, 1959); as a direct result of the relations of power between the racially dominant and nondominant groups of the society (e.g., Simpson and Yinger, 1965; Wagley and Harris, 1964); as something that starts at the point of contact between groups (Hughes and Hughes, 1952); and as a situation oriented and determined by socially prioritized roles and values (the classical Parsonian position; also Smith, 1965). Throughout the modern period and beyond, race-and-ethnicity research largely continued to emphasize the importance of macrosociological, or larger institutional (chiefly economic and political), forces operative in each national context, as the proper framework of explanation. This general tendency did not entirely disappear, in spite of the important analytical shifts occurring as the postmodern period rolled on.[3] On this issue, it is fitting to cite here a recent commentary to the effect that research on race relations has "often underlined the structural character of racism" (Staudigl, 2012: 36).

With this said, the postmodern era of the 1980s and 1990s also saw the flowering of other theoretical streams, such as cultural studies and critical race theory, which brought into sharper focus the role of nonstructural, or symbolic, factors, in the spheres of race and gender relations. It is to these more recent currents of thought in race research that we now turn.

CULTURAL STUDIES AND RACE

Cultural studies are an area of social inquiry that developed and expanded during the second half of the twentieth century, concomitantly with the rise of postmodernism. It is a broad-based, interdisciplinary, methodologically eclectic, and somewhat amorphous research orientation, something attributable to the fact that it developed out of the large-scale appropriation of materials and procedures from an array of fields of study, such as philosophy, sociology, anthropology, political science, linguistics, and literary criticism. In being coterminous with the postmodern movement, it also makes culture, as does postmodernism, the focal point of social analysis. The analytical starting point for culture is found in late nineteenth-century anthropology, as exemplified by the work of Frazer and Tylor. Early sociological thought in the United States also had a "profoundly cultural bent" (Long, 1997: 2–9), as evidenced in the work of writers like the Lynds, Park, Whyte, Becker, and Liebow. The scholarship of the American scholars was carried out in the intersection of sociology (strictly defined) and social anthropology, which enabled them to engage in a more holistic treatment of society and culture.

The cultural studies perspective expectedly makes culture the pivotal context for understanding social reality, with a direct focus on how cultural practices and arrangements are related to, and foster, social domination. This has been the central feature of this mode of inquiry as regards its adoption in the academic world proper, but also, and more pertinently, beyond the borders of academia. This means that its basic premises and concerns are brought to the broader political arena, in conjunction with the increasing representation of groups formerly marginalized from the society's political life, and with the society's effort to address, formally and informally, the grievances of these groups. Thus, culture, as a theme of research, "has replaced society as the general subject of inquiry among progressives" (Sardar and Van Loon, 1997: 3; see also Long, 1997: 1). The earliest cultural studies came out of England, dating from the years following the Second World War.

Clearly, too, these considerations reveal the political agenda—the critical and emancipatory thrust—of cultural studies, inasmuch as this particular interpretive orientation is invested in the project of social reconstruction, and seek to clarify how cultural arrangements and practices are related to power. To that end, it engages in the moral assessment and criticism of prevailing social institutions and practices by probing into their political genesis and dynamics from a cultural standpoint. Thus, in accordance with this methodology, the attack on race-based inequality and injustice must be undertaken via the understanding of how the relations of power between dominant and subordinate racial groups not only bear on, but also shape and maintain, discriminatory social practices and arrangements and, therefore, racial inequality.

In the context of race and ethnicity and, specifically, the operation of power, the confluence of postmodernism and cultural studies is readily ascertained in the fact that the cultural studies approach, like the postmodern approach as a whole, "sees power saturating everything, and often moves very quickly between large registers of social hierarchy (race, class, gender)" (Long, 1997: 7). Both stress the social grounding of knowledge claims and value orientations, and characterize the latter as resulting from historically specific power arrangements and hierarchies. Additionally, like postmodernism, cultural studies is marked by its particularizing mode, regarding its emphasis on the need for research on race relations to seek to identify and address the particular circumstances of each racial minority group or subgroup, the underlying assumption being that the life situation of members of each oppressed group is affected differently (from the situation of every other oppressed group) by the forces of the environing society. This clearly particularizes the nature of societal oppression not only in regard to its impact on racial groups versus all other social minorities but also across diverse racial minority groups. A number of variables figure into this equation, accounting for this variation: gender, race, class, age, sexual orientation, the group's specific historical and cultural background, and so on. Finally, reflecting the postmodern conception of culture, cultural studies treats it as "the entire range of a society's arts, beliefs, institutions, and communicative practices" (Grossberg, Nelson, and Treichler, 1992: 4).

The cultural studies approach shares some common ground with phenomenology in the sense of both approaches having a basic interest in directly experienced reality (the phenomenological *umwelt*), or the structures of the cultural world, and treating culture, as a driving and transformative force on everyday life and social relations. However, these two analytical frameworks diverge in that phenomenology generally understood, but particularly its classical (Husserlian) version, makes its central task to *describe* things as they appear and are experienced, and to focus special attention on consciousness. The cultural studies perspective, on the other hand, does not stop at the mere description of these things. Rather, it is invested in the project of social reconstruction and seeks to establish the connection between cultural practices and relations of power. This reveals its political thrust.

A *critical* phenomenology would, therefore, be required to exhibit the same concern, that is, while maintaining the same focus on consciousness and intersubjectivity, to investigate how the operation of intersubjectivity, such as (to use the phenomenological lexicon) related to the community's stock of knowledge and its correlative schemata of typifications, expresses the exercise of social power, as couched in established, institutionalized intergroup arrangements.

CRITICAL RACE THEORY AND PHENOMENOLOGY

Finally, we turn to the area where the bulk of the "phenomenology of race" scholarship has been elaborated over the last quarter-century, namely, the philosophical research area denominated critical race theory. It draws heavily on critical theory and, therefore, shows a critical orientation toward social reality, which distinguishes it from the earlier or canonical work in phenomenology, termed classical phenomenology. It is represented by the theoretical contributions of Husserl, Scheler, Heidegger, Schutz, Sartre, and Merleau-Ponty. The designation *classical phenomenology* apparently began to appear in the literature as a more formal designation in the 1980s (Welton and Silverman, cited in Salamon, 2018), so as to distinguish the early, pre–Second World War works from the growing number of phenomenological analyses oriented toward a critique of domination; in other words, from the nascent version of phenomenology now established as *critical* phenomenology (also named *political* phenomenology; see, e.g., Zeynep, 2017).

Critical race theory had its formal beginnings as a movement in legal studies, during the 1980s, but has, since that time, been practiced across different fields of scholarship. In much the same fashion as the feminist revisionist

project on gender, critical race theory has relied on the resources of the phenomenological canon to address various aspects of race and racism (see, e.g.,
the anthologies of Bernasconi, 2001, 2003a, 2003b; Lott and Ward, 2002).

Critical race theorists have dealt predominantly with nonstructural or nonmaterial (i.e., ethical, legal, cultural, ideological) aspects of race. However, a
general distinction may be established between those who tackle "structuralist" (i.e., sociological, anthropological) themes, such as, for instance, Dumont
(2001), Visweswaran (2001), and Sheth (2009), and those who deal more
directly with social meanings and attributions. In the latter group—the dominant camp in critical phenomenology—the pride of place must be granted to
Frantz Fanon's pioneering contribution in his 1952 publication of *Peau Noir,
Masques Blancs* (*Black Skin, White Masks,* 1967). Fanon dissects the idea of
race, racial identity, and the practice of racial injustice in ontological terms.
His background in psychoanalysis informed his social ontology and was
largely responsible for his employment of phenomenological ideas toward
an elaboration of the phenomenology of being *racialized.* In more recent
decades, one may mention, for example, the work of Bernasconi, who has
over the last couple of decades written extensively on race within philosophy,
and on its impact on philosophy, from both historical and theoretical perspectives (the edited works cited above; also, e.g., 2005, 2008, 2012a, 2012b); of
Appiah and Gutmann (1996), who deal with the interrelation of race, culture,
and identity; of Mills (1997, 1998), who looks at the connection between race
and social power by addressing the ontological and epistemological foundations of race relations; and Gordon (2002) who relies on the language of a
Sartrean existential phenomenology, specifically Sartre's idea of *bad faith,*
to address the problem of (what Gordon calls) anti-black racism. For Sartre,
the condition of bad faith reduces the person to pure Object—the *in-itself.*
Looked at from the perspective of dominant social groups, their reductionist
conception of subordinate-group members that these groups have is an exercise in bad faith and serves as a mechanism of social domination. Gordon
rejects the essentialism and reductionism of bad faith and postulates that
the interests of oppressed individuals are best served when they seek refuge
neither in being the overdetermined social Object nor in the absolutism of the
pure or transcendental Subject. Fundamentally, people make choices within
the parameters of *situations*—that is, within the space of social ascriptions,
such as their racial situation and racial status, but these choices can also be
swayed toward self-alienation (in a roughly parallel fashion to the case of bad
faith in Marxian terms, or *false consciousness*). What is incumbent upon the
minority persons involved is a transcendence of their social situation without
necessarily negating it, a *transcendence from within.*

The earliest instances of phenomenological thought being channeled toward
the critique of domination, as linked to substantive sociological problems, are

found in the middle of the twentieth century, when thinkers such as Jean-Paul Sartre, Simone de Beauvoir, and Frantz Fanon put forth critical investigations of human inequality based on race, ethnicity, and gender, at the level of existence. Maurice Merleau-Ponty, a philosopher from the same period, and of equally towering stature, has been widely used by critical philosophers in recent decades, but his work did not explicitly articulate a critique of social domination and inequality in the manner of the thinkers mentioned above. Rather, it addressed the "embodiment" or naturalization of subjectivity—that is, the body as the focal point of analysis (the idea of the body-subject, or *corps propre*) in relation to the self, other fellow human beings, and nature.[4] Sartre, on the other hand, penned essays that were directly oriented to the question of race and racism, from a phenomenological-existential standpoint (e.g., *Réflexion sur la question juive* [1944], *Orphée Noir* [1948/1964–65], and the 1940s newspaper articles *Le Problème Noir aux États-Unis* and *Ce que J'ai Appris du Problème Noir*). Simone de Beauvoir, with her landmark work *Le Deuxième Sexe* (*The Second Sex*, 1949), focused on human inequality based on biological sex status and examined the ill effects of patriarchy over the social condition and the selfhood of women.

Some additional considerations on Fanon. His work has arguably been the most sought-after source of inspiration for critical phenomenologists of the current period when they address issues of race, ethnicity, gender, or sexuality. One writer (Staudigl, 2012: 30) characterizes him as a pioneer in the phenomenological critique of race, a reasonable characterization given the time and circumstances in which Fanon produced his work. Earlier phenomenologists in the classical tradition (Husserl, Heidegger, Merleau-Ponty) had dealt with inequality, but in more general terms, that is, they sought to explicate inequality *as such*. Sartre, for instance, examined the antinomies of human existence (e.g., the relation between *being* and *nothingness*), and Merleau-Ponty looked at the body-consciousness relation. (Sartre's theoretical interests, however, as indicated above, also reached substantive areas of social life like race and ethnicity, as evidenced in his essays on race and ethnicity. In fact, he is generally considered to have inaugurated the phenomenological discourse on *négritude* and race-based inequality proper.) Fanon, in contradistinction to the canonical writers in phenomenology, was fundamentally invested in the critique of race-based oppression, and he drew on psychoanalytic and phenomenological theory to accomplish that task. More precisely, he explored the dominance of "white" European colonizers over "nonwhite" non-European populations, and the damaging psychological effect this process had on the selfhood of the colonized.

The thrust of Fanon's critical phenomenology was his desire to expose, which he did in the most compelling fashion, the way in which colonialism locks the colonized nonwhites into the *otherness* of racial difference. This obviously does not involve a racial difference in a strictly and neutrally descriptive sense (as has been noted; Macey, 1999), such as in being simply *un homme noir*, or a *gens de couleur* vs. *un homme blanc*—a distinction of skin color which would apply to himself as a Martinican, and to the majority of the people in the French and British West Indies. As he explains it, racialized black people are perpetually locked into the otherness of being the socially constructed *nègre*, this human type that emerged in the course of the last three centuries, the child of colonialism, which came to serve as the pivotal element of the ideological defense of colonialism. More precisely, colonialism was invariably justified by its practitioners in reference to the latter's assumption of the innate social, moral, cognitive, emotional inferiority of the colonized nonwhite populations—in Fanon's discourse, of the *nègres*—of their barbarism, their infantile dependency, their moral deficiency, their unfitness for freedom, which thus legitimized their life under European tutelage. Being a *nègre*, therefore, expressed racial essence, and a perpetual prison.[5] Seen from this angle, colonialism strikes at the very ontological foundation of the colonized. It reconstructs their identity from the outside, in a way that produces their de-personalization, the obliteration of their Self, their placement into "a zone of nonbeing" (Fanon, 1967: 8).

This phenomenon described by Fanon was common to practically all natives of the West Indian island societies, where the populations are predominantly formed by people of African extraction. It has been the case that people from these regions who have migrated to countries in North America or Europe have been confronted with a revision of their basic status and identity—that is, there is a shift from their dominant conception of themselves as members of a particular *ethnic* group (e.g., I am Cuban, I am Martinican), to a new dominant status and identity imposed by the host society, which is that of being irrevocably transformed into a member of a particular *racial* group (i.e., I am black). The social construction of the subordinate element in pluralist, multiethnic settings is a well-recognized phenomenon. It shores up and perpetuates power inequality between the hegemonic and subordinate racial groups. Typically, institutional processes together with cultural norms and expectations lead members of both groups to reaffirm and thus maintain this type of minority identity in everyday life, which in turn strengthens the privileged position and sense of superiority of the dominant group.[6]

Fanon attempts to unveil the operation of meanings and other subjective processes triggered by the experience of colonization, and their effect on the consciousness of colonized persons as they seek to build an identity. His interpretations apply to colonialism in the general sense, that is, to its historical operation anywhere in the world, including geographical settings where racial considerations would not have been a factor (e.g., the eighth-century Viking invasion and colonization of northern England). However, they are especially pertinent to the present study because they address the dominance of a European group over populations codified as nonwhite—in this case, West Indian people of African extraction. They treat, as the focal point, the structure of the postcolonial self, and its dysfunctional aspects, stemming from the corrosive legacy of colonialism. In this respect, Fanon looks at the process of self-alienation—in other words, how former colonials are dehumanized as they embrace an identity construed and imposed on them by the colonial power, which negates their fundamental autonomy as persons. The denial of the colonized self by this imposed identity is achieved through the assignment of *otherness* to it—otherness manifested as racial otherness—at the same time that *white masks* are adopted by those who are depersonalized in this way. He says, in connection with this, that "white civilization and European culture have forced an existential deviation on the Negro" (1967: 14). (The story of the colonization of West Indians is yet another historical instance and theoretical problem that implicitly, or perhaps not quite so implicitly, direct our attention to the anthropological question of assimilation, its forms and degrees, versus pluralism.)

In the last quarter-century or so, a new generation of scholars, writing mainly from a feminist and phenomenological perspective, have drawn on the standard texts of classical phenomenology in order to address the dynamics of power in society in the context of the intersectionality of gender, sexuality, ethnicity, and race. This has been done, for example, from the standpoint of the alterity (*otherness*) of color, whiteness/nonwhiteness in reference to corporeality and social meaning (e.g., Ahmed, 2007); of corporeality and social identity (Salamon, 2010); of the notion of multiple selfhood, the simultaneous existence of racialized or genderized persons in the spaces between various identities (Ortega, 2016); of race and colonialism, temporality, and the problematic nature of the *vision racialisante* (Al-Saji, 2017); of the idea of whiteness as property (Guenther, cited in Salamon, 2018); and so on.

We will now briefly consider the work of two other phenomenological writers, Michael Barber and Michael Staudigl (2012), who concentrated more directly on race and (anti-black) racism. Barber (2001) appeals to Schutz's because-motive formulation in order to clarify the redeeming quality and emancipatory potential of an amnestically retrieved, socially construed, and determined minority identity—that is, blackness or *négritude*. In this perceptive analysis Sartre's positive treatment of *negritude* in *Orphée Noir* is analyzed as not having necessarily been a defense of racial essentialism (and all of its mystifying aspects), but, rather, an attempt to show the social and psychological value, for oppressed black populations, of the idea of *négritude*. The main argument has it that the harmful effects of racism on its victims (e.g., their negatively constructed self, which is internalized through the process of socialization) can in fact be countered by the affirmation of their *otherness*—that is, of blackness, inasmuch as this emphatic, even enthusiastic, affirmation of their selfhood, as constructed by the society, bears the quality of resistance and the promise of liberation. That is to say, the anamnestic recovery of the group racial "soul," so to speak, has an emancipatory potential and serves moral purposes, but, as this author notes, it contradicts "scientific verities," or the objective (scientific) accounts of race and ethnicity, which act as a corrective to it. The latter, it is argued (2001: 101), "will never replace" the former. This is a complex issue, that of the minority group reaching empowerment by turning negative societal attributions around, and using them as a basis for the consolidation of group identity, cultural life, and more effective social representation—that is, making the best of a bad situation. Certainly, it is difficult to dismiss the social, political, and psychological benefits that the minority group may gain from assertively embracing the collective minority identity, as generated by the society-at-large. On the other hand, some analysts (e.g., Franklin, 1997) have issued *caveats* on this issue, warning against the dangers of the crystallization of the minority identity and status.[7] For now, and given the frame and orientation of this study, it should suffice to simply point to the double-edged-sword aspect of this situation.

Staudigl (2012) presents a characterization of racism as a phenomenon of "negative sociality," which means that, rather than being something contingent or random, the product of some random "deficiency" or malfunction of institutional structures, it results from the normal operation of the social system itself—this "negativity" becomes, in fact, a functional requirement for the operation of the system, thus playing "a constitutive role for the accomplishment of the social order" (2012: 25–26). Negative sociality is thus inculcated in individuals through the regular mechanisms of socialization, as part of how the larger system normally operates.

In sum, and concerning the issue of the potential critical orientation of phenomenology, some analysts (e.g., Salamon, 2018) have proposed that this orientation is *already present*—that is, it is inherent, in phenomenological practice, or in its description of what is observed, and therefore, the work of description and that of critique are not mutually exclusive but rather, integrated. Phenomenological description is therefore, in and of itself, a critical practice from this standpoint. It reveals reality on a level deep enough to allow us to see, to make evident, what is already empirically visible to us, but because it is "so close, so immediate, so intimately linked to us . . . we do not perceive it. Whereas the role of science is to reveal what we do not see, the role of philosophy is to let us see what we see" (Foucault, quoted in Salamon, 2018: 12–14).

The specifically phenomenological manifestation of philosophy, as employed by the aforementioned writers, constitutes, in any case, a phenomenological practice that explicitly transcends the boundaries of pure description and advances toward a questioning of existing conditions, thus addressing the relation between the lived experience of individuals and historically established power arrangements. In other words, it amounts to a critical phenomenology. Such an approach reaches deeper than empirical ones in excavating and explicating the meaning of social action, the *meaning-structure* of the social world. This is the task to which phenomenology devotes itself: a *radical* analysis of meaning, reaching the latter's roots and genetic development.

THE SCHUTZIAN TURN IN CRITICAL PHENOMENOLOGICAL DISCOURSE

Sociological interpretation, according to Mannheim, is valuable because it allows us to go beyond the level of immanent, or intrinsic, understanding and explanation of reality, by engaging in the extrinsic analysis of it. This in turn will enable us to identify "those meaningful existential presuppositions" that remain inevitably beyond the reach of intrinsic interpretation (Wolff, Introduction, in Mannheim, 1971: xiii). This general principle does not apply to positivistic sociology, which occupies itself mainly with "quantitatively-determined functional correlations," but to interpretive sociology, such as elaborated in the present study, a phenomenological analysis of a concrete sociological problem.

Sociology addresses society in its manifold aspects as its primary subject-matter, but must do so with clarity and precision, not to be obtained, in this case, from empirical thinking, but from philosophy. The benefits from this collaborative relation are mutual. Sociologists, says Ferguson (2006: 1) in very effective terms, "must concern themselves with [some] philosophy if they are to produce incisive *sociology*; and philosophers have to attend to [some] sociology, if they are to realize the promise of *philosophy*."

It is in association with philosophical thought that the study of inequality and power in society is addressed here, in the particular sphere of race relations. The research on race and ethnicity of the last half-century has been reviewed above, including the recent scholarship in the critical phenomenology of race, which relies heavily on the work of the canonical writers. This study draws more directly on the social phenomenology of Alfred Schutz. Schutzian phenomenology constitutes an elaboration on Husserl's principal theoretical ideas applied to the study of the social world, but it eschews Husserl's monadic position, according to which the construction of reality is elaborated in the individual consciousness—the pure consciousness—in conformity with the latter's formal and invariant properties. In other words, Husserl's emphasis on the centrality of pure or transcendental reality, and the bracketing of concrete reality, and Schutz's focus precisely on this mundane reality, on the world of everyday life, do not go together. Schutz places much greater emphasis on the *social* construction of reality, to the effect that the circumstances of group life—the intersubjectively shared web of (behavioral, linguistic, interpretive) *typifications* that make up the *stock-of-knowledge-at-hand* of society's members—structure our relationships with others, and form the world of everyday life, the *lifeworld*. (The conceptual architecture of Schutz's work will be discussed in the next chapter.)

Schutz's social phenomenology, as Wagner (in Psathas, 1973: 84–85) maintains, lends itself well to the analysis of "all levels of sociological concerns and can cover the scope of sociological problem areas." This means that it reaches into not just the more conventional areas of social-psychological concern, which have to do with intersubjective relations, questions of meaning and identity, and so forth, but also the substantive areas and problems of the social world, those larger and pressing problems that demand immediate attention. Schutz remarks that phenomenology *qua* methodological approach can be utilized "with the greatest success within the empirical sphere," but it must be kept in mind that the primary interest of the phenomenological researcher is not in the empirical object of study itself, but in its *meaning*, "as it is constituted by the activities of our mind" (1945a: 92, 94). The meaning of social phenomena is to be found in the context of ideal-typical action grounded in "varying degrees of anonymity" (1997: 9), by seeking its roots in the "fundamental facts of conscious life"—which is to say, in the realm of consciousness and intersubjectivity. It is up to the researcher, therefore, who wishes to provide fresh insight into group-based inequality, to utilize in an effective way the heuristic potential of social phenomenology toward that goal. In basic terms, the standpoint of this investigative approach is that the object of study—in the specific case of this analysis, race and ethnic relations—which is a phenomenon of the *social* world—cannot be treated, as is normally the case, as if it were a phenomenon of the *physical* world, causally determined by physical events. Whereas the occurrence of natural phenomena (e.g., why rain falls) can be understood only in reference to certain regularities ("laws") that have been established as the foundation and driving principle behind everything that happens in nature, where the social world is concerned we aim at a deeper understanding of it, which can be attained only by concentrating on "the categories of human action," namely, human motives, means and ends, deliberation, and planning (Schutz, 1970: 110).

Schutz focuses particular attention on the aspect of meaning and motives in his explanation of social life. More specifically, he distinguishes between the objective and subjective meanings of things, and between the types of motives that drive human action, which he classifies as *because-motives* and *in-order-to-motives*. The because-motives, in particular, will have paramount importance in the present analysis because, as will be explained later in greater depth, they ultimately have to do with the constitution of the Self, as informed by the person's historical background. In the context of dominant/ minority race relations, the temporal flow and effect of society's typifications—its dominant meanings and practices, taken for granted by social actors—not only account for the constitution of the self of individuals but also, in the case of racialized minority persons, may bring upon them very deleterious consequences. As such, these concepts will be the cornerstone underlying this project, which involves the way race-based inequality impacts on the consciousness of racialized individuals, and affects their lives (Schutz, 1997; Schutz and Luckmann, 1973, 1989; see also, e.g., Swingewood, 1993: ch. 9; Münch, 1994: 145–149).

Finally, the resources of Schutz's social phenomenology will be channeled in this project toward a critique of social domination, in reference to the domain of race and ethnic relations. Consonant with the phenomenological approach, Schutz's description of the dynamics of social relations reaches unparalleled completeness and acuity of detail, but this study aims to expand the descriptive project by applying his ideas to the critical discourse on intergroup (race-based) inequality. Schutzian analysis has often been said to suffer from a lack of political sensitivity, as it describes everyday life and its operation through a complex of typified patterns of behavior and thought. Some phenomenological analyses (e.g., Lengermann and Niebrugge, 1995; Camara, 2014) have addressed this issue and attempted to fill this lacuna by identifying the connections between typifications and social power.

NOTES

1. With reference to Great Britain, this took the form of the Windrush Generation migration, as noted earlier, resulting in a large-scale demographic shift that added massively to the ethnic-racial diversification of the English population, thus in turn reviving the consciousness of race and its vital relevance for social organization in that society.

2. The replacement of the postmodern focus on broad binary oppositions in intergroup life, which tend to bypass the particular concerns of particular segments within the larger minority group or community, with the endless postmodern fragmentation of the minority community into subgroups, is very problematic. In time this turns into a case of *ad infinitum* subcultural differentiation of the minority group, which in turn tends to create tensions and rifts among the multiple minority subgroups. Under such circumstances, it is likely that the main concern(s) of the minority group may shift progressively away from the source of their oppression (e.g., institutional racism, patriarchy), and toward the bureaucratic organization of the minority subgroups—that is, away from a direct focus on the integration of the group's resources to combat the

source of harm to the minority segments (e.g., racism, sexism), and toward the question of who belongs properly to which minority subgroup, of working out the proper agenda for each specific subgroup, and so on. Ultimately, this may dull the sensitivity of the minority collectivity to their great commonizing factor, that is, their collective victimization by racism or sexism (or some other social criterion), and to the priorities to be addressed as they struggle for emancipation.

3. This trend may be evidenced in the work of a considerable number of authors who have turned their attention to the historical background of minority ethnic groups, their experience of structural assimilation, the concrete effects of institutional discrimination against each minority group (e.g., Burkey, 1978; Feagin and Feagin, 1993); the application of economicist frameworks of explanation to the problematic of race (e.g., Banton, 1983); remediation strategies for dealing with the various levels of impairment caused by institutionalized discrimination (e.g., Ezorsky, 1991; Guimarães, 1999); or contrasts in the ethnic developmental history of different multi-ethnic societies (e.g., Yetman and Steele, 1975; Marger; 1991; van den Berghe, 1995; Schafer, 1996).

4. Maurice Merleau-Ponty's phenomenological approach, which is deeply informed by Husserl and Heidegger, cannot be left out from this basic list of early influences, but his position differs fundamentally from that of Fanon and Beauvoir. Merleau-Ponty's phenomenology of perception presents *the body* and its sensorial apprehension of the world, rather than consciousness, as the primary site of knowing the world. This means the privileging of sensorial perception as the main avenue to the understanding of reality versus what he considered to be the "intellectualism" that has historically prevailed in Western culture—specifically, the monolithic dominance of consciousness as the source of truth, a phenomenon traceable to the ideas of Plato and Descartes. He favors instead a more primordial, "pre-intellectual" position for understanding the world and reaching truth about reality, because the latter is given to us directly, through the senses. This standpoint diverges from the phenomenological orientation favored in the present analysis.

5. We will retain the French here, since the English equivalent "a black man" is more of a descriptive term, and does not convey the special ontological dimension contained in the French, as used by Fanon.

6. Genovese informs us that planters in the U.S. South during slavery times normally discouraged their slaves from learning and speaking good English. The expectation was that bondsmen speak the slave dialect, and they were actually punished if they did otherwise. The explanation here was that the cultural marginalization of the Africans reinforced their servile status.

7. Franklin (1997: 18) stresses how the preservation ad infinitum of the minority status in U.S. society turned into the very source of imprisonment for minority ethnic communities. As he states it, "The ethnic grouping that was a way-station, a temporary resting place for Europeans as they became American, proved to be a terminal for blacks who found it virtually impossible to become American in any real sense."

Chapter 3

The Foundations of Alfred Schutz's Social Phenomenology

We begin with Alfred Schutz the scholar. He is known for his pioneering studies and insights in social phenomenology—the phenomenology of the *lifeworld* (*lebenswelt*), or the world of daily experience. A scholar of broad intellectual interests and endeavors, Schutz became thoroughly grounded in international law, philosophy, political science, and economics at the University of Vienna in the years following the First World War. During that time as well, he developed a strong interest in music, as both practitioner and theoretician; but his writings on the phenomenology of music are contained in only four essays, covering the period from just before the Second World War to the 1950s (Skarda, 1979).

His illustrious academic career as a philosopher of social science started when he was in his early thirties, with his magisterial work *The Phenomenology of the Social World* (*Der Sinnhafte Aufbau der Sozialen Welt*, 1932), produced as an effort to go beyond Max Weber's sociology of understanding, specifically Weber's subjective theory of action, which Schutz found to have significant problems in its treatment of meaning. In the larger and more fundamental sense, Schutz's intent with the *Phenomenology* was to establish a philosophical foundation for the sciences of society. This work, widely acknowledged to be his *magnum opus*, combines Husserl's transcendental phenomenology as a point of departure, the philosophical vitalism of Henri Bergson, specifically his concept of *durée* (i.e., duration, or inner time), and the influence of William James's notion of *stream of consciousness*.[1]

The early development of Schutzian phenomenology in the first part of the twentieth century coincided with the steady expansion of the field of sociology and other social sciences, and both events were fundamentally related to the *methodenstreit*,[2] the intense late 1800s interdisciplinary debate in the German-speaking academic world, which revolved around the important question of what should be the proper boundaries, aims, and methodology for the social sciences. This debate raged long and intensely, well into the 1900s, and its impact spread beyond the borders of German *academia*. To a significant extent, it still finds resonance in the present time, in the activity and thinking of academicians in the human sciences everywhere in the Western world.

Schutz's phenomenological account of the structure of social life directs our attention to the world of intersubjectivity, and starts, as noted, from the concept of the *world of everyday life*, which is treated as an *interpreted reality* (Ferguson, 2001: 243). This conception of social life implies that, in the project of understanding and explaining social life, the greatest attention is deserved by cultural structures, specifically as concerns aspects of consciousness and the world of meaning within which social actors engage in direct, face-to-face relationships with one another. In this respect, Schutz's work is closely aligned with the larger tradition in the German-speaking world of *verstehende*, or interpretive social thought (Berard, 2010: 129; Staudigl and Berguno, 2014),[3] in particular with the work of Max Weber. This orientation is also represented by the work of such German scholars as Ferdinand Toennies, Wilhelm Dilthey, Johann Gustav Droysen, Heinrich Rickert, Georg Simmel, and Werner Sombart.

The emphasis placed by Schutz's phenomenology on the subject of consciousness and intersubjectivity, as the logical framework for explicating the meaning-structure of the social world, means that this is an attempt to explicate culture in its own terms, rather than in the reductionist terms of its socio-structural origins, or as an epiphenomenon or collateral product of structural factors. The focus on culture, with special reference to aspects of meaning and intersubjectivity, is of first importance here not only because, in a more general sense, it draws our attention to the underlying reasons why structural arrangements persist over time, but also because, for the particular purposes of this study, it sheds critical light on the operation of power inequality between majority and minority (racial and/or ethnic) groups. The insights of Schutz's social phenomenology should be valuable in this connection, insofar as they reveal and call into question the presuppositions, foundational ideas, that actors have about their life in the social world. As Zaner (Introduction, in Schutz, 1970c: xii) puts it, this investigative approach is characterized by "the effort to make explicit precisely what is implicit and taken for granted by the very nature of commonsense life- to make its foundational presuppositions explicit for the sake of disclosing its structures, analyzing its strata, revealing its interconnected textures."

The present analysis will attempt to show his this strategy lays bare dimensions of intergroup inequality that are normally bypassed in the conventional literature.

Schutz's impact on and contribution to the development of phenomenological research in philosophy and sociology in the United States has been monumental. In this respect he embodies the model of the philosopher-sociologist *par excellence*, in that he contributed perhaps more than any other social thinker to the bridging of the sociological and phenomenological traditions, not only in terms of utilizing the resources of phenomenology to open up alternative avenues of thinking for sociologists, but also, and more importantly, as indicated above, to build a philosophical foundation for the social sciences.

Schutz expanded the Husserlian formulation of a transcendental phenomenology by converting it into a phenomenology of the social world. Thus, Schutz's version is not solipsistic, as would be the case with Husserl's, but advances beyond what Husserl himself referred to as his monadological phenomenology (reflecting Leibniz's influence; on this point, see Altobrando, 2015) to become a theory of *inter*-subjectivity. As Wagner (*in* Psathas, 1973: 66) expresses it, "The individual is linked to a social world transcending the spheres of his own activities and his direct acquaintances with others," a world mediated through the objective element of language and all of its typified aspects and features." To that, Gurwitsch adds that subjective meaning arises "out of the total contexture of our experience of social reality and our life within it" (1962:68), a statement that unquestionably underscores the influence of culture on social action.

Schutz and Weber are of the same mind regarding the idea that the social world can be comprehended only "in an ideal-typical way" (see Schutz's comments on this issue, 1997: 226), but they part company when Schutz characterizes Weber as not caring sufficiently to embark on a deep analysis of the meaning-structure of his own concepts, such as, for instance, *meaningful behavior*. Therefore, Schutz attempted to overcome Weber's more superficial treatment of subjective meaning by incorporating and systematically examining the temporality or historicity of meaning, by taking into account its genesis and development in the mental life of the social actor. This involved looking at meaning from the point when it emerges initially, as the actor engages in a particular course of action—the moment of action-in-progress (*Action*), to the point of the completion of the action (the *Act*). Other related aspects of meaning operative at the level of intersubjectivity remain unexplored by Weber, and Schutz insists that those too are essential and need to be included in a comprehensive investigation of the question of meaning in the social sciences (1997: 6).[4]

THE EPISTEMOLOGICAL LIMITATIONS
OF TRADITIONAL SOCIAL SCIENCE

The phenomenological critique of the shortcomings of traditional empirico-quantitative social science is extremely cogent and, ultimately, leads us to wonder whether social action at its core can be truly understood through traditional approaches of research. As one analyst (Walsh, in Schutz, 1997:xv) put it, we are faced with the fundamental question "of whether and to what extent the social sciences can provide us with a genuine understanding of human beings." The problem at hand has mainly to do with the fact that the traditional scientific approach reduces human experience to only that which can be observed "scientifically," and measured quantitatively, while the intersubjectivity of thought and action of actors in the social world is simply taken for granted. The result is a mass of data that is basically abstracted from human social life, amounting to what Schutz called "a kind of intellectual shorthand" (1970b: 110), something disconnected from "social reality as experienced by men in everyday life" (Schutz, 1970a: 11–12). The different aspects of intergroup life—cultural symbols and meanings and their sharedness by the members of society, language and all other communicative practices, the society's conceptual *armamentarium*, the existence and operation of institutions in the social world—the existence of all of these things is acknowledged, but treated as natural and unproblematic. This generalized tendency reaches, in fact, even into the versions of sociology (and social science in general) that favor qualitative thinking and research orientations, such as the so-called sociologies of everyday life (e.g., symbolic interactionism). Yet, the fundamental questions about the underlying processes of consciousness—namely, how meaning emerges; the nature of intentionality and how it operates; how social actors are motivated into particular courses of action, and so forth—remain unanswered. Schutz addresses this problem thusly:

> How does it happen that mutual understanding and communication are possible at all? How is it possible that man accomplishes meaningful acts, purposively or habitually, that he is guided by ends to be attained and motivated by certain experiences? Do not the concepts of meaning, of motives, of ends, of acts, refer to a certain structure of consciousness; a certain arrangement of all the experiences in inner time, a certain type of sedimentation? And does not interpretation of the other's meaning and of the meaning of his acts and the results of these acts presuppose a self-interpretation of the observer or partner? How can I, in my attitude as a man among other men or as a social scientist, find an approach to all this if not by recourse to a stock of pre-interpreted experiences built up by sedimentation within my own conscious life? And how can methods for interpreting

the social interrelationship be warranted if they are not based upon a careful description of the underlying assumptions and their implications? These questions cannot be answered by the methods of the social sciences. They require a philosophical analysis. And phenomenology—not only what Husserl called phenomenological philosophy but even phenomenological psychology—has not only opened an avenue of approach for such an analysis but has in addition started the analysis itself. (1945: 96–97; see also Habermas, 1989: ch. 3)

In more substantive terms, the unswerving adoption on quantitative methodologies has had a particular effect on the analysis of intergroup relations, such as based on race and ethnic status. Over the last several decades, the reliance on racially binary assumptions and conceptual schemes has systematically characterized investigations in this area, resulting in an analytical reductionism that levels the interethnic experience and presents its cross-national variations in strictly quantitative terms. This quantitative or statistical lens may be deceiving, insofar as it typically fails to reveal the day-to-day existence of groups and the meaning-structure of social behavior, only allowing for the apprehension of the variations between polyethnic systems in terms of *more or less*—that is, of evaluating the nature of these variations in terms of the extent to which they correspond to a given dominant national model of interethnic life. Moreover, this statistical model of measurement normally comes together with the imposition of a particular analytical-conceptual scheme as a *lingua franca* for the study of societies with the *most diverse* interethnic configurations. Such an approach constitutes a form of authoritarian epistemology, a cultural colonialism through which the historical and structural particularity of each multiethnic society is summarily ignored. The present analysis aims to challenge this pervasive orientation.

The foregoing considerations should underscore the idea that the social world cannot be studied through the application of the same investigative methods as those of the natural sciences. In fact, it must be studied by recourse to a methodology whose particular devices are "foreign to the natural sciences" (Schutz, 1970a: 11). Our intent here is not to engage in an extensive analysis of the methodological issues surrounding the investigation of social phenomena, for this would surpass the frame and purpose of this project, but to place into relief the heuristic fruitfulness of phenomenology, on two interrelated levels: the first, in terms of showing the great importance of symbolic material for grasping the dynamics of social action, and how this symbolic material is primarily grounded in intersubjectivity. The second, more directly pertinent to the substantive social issue addressed here (namely race and ethnic relations) in terms of highlighting the fact that the structures of consciousness of subjects are formed *contextually*, which means in reference to the particular life experience of the subjects involved. Some very important implications for the nature of intergroup life flow from this idea. In this regard, Schutz considers all these phenomena of consciousness (meanings, motives, ends, acts) to be "a certain type of sedimentation," resulting from the life experience of social actors. Again, this reaffirms the principle that the workings of consciousness, the mental life of individuals, rest on the accumulation of cultural material—norms, definitions, prescriptions, values, and so on, which is passed on to them and internalized by them via the process of socialization. This in turn conditions how they understand their world of experience, conduct their relations with others, formulate courses of action, and so forth.

Writing in the same vein, Zaner (in Psathas, 1973: 41) stresses the cardinal importance of the phenomenological standpoint for probing the social world for its fullest significance. "If we would understand the social world," he says, "it is to the social world itself that we must turn for instruction, for our clues to develop our hypotheses and theories, as well as our sundry lines of activism and direction for social change." Our common life in society—in the lived world—and all of its manifold aspects must always be the focal point of social research. These constitutive aspects of our lived experience, in fact, "*all forms* (emphasis mine) of the social world"—such as, in the present analysis, the concrete case of race relations—can and should be investigated, as Tymieniecka has put it (1962: 107), "within the framework of the constitutive investigation of the lived-world."

Social analysts would be in general agreement on this last point, although they might also find it too general—that is, the question might still be raised as to what specific aspect of the social world should be focused on, and through what specific methods of analysis. Schutz clarifies this issue by first drawing our attention to the fundamental distinction between the natural world and the social world, which is that the study of the latter cannot be handled as if it were the study of the former, because natural phenomena are not driven by meaning, whereas social phenomena are. Meaning, therefore, becomes the primary *locus* of the distinction, and the necessary focus of analysis. In his words:

> [In the natural sphere] we collect facts and regularities which are not understandable to us, but which can only refer to certain fundamental assumptions about the world. We shall never understand why the mercury in the thermometer rises if the sun shines on it. We can only interpret this phenomenon as compatible with the laws we have deduced from some basic assumption about the world. Social phenomena, on the contrary, we want to understand and we cannot understand them otherwise than within the scheme of human motives, human means and ends, human planning—in short—within the categories of human action. (1970b: 110)

The implications of this idea, namely, the crucial importance of the world of *meaning* for understanding what goes on in society, for the analysis of race and ethnic relations should be quite obvious, as noted above. It comes down to the question of whether the larger social community under observation has been historically organized on the basis of institutionalized integration or separatism. The contact between members of racial and ethnic groups whose lives may have been linked to separate meaning systems on account of their having lived in separate and different cultural spaces within the same national community will likely be accompanied by problems of communication, compromise, harmonization of group interests, or even more serious problems of intergroup life.

Schutz's exploration of what makes social interaction possible clearly suggests, first, that the social scientist must see himself or herself as a fellow human being with a consciousness formed like that of other persons, since it is the product of accumulated living experiences with other beings like himself or herself; and secondly, that the partners in the social encounter will have the ability to grasp the meaning of the Other's conduct, or engage in what Mead termed *taking the role of the Other*, which presupposes their sharing a common cultural experience. Given this, Schutzian phenomenology stands in sharp contrast to the premises and *modus operandi* of conventional science, which treats human subjects as *objects*, whereas phenomenological inquiry starts from the idea that human beings in the social world relate to their fellow humans as *subjects*, that is, as other beings like themselves, with whom interaction—what Habermas construes as the "communicative experience" (1989: 106)—is carried out on the basis of *shared meanings and perspectives*. Therefore, they must be studied as such. The process of interaction takes place at the level of intersubjectivity, which requires, methodologically, that the investigative effort be directed to what is going on in that domain, or, phrased differently, that it be directed to how social actors interpret their social experience, to the complex of meaning that guides their behavior in the world of experience. In connection with this, the researcher develops scientific constructs of the common-sense constructs, which represent "a structure of intelligible intentional meanings" (Schutz, 1997: 7) developed by the subjects under study.

The task of interpreting how others interpret the world becomes a double-hermeneutical exercise, whereby the interpretive effort is carried out on two levels: the level associated with the first-order constructs, or the interpretations that social actors bestow on their world of experience, and the level associated with the second-order constructs, or the interpretation on the part of the social analyst of the common-sense interpretations of the subjects under study.[5] This satisfies methodological requirements, and constitutes an objective (scientific) account of "typical subjective processes of personal ideal types" (Schutz, 1997: 224).

THE MOTIVATION ASPECT

The ideal-typical interpretation of the social world presupposes the methodological correctness or adequacy of the ideal types used—that is, they should have been constructed in such a way as to receive "positive verification," in terms of being "both adequate on the level of meaning and causally adequate," which means consistent with past experience (i.e., the verification procedure of traditional science), and with the researcher's overall ideal-typical construction of the subject (individual or collective subject) under observation (Schutz, 1997: 228, 231–232). An example should be useful. Rivaldo, the young man from Recife, is on his way, one summer afternoon, to visit his aunt Tarcila who lives in the Espinheiro neighborhood, and expects that she will serve him guava paste with a slice of cheese when he arrives. He knows from experience, and from his knowledge of the historical custom and expectation in his community and part of the country, that visitors are typically served a plate of sweets or some other snack dish when they arrive, and he himself has had this experience several times in the past. His aunt, for her part, expects that her nephew will likely stop by to visit with her, given that she learned that he would be in the neighborhood, and he has engaged in that behavior (i.e., he has visited her) every time he is in the area where she lives. This pertains to the causal adequacy of this course-of-action pattern, insofar as the social actors involved are gifted with consciousness (and thus have internalized the community's rules and expectations for behavior in this particular situation), and will likely interact in this fashion again and again, thus maintaining this pattern of repeatability over time.[6] They are, in Schutz's lexicon, *homunculi* or *puppets*, meaning, typified social actors to whom particular motives, goals, and so forth—"systems of relevance"—are imputed, by the social scientist (Schutz, 1970a: 17). These typified social actors all share and have access to the society's complex of traditional, standardized customs and practices. The young man in question here expects that his brief visit with his aunt will have a particular meaning for her, namely, that of a nephew who is visiting, and therefore will be met with a set of typical behaviors on her part, including the serving of a snack. She will in turn interpret his action as a nice gesture on his part (i.e., being attentive to her, mindful of the social obligations attached to his nephew role, etc.).

In Schutzian terms, when one discusses the motivational context that drives social action, one is talking about a two-pronged force. The motive (i.e., the "motivational context") behind the social action is the actor's expectation that her or his action-in-progress will be eventually completed in the Act. For the young man in the example above, the action-in-progress involves his traveling on the bus to the area of the city where his aunt lives. He intends to visit her, and have a pleasant get-together with her, enjoying some conversation and sweetmeats. The enjoyment of this snack in her company is the completed Act, which, in the actor's consciousness, is projected or anticipated to occur in the future. The projected or phantasied completed Act, which imparts to the action-in-progress its orientation, is the actor's *in-order-to motive* (Schutz, 1997: 88), which, as suggested, is oriented to the future. The *because-motive* is oriented to *the past*, to some specific reason that accounts for the action—as in, for example, Rivaldo went to visit his aunt because he is interested in being seen by her as a family-minded, considerate, friendly nephew. There is a background to draw from, and be oriented by, namely, his earliest years, back to the time when there began to operate in his consciousness the recognition of his role as a member of the family, and a nephew to his aunt. Schutz characterizes this latter type of motive as the true explanation of the action, in the sense that it explains his action in terms of a larger context of his life history, his biography, as a nephew and member of the family. So, the two motives, as discussed here, appear to be distinct from each other—that is, the because-motive in this example is a "genuine" *because-motive*; as such, it is distinct, therefore not interchangeable with the *in-order-to-motive* (Schutz, 1997: 91), even though they form a unity. They are two sides of the same motivational coin, so to speak. One is oriented to the action project as such—as in the example just provided, in relation to which the meaning-context of the action is linked to the projected or anticipated situation, namely, the meeting between Rivaldo and his aunt Tarcila. The other is oriented to the actors' history or past experiences, the latter being temporally prior to the action-in-progress, that is, the action that is being engaged in. This motivational framework thus constitutes the meaning-context of the action *qua* prelude to the completed act in the future.

I am driving to the supermarket to get groceries before closing time—this is the action-in-progress. The *in-order-to-motive* motivates this action. If one is asked: "Why are you going to the supermarket?" one says: "In order to get groceries." The *genuine because-motive* comes into play here as the motivating force in the sense that it is propelled by knowledge from *the past*, that is, from the actor's prior experience. This is knowledge gained in the past regarding the fact that the supermarket will be closed if one arrives there after 5 pm. But one will not be directly conscious of this connection as one proceeds to that destination.

Both types of motives are connected with the past. The *in-order-to motive* is clearly based on the fact that a certain action has been engaged in before, yielding a particular outcome, which then serves as the basis for my decision to engage in the same action at the present time, in order to achieve the same outcome or result. I noted earlier that this involves a "technical" or "instrumental" aspect. The reasons given by social actors in expressing their *in-order-to motive* for a particular action involve this instrumental aspect: Thus, for instance, "We marched down the street in order to protest the Governor's policies" presupposes, first of all, a connection with the past, in the sense that prior experience would have established, for the actors involved, the efficacy of a protest march toward the accomplishment of certain goals. Secondly, the protest march is a particular "technical" approach, a particular "methodology," broadly construed, used by groups to reach a given objective. The *in-order-to motive* does entail all of this. However—and therein lies the key distinction—it does not provide an explanation, also drawn from the past, as does the *genuine because-motive*, for *why* the protest march is being carried out.

When institutional discrimination infiltrates the process of motivation, it becomes very problematic for the people involved, as concerns the pragmatic selection and determination of appropriate courses of action, and so on (Schutz, 1997: 96). As a rule, social actors are exposed systematically and regularly to the society's expectations, values, and standards, and are directly and indirectly pushed to live up to these determinations. For example, members of modern societies are expected to become educated as a means to upward social mobility. The actor's grasp of this larger frame of motivation would stand for his or her grasp of the *genuine because-motive* behind the project of getting educated. Social actors normally take this particular motive for granted; it is part of the larger cultural existence of people, which is normally taken for granted, as anthropology reminds us. So, when the social actor is asked why she is getting educated, she is likely to reply, "In order to be able to apply for this or that job" (the *in-order-to motive*), rather than "Because I want to have access to upper social mobility in the society's stratification system" (the genuine *because-motive*). Had she resorted to the latter explanation, her partner in the interaction would have understood it. We would infer from this that both of them would have reasoned in the same way, by virtue of their sharing the same stock of knowledge, and the same type of life experience (i.e., a common past). This would have made it possible for them to know that education normally enables people to experience upward social mobility, and they would have witnessed cases of this taking place. Thus, when their interaction becomes centered on the *genuine because-motive*, there is *mutual* understanding between them, because their common prior experience and knowledge would have made them aware of the connection between education and social mobility. The past orients and elucidates the present; that is, the meaning-context of the present action is grasped, by the actor, in terms of a reference to the past, of a "backward glance" (Schutz, 1997: 93).

The scientific interpretation of subjectivity, specifically of the subjects' understandings of their social world, entails the careful ideal-typical analysis of the course-of-action patterns under observation, by means of which a whole gamut of "typical notions, purposes, goals" are assigned to the ideal or typified actor or actors. The theoretical social scientist, though a human being like the fellow human beings under observation, is separated from the latter, strictly *qua* observer oriented by an interest in grasping their reality purely at the cognitive level. In that capacity he or she relies on an array of ideal-typical constructs, formulated according to the standard requirements of scientific research, which are assumed to have a quality of invariance and systematicity, meaning that they are assumed to be universally applicable, across the manifold of empirical correspondents, so that the constructs of the population under study can be grasped. The application of this set of constructs to explain social reality can be checked at the empirical level, normally understood as referring to the "sensory perceptions of objects and events in the outer world," but also, and more importantly for this study, in terms of the "underlying motives and goals" driving and shaping human action (Schutz, 1970a:16–18). Schutz's position here converges with the larger emphasis in interpretive social science on the internal aspect of behavior, pertaining to the mental activity underlying the behavior, as opposed to its external properties, or its physical, sensorially perceived manifestations (see also Münch, vol. II, 1994: 147).

To be scientifically sound, the study of human beings in the social world must, and can only, be carried out on the basis of the systematic construction of *ideal types*, focusing on social actors as *typified actors*, which means that these Subjects will be analyzed as members of a collectivity who have, as a rule, uniformly internalized the same fund of cultural knowledge and determinations, and therefore, as people whose actions and thought patterns will be addressed in their typicality. The starting point of the research is the attempt to comprehend their lived experience in the lifeworld. This will be *indirect* knowledge of the social world because it is not gained from direct, face-to-face relations with individual social actors. This knowledge must be consistent with "pregiven knowledge of the social world," that is, with previous ideal-typical constructions. Therefore, patterns of social action must be explained in terms of "course-of-action" ideal types, and of the *motivations* that account for the complex of subjective experiences (of the subjects) studied (Schutz, 1997: 224). The scientific explanation of a collective pattern of action through these ideal-typical frameworks, as undertaken by the phenomenological analyst, constitutes, in Schutz's masterly conception, "objective-meaning contexts of subjective-meaning contexts" (1997: 241). This level of objectivity and anonymity is the required standard of all science, and, in proceeding in this way and reaching this final stage—that in which social actors are understood objectively and anonymously, the interpretation becomes applicable to the entire collectivity.

The phenomenological analysis of the social world, as we have seen, calls for an exploration of what is happening in the consciousness of the research subjects that has driven them to the action pattern that represents the phenomenon under investigation. This establishes not only the basic position of the interpretive disciplines, based on subjective interpretation, but also the great importance of the focus on the typified, shared patterns of human behavior displayed by the individual actor, which are generalizable, or typified, at the group level—at the level of "everyman"—through the process of socialization. (The Schutzian *homunculi* or *puppets*—his term for ideal types—are constructed similarly and in a logically consistent way through the encompassing, community-wide reach of socialization.)

Schutz offers a strong *caveat* against the unswerving and unrestrained adherence of the quantitative or empirical sciences to mathematical language as the principal epistemological framework for understanding social reality—which amounts to a tendency which may be referred to as the mathematization of the social world—a problem already much theorized in the scholarship of recent decades (see, e.g., Bouleau, 2011). He warns (1945a:78) that Husserl, a trained mathematician himself, had already recognized the limitations of mathematics in making sense of the human experience in the world. Habermas (1989: 56) likewise maintains that social phenomena need to be investigated hermeneutically, when he says that "the methodology of the sciences of action cannot avoid the problem of understanding meaning, of hermeneutically appropriating cultural tradition." He points to the pivotal importance of the "intersubjectivity of experience" to the effect that the "facts" of social reality are not only to be understood in reference to symbols, but also in terms of being structured symbolically. The "access to [the] data" of the social world is achieved not only through the empirical observation of events, as done in conventional scientific research, "but at the same time through the understanding of contexts of meaning" (1989: 92). Meaning is action-orienting, in the sense that it has a direct and powerful normative effect on social behavior, and it is also the indispensable heuristic framework for grasping the dynamics of this behavior, a point in reference to which the subjective definition of reality (as addressed by W.I. Thomas in his well-known *Thomas Theorem*)[7] is immediately pertinent.

Pushing aside certain contexts of social behavior in which the measurement and interpretation of this behavior may be achieved in reference to "theory," that is, by recourse to sciences that operate in what Habermas refers to as the "normative-analytic manner," whereby social behavior can be interpreted on the basis of either immediate or direct observation, or its meaning is inferred from larger abstract processes (e.g., the distribution of commodities in the marketplace, voting patterns in pluralist social systems). That is to say, in the latter case the behavior of individuals is treated as being predetermined by the working out of these formal laws that govern the operation of institutional processes. One additional case of the application of formal theoretical schemes to the measurement and interpretation of human behavior may be seen in the human sciences, in which human behavior is reduced simply to a pure mechanical, ahistorical, stimulus-response situation (i.e., the case of the behavioral sciences). The assumptions driving this methodological approach are, obviously, in complete disregard for intentionality, which means that there is nothing in the space between the stimulus and the response that interferes with the effect of the former on the latter.

In this connection, the interpretive sciences have a sharply contrasting stance. According to Cicourel (cited in Habermas, 1989: 104), in order to properly and precisely measure the social process as such, or the patterns of social behavior of individuals and groups, the need for a "theory of culture" arises, in other words, a theoretical approach that targets the role and effect of meaning in "the common-sense world of everyday life." This involves a network of sociocultural meanings that are bounded, insofar as the actual *content* of these meanings is concerned, because they pertain to specific groups or collectivities, and thus do not operate across collectivities.

On the other hand, the application of such a cultural theory to the study of the social process—the nature of collective (intergroup) behavior—takes on an *invariant form*, in the sense that social acts in every society are always informed by, and will always conform to, these shared meanings in invariant ways. Habermas writes about these invariant properties and rules that guide social interaction, placing into relief the critical role of language, or communicative practices, the primary vehicle for the articulation of intersubjectively shared, culturally determined meanings. Social actors are normally unaware of the underlying and invariant rules and properties that account for how they conduct their daily interactions with one another. It is all part of the taken-for-grantedness that characterizes the life of individuals in the everyday world. They are certainly keenly aware of the specific behavioral prescriptions, the dos and don'ts that apply to their respective communities For the social analyst, the knowledge of these invariant rules and properties and how they work their effect into social interaction is best reached through "phenomenological reflection" (1989: 105).This aspect relates more broadly to the dualism of form vs. content of social action. The content of social rules and practices varies strikingly across societies, while the underlying rules that account for *how* social behavior, communication, and the internalization of cultural meanings take place remain invariant to the actual content of these social structures.

Schutz's remarks that phenomenology *qua* methodological approach can be utilized "with the greatest success within the empirical sphere" (1945: 92) are linked to his insistence that the phenomenological researcher must direct attention not to the empirical object of study as such, but to its *meaning*, "as it is constituted by the activities of our mind" (1945: 94). In this way phenomenology reveals the dynamics of intergroup life at a deeper level than what is revealed through empirical-quantitative methods of analysis, or through a straightforward cultural determinism, *à la* Durkheim. The subjectivist thrust of Schutz's work focuses instead on the more dialectical relationship between the individual and the sociocultural milieu, whereby the cultural elements are negotiated, reworked, redefined—an "acting back" on the force of the collectivity. We would essentially not err in bringing this Schutzian version of the individual-society dialectic into correlation with the relation between individual consciousness and societal demand in the process that Mead referred to as *self-interaction*.

The implications of the foregoing considerations for the harm that is brought upon social segments systematically subjected to institutional discrimination (such as, for instance, based on racial status), in the wider society over time, should be crystal clear. This situation wreaks havoc with the mental life, and consequently the relation to the social world, on the part of the actors involved. This aspect will be addressed more fully later. The social marginalization produced by the society's differential treatment of some of its constituent segments adversely affects the members of the segments regarding their interpretation of the world. This contrasts with the experience of social actors in general, who live under normal circumstances (i.e., who are not subjected to institutionalized social oppression). In the case of the former group, racial inequality creates a cleavage between their project of social integration, on the one hand, and that of trying to live in accordance with the requirements and determinations of subcultural life, a rather schizophrenic situation.

We may add some comments here along the same lines, with reference to the aspect of the motivational context of social action, as addressed above. Let us imagine a scenario whereby members of certain social segments who have been historically and formally barred from the society's educational mainstream on the basis of some ascribed status, such as race, and are confronted with the same query posed to majority-group members: "Why are you getting educated?" Our subjects in this example are immediately thrown into a cognitive predicament. Specifically, being members of, and living in, the larger society, they cannot possibly remain immune to the general emphasis placed on the practical value of education as a means to social mobility. Yet, they are daily negated access to the educational mainstream, or in the instances when they do get access to it, the promise of education in translating into social mobility does not always materialize, it is daily thwarted by discrimination, and therefore does not apply here. Thus, these individuals cannot automatically refer to this goal as the primary motivation—the *genuine because-motive*—for their action, for their effort to get educated, and respond in this way. They may say, "I am working for this degree because a job I am applying to requires it." This is the more immediate in-order-to-motive, geared to the present circumstances—whereas the other type of motivation, the genuine because-motive, is grounded in the past history of the actor(s), which, in this case, is a history of systematic denial of opportunity, educational and otherwise, and thus cannot account for the effort of the actor in the present time to become educated. This situation represents marginalization at the level of intersubjectivity, which, when we consider the awareness of these individuals of being formal members of the society (i.e., through their citizenship status), leads, again, to turmoil in their mental life, specifically in terms of cognitive dissonance as concerns their social identity, with all the attending problems of psychological distress, alienation, resentment, and animosity.

A REVIEW OF SCHUTZ'S FOUNDATIONAL CONCEPTS

We will now turn to a more detailed exposition of Schutz's main concepts and ideas, and show in which way they apply to the substantive social problem taken up here, namely, race and ethnic relations. We must begin with the notion of *lifeworld*, Schutz's master concept, the starting point of his phenomenology. As has been indicated, this refers to the world we all live in everyday—the *social* world—not the physical world, notwithstanding the fact that the world of daily living has a physical structure. Our lives hinge on our functioning in the *lebenswelt*, the world of interaction broadly construed as the larger complex of meanings, emotions, values, communication: the context of *life*. The world "of action," says Natanson (1968: 221), or "the common-sense world," as referred to by Gurwitsch (1962). The latter writer adds that this is also the world of the *natural attitude* (more on this concept later), quite simply, "the world in which we find ourselves at every moment of our life, taken exactly as it presents itself to us in our everyday existence" (1962: 51). As noted earlier, in the Schutzian phenomenological system, reality is *socially* constructed, rather than being something that exists in the transcendental or pure consciousness, as Husserl would have it. Thus, social reality and the complex of meanings associated with it result from the operation of intersubjectivity, as human beings organize and negotiate their common existence, or take their bearings, in the lifeworld on the basis of these meanings. As Landgrebe (1940: 46) affirms it, "The lifeworld is not only a world for me, the single individual; it is a common world, a world for a particular human community . . . [furthermore] . . . a world fashioned and cultivated by the [human beings] who live in it."

In the light of these considerations, it is reasonable to infer that in cases where social groups have historically lived side by side within the same environing community, but not necessarily being part of an integrated world of "customs and usages," or not sharing the same fund of cultural knowledge as the remaining population, this results in the separation and differentiation of their "surrounding worlds" (Landgrebe, 1940: 46). This means a division within the larger sociocultural environment in which they live. Clearly, this leads to a problem of meaning for these groups, in the sense that they will be guided by divergent meaning systems, a situation that becomes all the more problematic when the interaction between the groups involved occurs under circumstances of asymmetry of power, or in the context of dominant/subordinate relations.

The prevalence of meaning in the lifeworld rests on the daily reliance of social actors on what Schutz treated as *typifications*, which are collectively acknowledged, collectively based (and historically variable) habitual or typified cultural objects and practices, behavioral and linguistic patterns, and interpretations. These in turn make up the group's *stock of knowledge-at-hand*, or the commonly shared complex of knowledge and understandings used by social actors for orienting themselves in the everyday world. These two concepts are of utmost importance in Schutz's theoretical system, and will be revisited later. Understanding how social actors construct reality, and structure their collective life—that is, social arrangements and practices, patterns of interaction, and so on—on the basis of intersubjectively shared typifications is, at root, the paramount concern of those who seek to understand society. Culture as such, therefore, amounts to a vast complex of typifications.

The chief aim of the present study is to understand a particular form of social action, manifested as race and ethnic relations, in large, pluralistic societies of the modern time. To that end, it brings the insights of Schutzian social phenomenology to bear on the conventional analytical treatment of this problem in the race-and-ethnicity literature. As concerns the *political* potential of the phenomenological approach, or its possible utilization as a critique of domination, the fact that it dissects the meaning-structure of human relations at the foundational level brings to light certain critical aspects of intergroup inequality and oppression which, as noted earlier, have been left largely unexplored in the traditional literature on race and ethnic relations. In so doing, the phenomenological standpoint can be directed toward amplifying the political discourse on race and ethnicity, thus making a significant contribution to it. In relation to this, we can appeal to Chomsky, reversing Marx's *dictum* to the effect that in order to change the world one had better try to understand it.

THE CONSTITUTION OF MEANING

It may be stated that meaning is the central element and driving force in the interpretive sciences, and it functions pre-eminently in that capacity in Schutz's social phenomenology, more precisely in reference to his theory of social action. We are primarily interested in showing how the question of meaning is directly relevant to the discussion of intergroup relations and inequality. It is, first of all, the element that shapes the construction of the self of individuals, as they engage in the process of accounting for their actions—for how they express their selfhood to others—by reference to their past (the because-motive). In order to accomplish this reconstruction of their past lives as the basis of explanation for their present lives, in this deriving a sense of selfhood, individuals rely on the society's fund of general knowledge and on the complex of society's typifications. They rely on typical meanings and understandings as well, as they seek to communicate and interact with others.

Regarding this latter aspect, or the mechanics of social interaction, meaning is the indispensable mediating mechanism that determines the outcome of social encounters and relationships. In other words, the emergence of mutual agreement or conflict between interacting actors or groups depends on whether the parties involved will be able to reach mutual understanding of interests, intentions, projects, and so on, on the basis of commonly shared meaning. This being the case, social relations will be characterized either by mutual understanding or by mutual conflict, in the degree that meaning is/is not shared by all the parties involved. Sharedness of social meaning affords each party in the interaction the ability to grasp the subjective intentions of their interacting partners, with a substantial degree of accuracy, to the point of being able to predict their reactions. If social meanings are within the reach of everyone, the communicative exchange will work in the fashion of a two-way street, thus allowing for a *reciprocity of perspectives*, Schutz's conceptual designation for this process. The reciprocity of perspectives affords the partners in the transaction the ability to anticipate, through typifications, the subjective intentions, motives, dispositions, and goals of each other (see Gurwitsch, 1962: 67–68). On the other hand, in cases of social systems where institutionalized cultural separatism is systematically and formally enforced, this strongly affects the communicative process in those systems. The groups involved in the social encounter will likely be, in this case, affiliated with and oriented by separate meaning systems, which will most likely create problems for their mutual understanding, and may also eventuate in serious conflict.

In this exploration of the implications of social meaning, and its impact on what goes on in intergroup life, our main concern is to focus particular attention on the importance of the *integration* of meaning for the functioning

actors within a given sociocultural community. Schutz's great contribution
to the analysis of meaning, as we have indicated, was that of overcoming
Max Weber's insufficiently deep excavation of the meaning-structure of the
conceptual framework of his own theory of social action.[8] Schutz's contribution resides in incorporating the dimension of time—that is, of temporality or
historicity—into his explanation of how social meaning emerges and evolves.
This process is presented below, in much abbreviated form.

Schutz's theory of meaning starts by subjecting Weber's *verstehendesozi-
ologie* to critical scrutiny, in order to show that the Weberian analysis is not
incisive enough to get at the phenomenological foundations of the meaning
of social behavior, to provide a phenomenological description of the genesis
and development of meaning. Schutz does acknowledge Weber's merit in
maintaining that human behavior is meaningful or driven by intentionality, which definitely counters the conventional scientific-empirical position
and the latter's reduction of social behavior to its physical manifestations.
But Weber considers the meaning of social action as it is given, and fails to
proceed further in order to establish how it is created and developed in intersubjectivity. In other words, the Weberian treatment of meaning is not as full
or as dynamic as in Schutz, who provides a richer description of meaning by
framing it in its temporal context. In this effort, Schutz is greatly aided by
Henri Bergson's theory of the *durée*, and more significantly still (as Schutz
himself reveals, 1997: 13), by Husserl's analysis of the constitution of the
subjective experience. According to the latter, the meaning of human action
occurs as a sequence of distinct, yet integrated, *moments* representing the
past, present, and future. These moments involve the acting Subject's anticipation of the completed action, the ongoing action or action-in-progress, and
the accomplished act. Thus, a distinction is made regarding the meaning of
social action as it applies to these distinct temporal stages, specifically, the
meaning of action-in-progress (*actio*) and the meaning of the completed or
constituted *act* (*actum*). In the initial phase, actors engage in action in the
present, and anticipate, or engage in the *phantasying* of, the completed action
or Act (which is the goal) in the future. For instance, a person engaging in a
workout, and anticipating the completed or executed action—that is to say,
the actor entertains in consciousness the possibility of the completed workout, its execution, in the future. Natanson (1968: 224–226; see also Campbell,
1981: 204) highlights the aspect of phantasying in his discussion of the temporality of meaning in Schutz's work. This refers to a projection or anticipation, by the social actor, of an action-to-be-completed as real, which means,
in consciousness, its mundane or concrete manifestation is already visualized
or phantasied. It is visualized in future perfect tense, as in "I-will-have-done-
such-and-such"—that is, "I will have completed my workout," "I will have
cooked a meal," and so forth.

A completed action in the future [which becomes a social Act] is crucial because it reveals the property of *selectivity* operating in the Subject's consciousness, that is, the determination by the Subject regarding what merits attention, or what is to be treated as relevant (Schutz, 1970c: 4). This selectivity is in turn determined by the Subject's cumulative life experience; that is, all the interconnected events and situations which form a cohesive, integrated frame in the actor's life have serious implications for social action at all levels of human experience.

Phantasying is of first importance in the explication of the dynamics of social action, and therefore, ultimately, of intergroup relations—such as, for instance, in the case of ethnic and racial relations—because the projection of acts represents the foundation of the meaning-structure of the social world. It shows that meaning-structure to be *contextually determined*, and thus bounded, a condition that separates a *particular* meaning structure from that of other sociocultural worlds, ranging from the interpersonal or face-to-face relations to the larger, community-wide domain of "quite remote and distant fellow-men and their cultural realities" (Natanson, 1968: 226). The particular pattern of phantasying about a completed action is clearly a subjective process, but is fundamentally an aspect of intersubjectivity—an integrated process at the level of the collectivity—insofar as other social actors within the society, with varying life experience and "cultural realities" will, on account of their common life together in the same sociocultural context, share the same *schemes of relevance*—and therefore, patterns of cultural behavior. This shows the critical importance of the *integrative* nature of phantasying in the formation of cultural behavior. The question at hand is, what drives the projects of social actors? In this regard, the need to identify the motivational forces that drive the projects of social actors is of cardinal relevance for an interpretive sociology. Motivation, intentionality, are contextually (historically, geographically) determined—that is, the *in-order-to* type of motivation which is attached to future-directed action is predicated on the history of "past acts" (Natanson, 1968: 227–228) by social actors. But this warrants qualification. More precisely, as Schutz describes it (1997: 91–96) the *in-order-to motive*, which is immediately attached to the project at hand (e.g., It is freezing outside, so I will put on my sweater before I leave the house), involves a technical procedure (putting on my sweater), and it does have a connection with past experience, specifically the fact that I have stepped outside on a cold day, without a sweater, and felt uncomfortably cold. Therefore, I am putting on a sweater in order to avert this unpleasant experience of feeling cold. But the *in-order-to motive* still begs the question. It only addresses the technical or instrumental aspects of a process (thus putting on a sweater constitutes my "project") in order to avoid the physical discomfort of not wearing a sweater when it is freezing outside. But people will normally take the connection between the project and the outside temperature for granted. This assumption is buttressed by a reference to the past, although what happened in the past is not revealed. My behavior of putting on a sweater cannot be fully understood by reference to the cold weather alone; a consideration of the "total complex" of my experience (which includes having been outside in cold weather without a sweater) is needed. This will then allow me to rely on a *genuine because-motive*, and respond, if I were to be asked why I am wearing a sweater: "Because it is cold." This judgment takes me back to the past to retrieve and incorporate my past experience in this way. So, therefore, the *genuine because-motive* is *the real explanation* for my action. In this particular situation, it brings to consciousness the unpleasantness of my past experience in having stepped outside without proper protection from the cold. Thus, the because-motive has a pragmatic orientation. From this angle, the *past* moment determines the *future* moment.

More pertinently for the discussion of the problems of intergroup life, as in those related to race and ethnic relations, these relations disclose deeper layers of meaning, something that may be accomplished when we consider these relations in terms of their *genuine because-motive*. For example, past experience for members of minority racial groups in the United States is a powerful and lasting reminder of their difficulty in having the society address certain minority grievances without direct confrontations in the streets, clashes between those who feel wronged and the power structures. Their *in-order-to motive* for these actions may involve certain technical preparations, arming themselves, gathering a critical mass for the protest, marching in particular areas of the city, and so on. But the real explanation lies in the reference to a *genuine because motive*—that is, in the larger historical context involving the interaction between majority and minority groups in the society in question, that has led to the specific patterns of intergroup relations of the present.

For the purposes of this study, and the concern with elucidating the dynamics of intergroup inequality, it must equally, if indeed not more emphatically, be kept in mind that, without the systematic access by members of certain groups, over the course of their life experience, to the same stock of knowledge of the sociocultural community as dominant groups have, the conscious determinations, projections, or anticipations put forward by members of the former groups, and the complex of meanings they rely on, as they interact with others in society, will not be within the reach of—that is, will not be intelligible to—the members of the dominant group, and vice versa. For example, members of a given social group go out together for amusement, dressed in accordance with the habitual construction (within their cultural group) of being dressed fashionably. They will experience this outing together—the action-in-progress—and visualize its successful completion in the future, and have a specific collective sense of the meaning of the experience, which will be in conformity with the society's larger complex of the meaning of things, and so forth. However, their projection of coming across as being fashionably dressed may run counter to dominant conceptions, associated with the society's ruling group, of what being fashionably dressed entails. In other words, their attire may be viewed in a very different light. It may be associated, by members of another social group, with social deviance, not sartorial elegance. This situation would be problematic enough in itself, but is most significant when it occurs in terms of a dominant/subordinate intergroup relationship, with its attending implications of political inequality, dominance, and control.

According to Schutz, when a certain set of our experiences "show a specific cognitive style and are—with respect to this style—not only consistent in themselves but also compatible with one another," they become a *finite province of meaning* (1970b: 7). This definition indicates that self-contained, internally consistent cultural communities constitute finite provinces of meaning. In each cultural community of this type, as a self-contained sphere of meaning, the members bestow upon their collective experience of shared meanings "the accent of reality." Using Schutz as a frame of reference, we may say that the co-existence of dominant and (sub)cultural communities within the same society, as a corollary of institutionalized intergroup separatism, presents problems related to the absence of consistence and compatibility. This is the critical problem attending the relation between dominant and subordinate racial groups in social systems historically organized on the basis of cultural (and structural) separatism. And, since within the boundaries of a cultural community, the latter's members, oriented by the natural attitude, will take their specific life circumstances for granted, and moreover, will also take as a given their "unity and congruity," this will obviously translate into immediate opposition to all other models of cultural existence of other groups, whether groups inside the same environing society, or from other societies. These considerations extrapolate from Schutz's discussion of the actor experiencing shifts from one finite province of meaning to another within the same, unified cultural environment, to the discussion of actors being confronted with different models of group existence *within the same national community*. Thus, the finite provinces of meaning treated in Schutz's discussion—for example, "the world of dreams, of imageries and phantasms, especially the world of art, the world of religious experience, the world of scientific contemplation, the play world of the child, and the world of the insane"—are all part of the same, large world of daily experience, and integrated within the mental life of social actors, who shift back and forth between them. The complete taken-for-grantedness with which social actors relate to their *paramount reality of daily life* (the term that corresponds to the everyday world, borrowed by Schutz from William James)—that is, their taking the things and processes of everyday life to be natural and beyond any doubt—makes it virtually impossible that they will consider other lifeworlds valid, or the identical taken-for-grantedness with which members of those foreign lifeworlds relate to their daily experiences. Contact with unfamiliar cultural situations typically leads to anxiety, and that in turn to any number of reactions, ranging from fear to aggressiveness, from withdrawal to outright domination. This is based on what Schutz termed "the epoché of the natural attitude" (1945b: 551–553), which is expressed in the fundamental doubt, by members of a given cultural community, that their daily world of experience could be any different from what it appears to be to them. This familiar cultural attitude stands for the phenomenon known as ethnocentrism.

THE TYPIFICATION OF THE WORLD

As has been indicated earlier in this chapter, the social meanings and common-sense understandings, the standardized and shared patterns of daily life, prescriptive specifications for social behavior that we internalize and take for granted, and use daily to orient ourselves in the lifeworld, are designated by Schutz as typifications. Typifications integrate the social world, and have in fact been characterized as the very blood of daily life (Natanson, 1973: 16).They are, essentially, what culture is about, which means that culture amounts to a vast complex of typifications. Social constructions though they may be, typifications are understood by all as a *natural* phenomenon, as *givens*, a natural and logical part of daily life. This *taken-for-grantedness* that characterizes people's relation to conditions of the social world amounts to the *natural attitude*. It develops as social actors undergo the lifelong process of socialization, by means of which the internalization of culture, in its material and nonmaterial aspects, occurs at such a deep level as to acquire an ontological character. That is, members of the society come to equate their very existence with their existence-in-the-world-at-hand and all that this world encompasses. Thus, the natural attitude implies that social actors not only take for granted the manifold of concrete elements associated with their life in the social world, but its *naturalness* or taken-for-grantedness reaches into the most fundamental and inclusive level of their existence, that of *being in this world* as such. Gurwitsch (1962: 56) addresses thusly this attitude of unquestioning acceptance of the world around us: "Growing into our world and into our society, we have acquired a certain language that embodies the interpretations and typifications . . . that prevail in our society and come to be accepted by us as patterns to be followed unquestioningly." These typifications involve, as noted, a vast complex of culturally prescribed, constantly evolving, recipes for behavior and understanding, To take an example from the world of interaction in U.S. society: given the widespread popularity of the high-five gesture in the society-at-large over the last couple of decades, what does a typical member of the society do, in the midst of an encounter with another typical member of the society, and the second person, facing the first person, raises her or his outstretched hand over her or his head? Does the first person wonder in bewilderment about the possible meaning of that behavior? Does he or she try to duck and defend himself or herself from what, by all indications, suggests an impending attack? Or, does she or he complete the gesture in the socially prescribed fashion, by raising his or her own arm over his or her own head, in order to slap the palm and fingers of the other person, in a gesture signifying celebration or congratulation? In all probability, the third option will be followed. Such is the nature of typified social behavior in social communities everywhere.

The universally shared quality of the stock-of-knowledge-at-hand provides the conditions of possibility for the complete typification of the lifeworld carried out by its inhabitants. This is an important consideration. Universality is the focal point and paramount concern here. It stands for the fact that, as a rule, we understand the aspects of the social world, and relate to our fellow members in that world, in ideal-typical terms.[9] This has mainly to do with people's social performance or social functions, as they play a plurality of social roles. Thus, in riding an elevator I expect that others in the elevator will behave toward me and all others in the elevator in the way that socially derived recipes for public behavior demand it, and I will likewise pattern my conduct in the same typified fashion, that is, in the way "my typified partners expect me to perform it" (Gurwitsch, 1962: 66). This causes patterns of social behavior in general, as manifested in the multiple social functions that individuals perform in social life, to become standardized, to reach as point of universality, insofar as anyone who, for example, specializes in the functional requirements of being, say, a baker or a candlestick maker, is able to perform either function to the satisfaction of all those who use either service. This viewpoint fundamentally points to the undeniable preponderance of culture in shaping social behavior. This standardization of social procedure and social thought, again, becomes immediately pertinent to the discussion of intergroup relations in a context of political inequality, or asymmetry of power, a point to be pursued more systematically later. At this juncture, it should suffice to state that intergroup relations are powerfully impacted by formal or institutionalized cultural divisions within *the same* society, which normally keep the ruling and subordinate social groups, within that society, culturally apart, and, in most cases, physically apart as well. This precludes a *fusion of horizons* (Gadamer) between these groups. Instead, these structural divisions foster significant, intractable animosities between majority and minority groups. This problem, as can be clearly demonstrated in the concrete cases of societies afflicted with institutionalized cultural separatism based on racial status, are not always resolved through economic or political means, as argued by other interpretive positions. Gurwitsch (1962: 66) in fact draws attention to how this level of society-wide standardization of social meaning and practice, which facilitates the anticipation of the future actions and reactions of our "fellowmen," is something "without which no cooperation or social interaction is possible," meaning that the interlocking of the expectations and courses of action of the groups involved is not likely to take place.

THE STOCK-OF-KNOWLEDGE-AT-HAND

By this term Schutz referred, essentially, to the cultural legacy of the society, which we receive upon birth. It is that which forms, in the words of one analyst (Gurwitsch, 1962: 58), "the frame of reference, interpretation, and orientation for my life in the world of daily experience, for my dealing with things, coping with situations, coming to terms with fellow human beings." Münch (1994: 347) describes it as being made up of "typifications, skills, useful knowledge, and recipes for viewing and interpreting the world and for acting in that world." This in turn provides the appropriate *system of relevances* that will drive and orient social action, in dynamic fashion, or in terms of the historically constant renewal and revision of cultural directives. The entire process is grounded in the daily world of experience. Life in society is the ultimate determinant, in that the individual, as Munch reminds us, "can never escape the lifeworld in which he or she lives" (1994: 147).

Social actors interact with one another in everyday life on the basis of traditional or "common-sense knowledge," consisting of collectively created, established, and shared beliefs, norms, values, assumptions, which operate consistently through the generations and are internalized systematically by society's members through socialization. As already indicated, this refers to the *stock-of-knowledge-at-hand.* In the life cycle of the individual this knowledge is taken for granted, and it is the fund of knowledge on which social actors rely automatically before embarking on any given course of action. In this sense, it is treated as "foreknowledge" (see Habermas, 1989: 107–109). The latter point refers to the fact that the stock-of-knowledge-at-hand operates in a manner roughly parallel to that of *a priori* knowledge, but *only* in the sense of *being-there-before*, since it already exists in the actor's consciousness via socialization—it is, in other words, a social product. In that capacity, it precedes social action insofar as actors already have it at their disposal beforehand, living with it as they do, as part of their existence in a particular sociocultural world. The existence of a stock of knowledge comes out of the particular set of structural circumstances of human collective life. Once it is formed as a fund of interlinked values, understandings, meanings, it remains remarkably stable over time. Its pre-existence, however, vis-à-vis social behavior, as should be clear, does not mean that this knowledge is independent of *all particular experience*, as would be the case in Kant.

Just as we do not question the existence of the lifeworld, and our existence in it with our "fellowmen" who are human beings like ourselves, so too we take as a given the fact that our fellow human beings in the lifeworld not only have access to a stock of knowledge about social reality, like we do, but also their stock of knowledge is fundamentally *the same* as ours. This is part of our natural attitude toward the world we live in. These are not consciously made deliberations on our part; rather, they result from the experience of living in the lifeworld, and deeply absorbing or internalizing all of its features, to the point where these features become *natural* to us, intrinsic features of our existence as cultural beings. Thus, this collective dependence on culture on our part, as the very basis of *who we are*, reasserts the point that it has an ontological character, and that it conditions the operations of consciousness.

It should be understood that our taken-for-grantedness of the conditions of the lifeworld, specifically regarding the fact that our "fellowmen" have the same stock-of-knowledge as we do, does not necessarily mean that this applies to all the various kinds of technical knowledge and skills that serve to differentiate people in any given society—in short, that it applies to the division of labor. It does apply, however, to the *symbolic* level, or to all the *core* cultural beliefs and values, patterns of language and communication, basic ways of responding to the world, and so forth, that have to do with the society in question. This is of utmost importance when we consider it against the background of intergroup relations, and particularly with respect to the operation of asymmetrical power relations between social groups. It underscores the potentially problematic nature of the interaction between dominant social segments, on the one hand, and, on the other hand, minority social segments that have historically been kept physically and culturally apart, by formal determinations of the wider society, thus developing different modes of living over time. It is people's structural position in society, says Gurwitsch (1962: 60)—as a man, woman, member of the socially dominant group or a social minority, and so on—that will determine their perception of the social world, and give shape to their goals, plans, and purposes.

In connection with this issue, the question of anonymity will now be considered. The integration of social systems hinges on the condition of anonymity undergirding the interaction of members of the social system with one another. In other words, social interaction must entail the activities of each member of the larger community being connected with, or dovetailing into, the actions of every other member through a network of socially determined recipes for behavior and thought, made available through the process of socialization, and reaching the entire group. This establishes a network of interdependence, which is the basis of social integration. The anonymity aspect emerges from the fact that in every society individuals relate to others as other beings like themselves. Pushing aside our *contemporaries* (i.e., those with whom we coexist in the society at some given point in time), and with whom we have formed personal (i.e., *primary*) relationships, our connections with fellow members of the larger community occur essentially in reference to their social functions. For example, if I am waiting to be served at a restaurant, or at a bank, I am not interested in who performs those functions; I am interested only in having the service be rendered properly. What is important for me, in this example, is "the typical character of the occurrence within a typified situation" (Schutz, 1970b: 96).

The discussion of this issue so far has made plain the fact that the typification of action and thought in any social system stems from socialization. The latter ensures the development and establishment of social trust, and allows for prediction or anticipation of the courses of action of those with whom we interact. The cultural material transmitted to society's members through socialization, in turn, forms, as we have noted, the stock-of-knowledge-at-hand, which, as a rule, is available to everyone in the society, thus bringing about uniformity, and consequently, anonymity, in the social performance of society's members.[10] Social worlds, whether entire societies or smaller sociocultural communities within the larger society, act as frames of reference for the organization of the conduct and thought of the social actors who live in them. The social actor in turn expresses the determinations of society—that is, *the general*—through her or his individual conduct. Schutz tells us (1970b: 97) that it comes down to each particular sociocultural community being "centered in the self of the person who lives and acts in it." This is not a reduction of social life to individual reality. Rather, it brings to the fore the aspect of typification and anonymity, insofar as the individual—the *particular*—by virtue of having deeply internalized cultural materials to the point of naturalizing them, and thus relating to them as *givens*, and supposedly having done so *along with everyone else* in the same community (provided the community is culturally integrated)—comes to represent the *general*, that is, the group as a whole. When this happens (in the absence of internal cultural divisions in the wider society), anonymity has reached the level of completeness, and social actors in general become indeed interchangeable in their patterns of behavior and thinking. The latter are then expressed through "typical sequences and relations" (Schutz, 1970b: 98). Mead addresses this phenomenon in a parallel formulation, his discussion of the development of the Self. He postulated that when then person becomes old enough to be able to take the role of the *generalized Other* (the *game stage* of the development of the Self), this means that she or he is able to act and think like anyone else in the larger community. The assumption here is of the typicality of behavior and thought, and anonymity, that socialization brings to the world of social interaction, in any given community.

The confidence and assurance that we deposit in our stock-of-knowledge, the sense of consistency that we find in it, are not tested through the operation of natural laws, but through the ever-repeating patterns of routinized action. In other words, the regularity, systematicity, and *typicality* with which things occur in social life are the source from which we derive a reasonable expectation that things will repeat themselves—events, patterns of action, and so on—under normal circumstances. Thus, a confrontation, within the same community, with a different outcome, the inability to predict accurately the (behavioral) responses of others to typical interactive stimuli, creates cognitive dissonance, confusion, disorientation, and, likely, conflict, between the parties involved. Which is to say, if this typicality is not present, not shown in the actions of my fellow creatures (within the larger cultural community I live in and grew up in), this becomes a significant problem, which will hinder, if not render impossible, effective communication between myself and my partners in the interaction situation.

This has a twofold implication. First of all, it suggests the applicability of this analytical framework to the study of interpersonal relations. Schutz's application of Husserl's insights to the social world is fundamentally supported by Schutz's emphasis on the *We-relationship*, which is the cornerstone of social (vs. individual) life. The We-relationship (discussed more fully later) brings together the subjective and objective aspects of social life. Individuals engaging in a direct face-to-face relationship—for example, two people dancing the *xaxado*—will grapple with the harmonization or integration of the subjective and objective dimensions of that relationship. They are individual or separate subjectivities coming together in the We-relation. Each will bring his or her personal contribution—interpretation, in this case—to the situation. The actual encounter will determine whether the subjectivity of each—that is, each partner's subjective interpretation, or experiencing, of the situation—will find common ground in the objective properties of the group, namely, language, typifications, the stock of cultural knowledge. Thus, the objective elements, provided they are shared by the parties under consideration, will provide the conditions of possibility for a meaningful encounter. The parties involved will follow a set of typified or conventionalized procedures, or social recipes, regarding how to perform the dance, how to conduct themselves with reference to the other person, how to use the proper gestures, and so on, and they will assume that their behavior will be interpreted by the Other as according to typified, intersubjectively shared meanings, and so on. This objective dimension of this situation represents the *transcendence* of each actor's own stream of consciousness, and reaches into the socially shared stream of consciousness, which encompasses the group's stock of social knowledge. It thus represents the *dynamic* effect, in dialectical fashion, of the lifeworld—the culture of a community (Wagner, in Psathas, 1973: 64)—upon the behavior of its members. Secondly, this process operates at the macrolevel as well, such as regarding social problems involving the relations between groups (ethnic and racial relations, in the present study), because the same principles apply regarding the access of the groups involved to the society's stock-of-knowledge-at-hand, their sharedness of social meanings, and how these things minimize the possibility of estrangement, conflict, and so on, between them.

In closing, the stock-of-knowledge-at-hand, insofar as the operation of culturally determined meaning is concerned, may be said to exert a twofold effect on human group life. On the one hand, it enables social actors to identify and make deliberations regarding courses of action in response to what is of direct, or only peripheral, interest or concern. These are the situations, events, and so forth, of daily life, that are deemed to be relevant or not relevant by the group. Stated differently, this foreknowledge establishes the parameters of *intentionality* within which social behavior will take place. On the other hand, as we turn our attention to the sphere of interaction proper, the stock-of-knowledge-at-hand, as we have stated earlier, is the main axis on which turns the ability of social actors to foresee or predict, without necessarily being conscious of this process, the actions of other temporal beings like themselves, with whom they share the lifeworld. Internalized social meanings, norms, rules, expectations, and so on ensure, to a large extent, that society's members will respond to others in the way established and expected by the group. Fundamentally, this is what makes social interaction, hence, social life, possible.

THE WE-RELATION

The analysis of social relations hinges on the communicative contact between the actors involved, in what Schutz categorized as the face-to-face relation. This type of social relation constitutes "a basic structure of the world of daily life" (Schutz, 1945b: 544). The focus here is on the *interpersonal* phenomenon, but the basic premises undergirding this concept may be applied to the investigation of contact between social *groups*. We start from the idea that the lifeworld is integrated, or "unitary," in the sense that the reciprocal experiencing and apprehension of the Other's "conscious life" (subjective life) reflect the sharing of the criteria upon which the We-relation experience is based, at both the "pure" and the concrete levels of this relation (Schutz, 1967: 189). As stated above, this relation is foundational for our daily living with others, and in that sense it becomes the main axis around which intersubjectivity revolves, and, by extension, the lifeworld itself (Natanson, 1968: 228–231). It is about social actors encountering fellow members of the social community directly, in a face-to-face situation, which in turn presupposes their common temporal and spatial coexistence, or their being able to share "a common sector of time and space" (Schutz, 1967: 185).

The We-relation starts with the actors having a *Thou-orientation* toward each other. According to Schutz, this "Thou-orientation presupposes the presence of the fellow-man in temporal and spatial immediacy." Once this reciprocal relation is established, the mutual apprehension of each other's intentions, that is, of each other's subjectivity, will take place by means of the communicative material (i.e., words, gestures) being exchanged. These words exchanged, part of the common linguistic system utilized by the partners, are signs of the *objective* meaning-context of this relation, and of social interaction in the broader sense. It shows us how, at the most fundamental level, the condition of possibility for the mutual understanding of the Other's subjective intention and purpose lies in the *mutual sharing of experience*, which occurs in "the ongoing community of space and time" (Schutz, 1967: 185–186).

The common sharing of time and space are therefore obvious prerequisites before the correspondence inherent in the We-relationship can be established. Clearly, internal divisions in the lifeworld, maintained over time as an integral part of social organization, will ultimately impinge on and hinder the execution of this relation (although, as Schutz points out, at the initial point of contact with my fellow human being, when I become aware of his or her presence, I do not have knowledge of how that person is, what his or her qualities are). In any case, the common linguistic, and overall cultural, background of the partners, as noted above, is the element that provides the conditions of possibility for the interaction to be effectively accomplished. In the earliest stages of the relation, the actors involved do not have any certainty of their commonly shared background, stock of knowledge, and so on, but will act on that assumption.

As regards the substantive material involved in the We-relation—that is, the *content* of this relation—it is that which makes this a concrete social relation (Schutz, 1967: 187). The content takes the interactional situation further, insofar as it goes beyond the initial establishment of the Thou-orientation, which is to say, beyond the starting moment of the We-relation, involving only the reciprocal recognition of the Other's presence. The establishment of the concrete social situation, expressed in the mutual exchange by the actors at the *objective* level of meaning (which involves the common stock of knowledge, and that in turn the complex of behavioral, linguistic and ideational typifications), has cardinal importance for this study because it determines the nature of group-based relations.

The means through which we apprehend the "conscious life" (i.e., the subjectivity) of others who share the lifeworld with us encompass not only explicit verbal indications (input, stimuli), but also a whole array of other culturally determined elements, such as "movements, gestures, and facial expressions" (Schutz, 1967: 188), as well as linguistic inflections, mannerisms, and so on. This point reinforces what was stated above regarding possible convergences and divergences in the interpersonal contact.

The performance of social actors as they engage in the We-relationship, at both the interpersonal and collective level, rests on the mutual knowledge and confidence that each of the participants will be able to grasp the subjectivity of the Other, and that everyone will be drawing from the same set of objective (i.e., culturally determined) signs or symbols, such as words and gestures. Thus, as Schutz says, "our experiences of each other are not only coordinated but also reciprocally determined by continuous cross-reference. I experience myself through you and you experience yourself through me" (1967: 189). The taken-for-granted belief by social actors that their fellow social actors participate in the same sociocultural environment as they do, and therefore share this environment with them and experience and interpret it as they do, in a manner that is "roughly identical," sets up the intersubjective foundation of social relations and social life as a whole.

The idea of *cross-referencing* of the experiences of the interacting persons involved in the We-relationship is a constant process carrying the exchange along—it is done in an unmindful or not-conscious way. The assumption (by the partners in the relation) of sharing the same stock of knowledge about reality allows them to gain a sense of each other's motives (even if they do not know for sure what those motives are), and then to predict and anticipate (with a solid margin of safety, in most cases) each other's future conduct. This serves to guide their own pattern of action toward the Other. Schutz calls attention to the great importance of this *cross-referencing* aspect of the interaction for the overall structure of social relations (1967: 190).

Cross-referencing is made possible in reference to the presupposition, on the part of social actors, that everyone lives in a world of common experience (i.e., the particular society in which they all live), and therefore, everyone is "confronted with the same world and the same mundane existence" as everyone else—in other words, "we regard the lifeworld, as a matter of course, as identical for us and for our fellowmen and, quite in general, for everybody . . . [and therefore] . . . we orient our actions with regard to what we anticipate theirs to be, and we expect them to do the same" (Gurwitsch, 1962: 53). This passage by Gurwitsch not only articulates very clearly a key premise of Schutzian phenomenology, but also compellingly lays down the implications for intergroup relations within the same national community. Specifically, in situations of intergroup conflict in a given society, it may be the case that the anticipation on the part of one social group to the effect that the actions and intents of the other group will be the same as theirs is unfounded, because these opposing factions may have been living under different sociocultural circumstances. This applies to the case where institutionalized separatism is established in the society-at-large (although the groups involved may have shared, essentially, the same physical space in the society, and/or even participated together in its formal proceedings, such as the workplace and education).

Based on the foregoing considerations we may deduce that cross-referencing is an important component of the We-relation—whether at the interindividual *or intergroup* level—and its absence creates problems for the transaction. That is, the cross-referencing process is not viable or cannot be established when the interacting partners do not *fully* share the same community of time and space (owing to developments related to their socialization experience)—in more concrete terms, the same sociocultural community—because the stock of knowledge, the typifications, and so forth, to be relied upon by the social actors involved, will not be necessarily the same.

To recapitulate the basic aspects of the We-relation: In a relation *where actual contact between individuals occurs*, the necessity of a sharedness of the cultural material making up each side's general stock of knowledge is clear. In its absence, communicative chaos is likely to ensue. With the cross-cross-referencing aspect of the relation as a frame of reference, Schutz states that the interaction may unfold in a "unitary and integrated manner" if, and because, the processes of consciousness of one individual (or group) are "in synchrony with" each participant's own interpretive schemes (of the Other's "overt conduct") in the context of a shared, hence, objective, world of meaning. Or, stated differently, "the experiences of the world within reach" for the participants in the We-relation, will mutually (and "roughly") coincide. The general stock of knowledge of the participant individuals (or groups) in the interaction, with its complex or vast array of typifications, is the critical source of information that will guide the people involved in their conduct toward each other, and enable each party to "derive a typification" of the motives behind the Other's conduct (Schutz, 1967: 191–192). Such a task is clearly beyond the reach or ability of a stranger, an outsider to the sociocultural community, where the participants in this face-to-face relation are found—an outsidedness that may be construed literally, as in the case of immigrants, or symbolically, as in the case of socially differentiated and marginalized segments of the society's population. For example, in the concrete example of an outsider to a given society, this person might impute particular meanings and motivations to the actions of native inhabitants of that community which do not reflect the true intentionality, or motives, behind those actions. As Schutz puts it, the in-order-to motives of the Other's conduct cannot be accurately ascertained (in this specific situation), strictly on the basis of simple observation of the Other's "accomplished act." The outsider(s) will be forced to draw upon her or his original stock-of-knowledge for making interpretations, which will obviously lead to misinterpretation, confusion, frustration (a situation that the typical tourist is also likely to experience).

Regarding the world of *contemporaries* as such, the immediacy and directness of the We-relation that is experienced by the social actor with the partner in the face-to-face relation is not experienced in reference to her or his relation with the multitude of other social actors in the larger community. In the latter case, as Schutz points out (1967: 196–197), one's experience of others like myself out there in the society—one's access to the subjectivity of others in general—is achieved only by means of relying on "typical knowledge of typical processes . . . [based on] typical anonymous repeatability." In this case, one relates to others in general, whom one does not know, strictly in terms of a *They-orientation*. Put differently, this means that the circumstances of others like myself, my ability to apprehend the subjectivity of others like myself whom I do not know, will be done purely on the basis of typifications. I will, therefore, assume that a given physician, or plumber, or priest, whom I do not know, but shares fully my temporal and spatial context, will behave in such-and-such manner—that is, I impute to each of them "certain typical attributes" (Schutz, 1967: 195)—which will then allow me to predict, with a fair margin of safety, his or her behaviors, motives, and so on. As with our relationship to others in general, this relation is indirect, therefore anonymous, although we feel that we have some "entry" into their experience of the world (their subjectivity) because of our sharing a common (i.e., society-wide) stock of knowledge—which, in a broader sense, means that we share the same sociocultural environment. Inasmuch as, in this example, members of the separated groups will not have informal, friendship-type relations—rather, they will have only formalized asymmetrical relations (such as in, for example, the bureaucratic context of the employer-employee relationship)—within the larger context of sociocultural differentiation the interpretive schemes of the participants will remain invariant. The group-based anonymous quality of each group's apprehension of the other can only be changed by a confluence or integration of their respective, culturally determined stocks of knowledge about social reality. In the absence of this community-wide integration of cultural horizons of these groups, their apprehension of each other will remain purely as a particular "personal [or group based] ideal type" (1967: 197), and these ideal types will not correspond to the concrete individual (or concrete plurality of individuals).

The ideal-typical pattern of apprehension of the Other, inherent [in the anonymity] of the They-orientation is particularly important here, as we consider intergroup relations. The physical separation of entire categories of individuals within the same sociocultural community (i.e., institutionalized separatism) ensures that this act of apprehension of the Other be even further distanced from the actual nature of the individuals being apprehended, of their behavior, motives, and so on—even less identical, as Schutz (1967: 197) put it, with "a concrete Other or plurality of Others." This applies either to the case of individuals from either one of the differentiated social segments interpreting, or apprehending, the world of the Other in situations when the (social) segments are not in direct contact with each other; or to the case of members of either segment coming into contact (under circumstances of social and political asymmetry) with each other. An example of the latter case: the mistress of the English Victorian household engaging in a direct face-to-face encounter with her chambermaid. In both cases, the ideal-typical apprehension of the Other applies, and it is normally associated with a *stereotyped* grasp of the Other. This is, of course, a two-way street, in the sense that the ideal-typical apprehension of the Other applies to both the members of the ruling group and members of the subordinate group.

In the We-relation we are able to understand the subjective meaning of the Other by transcending our own stream of consciousness, in order to share in the socially constructed stream of consciousness, based on the group's stock of knowledge, typifications, and so on. In this way, we connect with the *objective* (i.e., socially determined, mutually shared) meaning of the Other's presence, expressed through linguistic responses, gestures, and so on, which then gives us access to the Other's subjectivity. We cannot objectify the encounter with the interacting partner, observing from the outside, so to speak; otherwise, the partner becomes merely an "object of thought," rather than a Subject (i.e., someone like ourselves). In this regard, we must suspend theoretical reflection on the relation itself, and remain, instead, in the natural attitude. This means that we suspend all doubt about it, proceeding unquestioningly toward the interaction situation, which then affords the ability to have a *lived*, continuous, mutually shared relation together—the reciprocal mirroring within a single, unitary experience, which Schutz refers to as an "interlocking of glances" (1997: 170). (These ideas are basically correspondent to Cooley's *looking-glass-self* formulation.)

Historically, members of nondominant groups, by virtue of their subaltern circumstances (hence, for reasons of social survival), tend to have a greater insight into the reality of the dominant class, than vice versa (on this particular aspect see Miller, 1976: 10–11). Thus, the subjectivity of the Other tends to be more readily accessible to members of subaltern groups, than to dominant-group members. The latter learn early on in their lives that they do not need to make the extra effort to reach the subjectivity of the subaltern Other. To them, the subjectivity of members of the non-hegemonic group is best left in the category of the quaint, the exotic, the inscrutable. This is an expression of dominant-group members, as they typically treat subordinate-group members not as subjects like themselves, but as objects, as objects of thought, perennially subjected to objectification through the gaze of the dominant element. This position taken consciously by hegemonic-group members is a classic one, demonstrated through history, and it serves their political interests by crystallizing the boundary lines (gender-based, race-based, etc.) erected by the society's stratification system, keeping clear the separation of dominant and nondominant groups, and thus perpetuating the *otherness* and inferiority associated with the traits of the latter groups.[11]

In connection with the aspect of social actors interacting and sharing the same stream of consciousness, as indicated above, when we bring the element of *power* into the equation it becomes clear that, as concerns the relations between social groups which stand at different points in the scale of political stratification of the society, and therefore relate to one another on the basis of this inequality of power, members of the dominant group do not necessarily have to endeavor to transcend their own stream of consciousness in order to merge with that of members of nondominant groups, quite simply because they will not be interacting as equals. Two points to stress here. First, given the typical physical separation between dominant and nondominant groups within the society, these groups will be oriented by separate and distinct stocks of knowledge. Secondly, dominant-group members normally remain within their own stream of consciousness, insofar as the whole array of social things that they have come to take for granted will be imposed on nondominant group members as *the real*. This is a central, constitutive feature of dominant-subordinate relations.

Keeping in mind the foundational requirements of the We-relationship, and the case of social systems in which entire groups have been kept, through formal and informal means, physically and culturally apart, different stocks of knowledge will emerge for these groups, and therefore, their interaction will be fraught with problems. First of all, the long-standing nature of their separation, and therefore, differentiation, will invariably lead to ever-greater stability and crystallization of the cultural boundary lines that separate them. Therefore, members of the majority and minority groups will have limited ability to apprehend the subjectivity of the Other, and they will naturally attempt to apprehend the subjectivity of members of the other group(s) through the typifications they are able to form, on the basis of this limited ability. The end result is, quite obviously, the proliferation of mutual stereotypes. These typifications will not change; that is, they will tend to remain invariant—meaning, the previous knowledge one group has of the other will tend to remain invariant—unless significant change in the society's intergroup life takes place. Until such a structural rearrangement of intergroup relations materializes, involving changes in the degree and patterns of assimilation of the social segments deemed nonwhite, the absence of mutual recognition and understanding of the majority and minority groups will continue, as will their problems of communication, and their tension-ridden coexistence in the society. Members of these groups will find it difficult to develop the we-ness inherent in the We-relationship, which calls for a mutual understanding of the objective meaning of the communicative "signs" being exchanged. For this to occur, it is imperative that the intergroup communicative experience be free from distortions of meaning. While it is true that this type of problem may even be said to inhere in intergroup communication as such, under normal circumstances, it is considerably aggravated by intergroup separatism enforced on the basis of some ascribed status, such as racial status (which, in the particular case of racially binary social systems [e.g., the United States], is construed as an essential attribute of the group, that is, in metaphysical terms, with attending implications of perpetuity (on this point, see Camara, 2003).

THE NATURAL ATTITUDE AND RADICAL REALISM

The world of daily life is treated in Schutz as the world of the *natural attitude* because we tend to take everything in it for granted. This is a point of utmost importance in Schutz's work. As Gurwitsch says, "The unquestioned and unchallenged certainty concerning the world at large underlies, supports, and enters into every particular mental activity." I refer to this as a world whose inhabitants practice what we could call a *radical realism*—alternatively, *a radical presentism*—whereby everything that *is* in the Here and Now attains absolute validity—a kind of apodictic truth—thus remaining entirely unchallenged: a world where there is no room for historical or spatial relativism. The latter would call for the objectification of cultural objects and practices, which is an extremely difficult thing to do from the standpoint of the natural attitude. The deeper we find ourselves immersed in it, the harder it is to transcend it, as would be expected. This situation ultimately converts into the phenomenon known sociologically as ethnocentrism.

From this angle, it may be asserted that the natural attitude is the foundation of radical realism, or a radical *present-ism* (the immediate implication of the latter being that these tendencies preclude, or at least hinder, the development and operation of the historical consciousness. A radical realism or radical presentism is an equivalent tendency that clearly stems from the same source. By implication, it could be said that the inability of social actors to imagine that anything could be different from what they know and/

or are familiar with would be equally applicable with reference to worlds of experience other than their own, and to the identical naturalness or taken-for-grantedness that members of other lifeworlds (other cultural communities) exhibit toward their own respective lifeworlds, as they appear to them. That is, this—the *alien* versions—would not have any validity to them, in the sense of not being *as real* as their own experience of living.

Normally, the objectification of aspects of the social world that people are generally inclined to engage in is reserved for the cultural ways, or *otherness*, of other groups, particularly groups of lower social standing than they. This is in fact something that is expressed rather spontaneously, namely, highlighting the cultural ways of other groups, followed variously by being amused, outraged, taken aback, and so on by them. This is the group feature we know as ethnocentrism in sociology and anthropology. It would be said, then, that ethnocentrism is linked to, and promoted by, the experience of the natural attitude, insofar as it tends to be expressed when group members are confronted with the cultural ways of other groups. It is also something that operates as a two-way street—that is, members of Group A reacting to the ways of Group B, and vice versa, from the standpoint of their respective standpoints in the natural attitude.

The natural attitude allows us to assume, as we approach a prospective partner in a direct relation, that the establishment of the We-relationship is within the realm of possibility. In other words, as we approach the concrete, face-to-face relationship, we will *always* assume (unless contrary signs are manifested, such as, e.g., we realize the other person is a foreigner, speaking a foreign language) that we can have access to the subjectivity of the interacting partner, and the same thing is assumed by the partner. My partner and I will further assume that we have had a common living experience, and access to the same stock of knowledge. We relate initially to each other, therefore, on the basis of anonymity, as discussed earlier. Thus, the face-to-face relation places the participants in the interactive encounter in a "common stream of consciousness" (Schutz, 1997: 167), whereby we relate to each other by remaining in the natural attitude, that is, by apprehending each other through the typifications of our shared lifeworld. The face-to-face relationship is a more direct We-relation. It requires that each partner "bring a whole stock of previously constituted knowledge" (1997: 169), comprising, particularly, knowledge of the typical reactions of people in general, and of the person we are interacting with additionally, in given situations.

A reference was made above to the way the dynamics of the We-relation, specifically its reciprocal reflections of the behavior of the participants, remind us of the relation described by Cooley (as noted above) and his version of the social grounding and evolution of the Ego in the context of the idea of the *looking-glass-self*. The intersubjective nature or orientation of social relationships is crystal clear here, inasmuch as we are focusing on how *others* are grasping our conduct, interpreting our inputs, as opposed to our simply focusing on our own conscious experiencing of them. That is, the orientation on our part is toward the subjective meaning of others (1997: 170), which, needless to say, operates in reciprocal fashion.

The effort to grasp the Other's subjectivity is mutual, but its successful outcome will revolve around membership in the same cultural system on the part of the participants in the relation. Therefore, it requires access to the same stock of knowledge, an aspect which, as stressed earlier, closely linked to the relations of power between social groups. This universal access to the society's cultural system makes possible communicative understanding and accord. In this connection, as Schutz is clear when he says that "it is . . . essential to the face-to-face situation that [all the partners in the interaction] have the same [physical *and cultural*—italics mine] environment . . . the same undivided and common environment" (1997: 170–171). These requirements concerning the operation of a direct face-to-face relation, the We-relation, apply on the large scale level, that is, at the level of intergroup relations as well.

ON THE OPERATION OF RELEVANCE

We have referred to the phenomenological analyst's interpretation of the interpretations that social actors produce of the world of experience where they live (i.e., of their common-sense constructs) as a process of double hermeneutics. This process is inherent in the phenomenological analysis, and it finds validity in the confluence between the analyst's own understanding of the research situation, and that of the actors in it that are being analyzed. This immediately draws our attention to the pivotal role of meaning in this process, and the need for social study to be oriented to the investigation of meaning, as embedded in what Schutz calls *the system of relevances*—or, as he referred to it in a different way, "the mind's selective activity" (1970c: 13) and "the selective function of our interest" (1945b: 549). More simply, this pertains to the array of problems or elements of daily life that we select in consciousness as essential, as ends or means, and direct our attention to, as we engage in social action. We are dealing here, then, with the question of selectivity of consciousness and intentionality. As actors engage in what Bergson termed *attention à la vie*,[12] as they embark on particular courses of action, they are being oriented by their *schemes of relevance*. These relevance schemes are, in turn, determined by their background experience, by the sum of the cultural experiences that mark their biographical situation as a whole—but ultimately, by the larger sociocultural world in which social actors live.[13] Natanson (1968: 223–224) states that the selection of acts to be considered in consciousness, the acts to be projected or phantasied, are directly conditioned by these relevance schemes. We select from the set of mental concerns that we have chanced our attention to, from the different "provinces of reality" in which we are always living and acting (Schutz, 1970c: 10–11), and select one that becomes predominant over all the other provinces, thus making the latter secondary in importance.

The political significance of these considerations should become immediately apparent at this point. Given that, in every society, intergroup relations are normally framed within the context of power inequality between the majority or hegemonic part of the population and the minority or non-hegemonic one(s), variations in the meaning systems utilized by these two major groupings for guidance in daily life are invariably entwined with processes of social domination. In societies structured in accordance with long-standing, formally established divisions by racial status, cutting across the society's institutional sectors, the typical pattern is for members of minority racial groups to be forced to function daily and simultaneously in two distinct cultural worlds, namely, the familiar territory of the racial subculture—in the varying degrees to which minority social groups are pushed to develop distinctively subcultural lifestyles in this type of society, *vis-à-vis* the larger or national cultural way of life. This is a rather problematic situation, with an obvious and largely detrimental impact on the lives of these minority individuals, at the social, economic, and psychological levels.

The foregoing considerations are intended to bring into sharper focus the political importance of this aspect of intergroup life, and the heuristic usefulness of a critical phenomenology in the analysis of power relations among social groups. This issue will be taken up again later, in greater depth.

THE DUALISM IN THE OPERATION OF RELEVANCES

The importance of this particular Schutzian concept—the idea of relevance systems—for the understanding of the dynamics of intergroup relations cannot be overestimated. In connection with this, a two-part question must be raised, about, first, *what* the members of sociocultural communities anticipate as the outcome of their relationships with others, and secondly, *why* specific outcomes are anticipated. The first part of the question is attributed to the influence of the stock-of-knowledge of the group in question, "the sediment of previous experiences." The second part is attributed to the relevance system "by which man with his natural attitude in daily life is guided." In other words, members of social groups will be socialized in particular ways, and led to internalize the society's stock of cultural knowledge—the society's particular complex of beliefs, values, attitudes, ways of living as such, which is not only very large but also constantly evolving—which affords them considerable ability to predict the outcome of events, the behavior of others, and so on. The anticipation of certain outcomes, of "certain occurrences," is related to self-interest—in this case, and most pertinently for present purposes, self-interest at the group level. The system of relevances that guide and determine the course of intergroup life is pragmatically oriented, or tied to practical interest—specifically, to the maximization, or privileging, of the interests of certain groups over those of others. This expresses the operation of domination at the level of group life. Schutz refers to the "fundamental anxiety" of human beings which leads them to attempt to maximize their well-being and advantage in their relationship with others, and, more concretely, to "attempt the mastery of the world, to overcome obstacles, to draft projects, and to realize them" (1945b: 550). Certainly, this is translatable at the level of intergroup relations, whereby particular groups achieve a position of dominance in the society, other groups assume the position of subordination, and this will, for each group, correlate with the system of relevances that will orient them in daily life, causing the former group to endeavor to maximize its privilege and interests by keeping the latter group under its control; and members of the latter group—the subaltern community—to be oriented by a set of relevances corresponding to its structural position in the society, geared to the maximization of the group's security and chances of survival.

A cardinal principle in Schutz's theoretical system, related to other basic components of that system discussed here, is the *reciprocity of perspectives*, a theoretical idea that is conterminous with that of the stock of knowledge, and the latter is socially produced and passed on the society's members via socialization. The interpretations of the world that individual social actors formulate by drawing from this stock of knowledge are therefore socially derived, which means that the society as such is the primordial source of knowledge about itself. This is what makes the reciprocity of perspectives possible, whereby social actors collectively think in conformity with the "*the general lines*" (emphasis mine),[14] for the purpose of orienting themselves as they make sense of the world around them. Thus, society's members in general, from this standpoint, become interchangeable, notwithstanding their diverse individual or group circumstances—such as biography, religious socialization, and socioeconomic position—which may flavor their functions and interrelations in society somewhat differently. At root, they will show as a group an "interchangeability of standpoints" and a "congruency of systems of relevance" (Zaner, 1973: 18), and thus be able to place themselves in the shoes of every other member.

The direct application of the Schutzian notion of relevance schemes to the specific context of social action undertaken by racial groups in a given multiethnic society brings to the fore the question of how the selection of the specific *social acts* to be entertained, or projected, will take place. Or, to phrase it differently, how particular action projects will be selected. From the standpoint of the principle of relevance, the mind delimits a *field of consciousness*, on the basis of practical interest,[15] where *theme* and an encircling or surrounding *horizon* converge. The *theme* is the specific nature of the task I am engaged in at the present moment, such as, for instance, writing a letter to a friend. The *horizon* is the array of elements of my life at the present moment which are pertinent to, or come to bear on, my task-at-hand, thus making it "thematic for me," because I have turned to it, or directed my attention to it. The convergence between these two elements occurs in the particular area of consciousness where certain aspects of reality have been selected by our consciousness, and become the target of our attention. They have, in other words, become relevant (Schutz, 1970c: 3–6).The activities of consciousness, and the selective property of the mind (which Husserl referred to as the *Ego's attentional ray*, or the determining mechanism for that which will be treated as relevant in the actor's mind; Schutz, 1970c: 4) relate strictly to the actor's cumulative life experience, that is, to all the interconnected events and situations which form a cohesive, integrated frame in the actor's life.[16] Within any given culturally cohesive community, social actors will function daily in various realms of reality, at the same time—that is, their lives are attached to and oriented by diverse contexts of relevance—and yet, as a rule, they are able to accomplish in consciousness a basic integration or synthesis of these various contexts of relevance. Schutz refers to this phenomenon as the "interplay of relevance structures" (1970c: 15), and actors are oriented in their daily lives by it. On the other hand, to reiterate the point made here in this section as we present each of Schutz's main concepts, in national communities characterized by the historical enforcement of intergroup separatism, based on ascribed status construed as essential condition of certain groups, this situation will ensure the permanent differentiation of the life experience of minority groups, *vis-à-vis* the national model. This will therefore prevent the convergence, at the level of the society-as-a-whole, of the directions taken by members of the groups involved, as they demarcate what will become thematic for them, or, as they establish a field of consciousness, among the various realms of their social reality, and follow that up with the corresponding social action.

PAST AND PRESENT IN THE DETERMINATION
OF SOCIAL MEANING

The reflections above are critically important in terms of their relevance for the concrete level of intergroup relations. They lead us to a consideration of Bergson's notion of *attention to life*, which addresses the individual engaging in the "bestowal of the accent of reality" on specific "finite provinces of meaning," toward the determination of the larger "field of consciousness" (Schutz, 1970c: 6–8). These aspects have direct impact on the question of social meaning, and the courses of action to be decided upon by social actors, whether individually or in groups. In his landmark 1945 essay *On Multiple Realities* Schutz had this to say about the regulative function of attention-to-life:

> *Attention à la vie* . . . is, therefore, the basic regulative principle of our conscious life. It defines the realm of our world which is relevant to us; it articulates our continuously flowing stream of thought; it determines the span and function of our memory; it makes us—in our language—either live within our present experiences, directed toward their objects, or turn back in a reflective attitude to our past experiences and ask for their meaning.[17] (1945b: 537)

We will take this further and connect the determining effect of the attention-to-life process to our fundamental reliance on the society's stock of knowledge. Campbell refers to the latter as the "inherited stock of knowledge" (1981: 202–203), and, because this fund of general knowledge is couched in the larger cultural environment, he places into relief the power of culture in orienting social actors regarding their choice of courses of action to achieve particular objectives, as well as regarding the specific objectives chosen themselves. This should be obvious enough from the fact that social actors rely on the cultural materials drawn from the stock of knowledge to form judgments, follow certain courses of action, and so on. The practical significance of this should be all the more obvious when this situation involves majority and minority groups within the same society, which have been kept historically segregated at the cultural level, through the force of the law and custom.

Yet, we are not dealing with straight social or cultural determinism here. Social actors, in Schutz's vision of social life, are not driven inexorably toward certain patterns of behavior and thought in the manner of puppets-on-a-string, *à la* Parsons.[18] It is certainly true that the individual consciousness is a *social* consciousness (Campbell, 1981: 205); the person's grasp and interpretations of the social world are grounded in the social-cultural legacy that has been bestowed upon him or her through the socializing process.

But, Schutz conceived of the individual-society relationship in dialectical terms. First of all, in order to retain his thesis of the subjective freedom of the individual, the actions of individuals must be free. The relation of each person to her or his experience in the lifeworld is ultimately grounded in his conscious grasp of that world, in the way subjectivity is impacted on by collective life (by intersubjectivity), and by the primordial sense of being-in-the-world. This naturally points to what the proper approach to understanding social life should be. Specifically, the explanation of social life should be oriented to the subjective meaning of social action, which means that social life unfolds through the interpretations given by social actors to the myriad situations and behaviors they are exposed to in the everyday world. Their interpretations are based, as indicated earlier, on ideal-typical constructions of these situations and behaviors, formulated on the basis of the stock of knowledge available to the members of a society. Dreher says that "all kinds of human action or their result [must be understood in reference to] the subjective meaning such action had for the actor" (2011: 504; see also Eberle, 2014: 14). On the other hand, this freedom of subjectivity is always exercised in the context of the intersubjective world, whereby subjectivity operates by means of taking account of the presence and operation of all other subjectivities like itself, which constitute this nonmaterial dimension of the lifeworld. We act and react on the basis of our interpretations of the possible actions and reactions of other fellow human beings, with whom we share the world of experience.

THE QUESTION OF TIME

We are not normally aware of the unifying, continuous nature of lived time, and the lived experience, as demonstrated in Bergson's articulation of the *durée*, and the importance of this concept for the idea of attention to life. The *durée* stands for the integration in consciousness of the social actor's lived experience—that is, of the *now-that-has-just-become-past*, the *now-as-presently experienced*, and the *now-flowing-into-what-is-to-be* (my terms; see Schutz, 1997: 47). This refers to our *inner time*, not to time as conventionally measured and divided up in the *outer world* (*cosmic time*). We are not normally aware of this, in daily life, while we are "immersed in the stream" (Schutz, 1997: 47), that is, in our stream of consciousness, which undergirds our life in the natural attitude. We cannot objectify it (engage in a "reflection" about it, to use Schutz's term), as we would be stepping out if it; we normally do not objectify our daily experiences and overall living in the lifeworld. Schutz speaks of the element of "remembrance," which allows us to relate to the now-that-has-just-been, and to separate it from the "irreversible stream of duration," from the continuous and ever-changing, rather than fragmented, flow of experience, whereby experiences "shade into one another" (1997: 51).

In those moments when the social actor reflects upon his or her lived experience, then this entails a departure from the pure flow of experience (the *durée*). I believe Schutz's remarks in this connection imply, *latu sensu*, the importance of the sense of history in determining what social meaning is. It is not something drawn from the experience being lived now, the "passing experience," but *always* in reference to the reflective glance (i.e., a glance at situations *already experienced*)—always in the sense of the possible "recoverability to memory" (1997: 53)

Thus, the meaning of social action is necessarily construed, from this standpoint, in reference to the past. (The real meaning of things is also addressed by Schutz in his discussion of the two types of motives.) For, as Schutz points out, "only from the point of view of the retrospective glance do there exist discrete experiences" (1997: 52), that is, the discrete experiences, events, situations occurring in the present time. Schutz did not deviate from this interpretation of meaning. In the mid-1940s, more than a decade after he first translated (in *Der sinnhafter Aufbau der sozialen Welt*, 1932) the Bergsonian conception of the *durée* into his own conception of subjective meaning, he stated, "Meaning . . . is not a quality inherent to certain experiences emerging within our stream of consciousness but the result of an interpretation of a past experience looked at from the present Now with a reflective attitude" (1945b: 535). This means that the experiences of the present take on a distinct meaning for the participants in them insofar as they are apprehended "in retrospection." The meaning of social things, therefore, is inexorably linked to, and retrievable *only from*, that which has already passed. Individuals and groups are, therefore, unavoidably bound to the pattern of their past lives, singly or together, whether at the interindividual or intergroup level, as concerns the definition of the meaning of their behavior—of social action, more broadly.

This is a very trenchant characterization of meaning as such, and of the meaning of social conduct. It clarifies the concrete problem of social conflict between different social segments, in terms of this conflict stemming from the impossibility of grasping the meaning of present (interindividual or intergroup) experience without recourse to past experience as the fundamental frame of reference. Such an approach, the lack of a reference to the past, could be said to represent, in a general way, the absence of a historical consciousness.

These considerations, which have centered on the idea of the *durée*, suggest the salient nature of the historical construction, in consciousness, of the meaning of things—in other words, the importance of the temporality of meaning. More specifically, we are not only bound to the *ongoing* stream of (social) experiences in determining the nature of the meaning of the experiences of the present (a point that has to do with the "fundamental unity in the time-constituting stream of consciousness; Schutz, 1997: 56), but, more importantly, the meaning of the situations presently experienced, of social action as such, is to be found in that which "is already over and done with" (1997: 57).

This chapter has pointed to how the key conceptual parts of Schutz's phenomenological system are interrelated, and to their potential usefulness for the explanation of dominant/minority relations in the sphere of race and ethnicity. We can draw these threads together and say that the social-phenomenological perspective as a whole offers itself as a valuable option for disclosing crucially important aspects in this area, pertaining to questions of power as well as the far-reaching effect of cultural integration in the larger society.

In the next chapter the discussion of because-motives shall be enlarged further, in connection with the constitution of the self. Subsequent chapters will deal with the elucidation of how race—racism as such, as expressed through negative attributions and discriminatory practices—has an injurious effect on the constitution of the self of members of racial minorities, leading to alienation. Attention will be devoted to how institutionalized racism is accountable for the pathologies of interethnic and interracial life. In this regard, the analysis will place into relief the way social organization built on racial bipolarity is normally associated with formally enforced intergroup separatism, and the cultural marginalization of members of groups designated as ethnic and racial minorities. The latter circumstance ultimately results in significant problems linked to the operation of social meaning for the individuals concerned, insofar as formal and informal separatism greatly limits their access to the society's dominant meaning system. The implications for social domination should be quite clear here. These individuals are pushed toward further entrenchment into a subnational lifestyle, further cultural differentiation and estrangement from the majority culture, greater obstacles to mutual understanding in their relations with majority-group members, continuing differential (i.e., unequal) treatment by the society's majority population, further seclusion into the racial subculture, further reinforcement of separatism, and so on.

NOTES

1. On the topic of James's influence on Schutz's treatment of time, see, e.g., Muzzetto (2006).

2. The *methodenstreit* hinged on whether the social sciences should develop and function as nomothetic sciences, or sciences based on empirical methods of research;

or as idiographic sciences, sciences based on the hermeneutic understanding of social and historical phenomena. The dispute commenced in the mid-1880s and lasted over a decade, although its impact was felt well into the 1900s. It was triggered by the operation of the empirically oriented Austrian School of Economics, spearheaded by economist Carl Menger, and involved, on the one hand, the scholars associated with the German historicist tradition and the general interpretive model of scholarship (e.g., among others, Ranke, Rosche, Knies, Stammler, Sombart—see Little, 2009), vs. the followers of Menger, most notably Eugen von Bohm-Bawerk and Friedrich von Wiser. Menger had fueled dissent and animosity between the two groups with his 1884 critical essay *The Errors of Historicism in German Economics.*

In the thought of Wilhelm Dilthey (1988/1923) inquiries into social phenomena are carried out in two distinct contexts: the *verstehende* sciences, or the sciences of understanding, which are oriented to "psychological" or "subjective" factors, and the *erklarende* sciences, or the sciences of explanation, which conform to the model of conventional science, and are oriented to "logical" and "objective" factors. This dualism, however, is not to be taken to represent an impassable gap between the two classes of sciences; that is, that they are mutually exclusive. Rather, these sciences operate much like two sides of the same coin. More concretely, Dilthey understood that the subjective understanding is also present in the nomothetic sciences, just as objectivity is also an orienting principle of the sciences of understanding.

Be that as it may, the differentiation between the two approaches to social inquiry holds, and the sciences of explanation have, over time, have shown a tendency to overemphasize methodological precision for its own sake, frequently at the expense of the understanding of the object of study, a classic case of goal displacement. Over the course of its evolution during the twentieth century and into the present century, sociology, and more specifically sociology in the U.S. context, has fallen into line with this dominant tendency, and with the Comtean ideal of a positivistic discipline. Yet, as Jonas (1959: 471) reminds us, it "requires a pre-sociological determination of its objects," that is, a more foundational (i.e., philosophical) grounding for identifying that which is to be investigated, establishing its operational procedures, and substantiating its claims. Otherwise, sociological praxis becomes entirely subordinate to the model of the natural sciences, which will in turn significantly limit the discipline's grasp of social reality.

From its inception, the *methodenstreit* had a significant administrative and political impact in the German-speaking academic world, which lasted into the twentieth century.

3. One may accept the distinction made by Little (2009), and argue that Schutz may have been a thoroughgoing hermeneuticist, without necessarily having fully endorsed the position of classical historicism, that is, the position that institutional life and human nature are always historically bounded or contextualized.

4. This process of formation of cultural meaning is integrated, in the sense that its moments in the past, present, and future form a cohesive or integrated whole, in parallel fashion to Cooley's formulation about the distinct *moments* of imagining in the process of self-presentation and development of the self.

5. On how the theoretical formulations of sociologists and other social scientists amount second-level interpretation, see Giddens (1984) and Habermas (1989: 107).

6. We need not extend the discussion of the mathematical calculation of the probability of the sequence of events occurring again, as this would go beyond the scope of this study. (Schutz, in fact, given the nature of the social world as opposed to that of the natural world, takes a dim view of the claim of rigorous causal assessment— which is to say, of rigorous quantitative measurement—of causal adequacy in the *social* sciences.) In any case, as Schutz claims, the pattern of repeatability of human action in social situations has to do, in virtually every case, with the coherence with *meaning-adequate* relations. He goes so far as to state that "insofar as it is a concept applying to human behavior. . . [causal adequacy] is only a special case of meaning-adequacy" (1997: 233–234). This means that causal adequacy is ultimately driven by coherence with culturally established practices and expectations that are solidly grounded in tradition and internalized by society's members through socialization, thus continuing to shape the course of social behavior and intergroup life. Important implications flow from these considerations regarding the patterns of intergroup life and the ability of researchers to explain and predict them. Clearly, too, it suggests the special importance of the cultural heritage of the community as the frame of reference for explaining the meaning of social action.

7. The *Thomas theorem* was the term given by Robert Merton to W.I. Thomas's *definition-of-the-situation* idea, to the effect that situations defined as real become real in their consequences. Facts do not exist independently and in a uniform fashion apart from the social actors who experience and interpret them. Thus, the objective meaning of situations, events, and so on, rather than being something that applies universally and across time, becomes, from this perspective, something entirely relative to how individuals experience these situations and events in particular times and places.

8. Schutz argues that, save for a few sociological thinkers, the various systems of sociology put forward in Germany during the first quarter of the twentieth century all delimited one area or level of meaning of the social world, and proceeded to explore it, but these versions of sociology failed to trace back the meaning-structures that each version had selected for investigation to this most fundamental level—that is, that of conscious life and intersubjectivity—involving the genesis and evolution of meaning ("processes of meaning-establishment"; 1997: 11), and its operation at the intersubjective level.

9. This is another aspect that finds resonance in the Meadian idea of the stages of the development of the Self. What Mead calls *the game stage* is precisely the time in our psychosocial development when we are able to relate to others on the basis of anonymity; that is, we can take the role of any other member of the society, a *generalized Other*, which essentially means we can act like everyone else in some specific situation. Thus, for instance, we can act as a friend to someone by taking on the qualities socially assigned to, and expected of, this role of "being a friend" to someone.

10. The progressive typification of social action within the various spheres of social life, at both the institutional and informal levels, amounts to the uninterrupted

process of functional specialization in modern society, which Max Weber termed the *disenchantment of the world* (*Entzauberung der Welt*).

11. A sterling example of racially based social conflict that reveals the absence of a reciprocity of perspectives among the society's formative groups, as a function of group-based political inequality, may be found in a recent (January 2019) incident in U.S. society. A group of high school students were in Washington, DC, to attend an anti-abortion demonstration, on the weekend of a national holiday celebrating Martin Luther King. There were other protest groups present, and subsequently a confrontation developed between the high school students and a group of Native American marchers, members of the Indigenous Peoples March organization. The students were of middle-class background, affiliated with the Catholic Church and Catholic education, and, most importantly, racially classified as white. Another group eventually got swept into the altercation, the Black Israelites. It is true that such factors as regional origin, socioeconomic status, and religious affiliation all play an important part in the determination of people's political, and overall ideological, position—and, therefore, they determine the viability of a reciprocity of perspectives across the board, among the various groups. In this case, however, as we consider the particular history of race and ethnic relations in U.S. society, the primary factor hindering the establishment of a reciprocity of perspectives is very clearly race. Once more, as in other similar incidents in the society over the years, racial status, with all of its implications of meaning, identity, social knowledge, and social power, acts as the overriding principle and division, across what would normally be perceived as a diversity of social segments. Thus, it reduces this apparent diversity to the dominant binary white/non-white dualism.

12. In developing this theoretical formulation Bergson sought to explore the relation between body and mind (1991: 172). It appears that, when Bergson says that the mind is affected by the sensations or stimuli from the external world, and that in turn leads to action, physical movement by the body—the "free act" is released from the person psychic structure Like an overripe fruit" (cited in Schutz, 1997: 67)—then these sensations or stimuli have to be those which flow from the concrete events in people's lives. "Stimulations received," Bergson says (1991: 173), "result in movements accomplished." In general terms, are we, following Bergson, for whom social behavior amount to the mind releasing specific types of action as "appropriate reactions" (1991: 173) to the stimuli from the external world, dealing with a psychic determinism? It seems reasonable to infer here that the description of what goes on in the mind of the social actor as she or he engages in an action, from its inception as action-in-progress to its completion as the already-constituted-act, whereby the "sensations and movements" condition our *attention to life*, may be put in more sociological terms to refer to the stimuli from the external world as representing the life experience of individuals in society, the body of accumulated cultural experiences, as signified by the stock-of-knowledge-at-hand. In other words, the behavior of individuals and groups in society will be conditioned by our attention to life, which is a mental state, clearly linked to and affected by our experiences in the everyday world.

13. There is a certain amount of determinism in this formulation. It is important to consider this determinism—a cultural determinism—in reference to how mental life operates, the choices social actors make, the resulting courses of action they embark on—and, ultimately, how this pertains closely to the discussion of intergroup life, how groups relate to one another, how intra-societal divisions affect this interactional complex, and so forth. Campbell asserts that consciousness and intersubjectivity are socially grounded. "Consciousness of daily life," he says, "is a social consciousness," which rests on the operation of typifications created and utilized daily by social groups (1981: 205–206). From this standpoint, it is only a short step to the specific context and patterns of race relations, as treated here. As Schutz says it, "By delimiting and determining the segment of our experiences of the world which . . becomes thematic, the intellect pre-delineates the lines *to be followed by action*" ([emphasis mine], 1970c: 5).

14. This emphasis on the *general lines* is meant to address the normal variations or deviations within the broad, yet distinct, pattern of behavior and thought characterizing each society.

15. This is the "the pragmatic motive." Schutz (1970c: 5) acknowledges the theoretical insights of Bergson and James on this point.

16. McCall (1983: 133) comments on the emphasis placed by *Daseinanalyse* on social learning and socialization, which in turn throws into relief the importance of the social world in the shaping of human behavior. Humans beings are *in* the social world, and not "[in] a Cartesian mind, boarded up in its own ideas and cut off from material [and social] entities." For some brief comments on the issue of the individual-*in*-the-world, refer to Binswanger (1962: 17–23).

17. Bergson's discussion of the *attention-to-life* concept reveals its organicist thrust and implications, by exploring the body-mind relation and aspects of psychic "equilibrium" (1991: 172–173). Schutz's appropriation of this concept takes it to a more abstract level, that of its operation in the realm of subjectivity. The present study relies on Schutz's conceptual focus on the operations of consciousness, and the purpose is to shed further light on social action in the more substantive area of race and ethnic relations.

18. Schutz's emphasis on the determining power of the lifeworld, the larger collective experience of social actors, on their action patterns, does not imply a cultural determinism of the Parsonian variety, with its reification of institutional structures, and these reified structures unilaterally conditioning the behavior of individuals. The main emphasis of a Schutzian social phenomenology, as concerns the nature of social reality, is that the latter is still to be found in the subjective experiences of social actors. At the same time, this interest in consciousness is not to be taken in terms of the argument being framed in psychologism, as already suggested. A considerable number of social analysts have, over the last half-century or so, taken a dim view of socio-psychological frameworks of investigation, which are often perceived to be vitiated by unregulated subjectivism, rendering them immune to quantifiability, and thus methodologically unreliable. Yet, the mainsprings of social behavior, as Schutz contends (1997: 239–240), are not subjectivistic in the sense of being purely oriented by introspection, or, as he put it, by "uncontrollable intuition, or metaphysical

revelation" (1945: 79), or a search for the idiosyncratic or the irrational. Rather, Schutz's reliance on subjectivity is tied to his foundational concern with the operation of *the social*, and with how individual actors experience it in their daily involvement with other fellow actors in the lifeworld. Therefore, the interpretive thrust here is not, strictly speaking, subjectivistic, but intersubjectivistic. What we are dealing with, then, is not with psychology *per se*, but with social psychology—Schutz's system most clearly keeps the researcher in the area of psychosocial relations, with primacy being granted to the *social*.

Additionally, the emphasis on subjectivity in Schutzian phenomenology assumes the rationality of the behavior of the individual actor, which is the prerequisite for satisfying the exigencies of the means-end framework in which action occurs, thus making possible the formal and objective construction of ideal types of social action. The ideal type, in this context, is a useful analytical device because it is causally adequate and adequate at the level of meaning (1997: 236).

In any event, the central notion here is that social reality is most directly and effectively grasped by interpretive, not positivistic, social science, inasmuch as this reality consists of the interrelations among human beings as *subjects,* thus being in this sense (as noted above) "psychological" and (inter)subjective. Human relations, though manifested concretely as social behavior and swayed by physical forces, are most fundamentally "psychical." Processes of intersubjectivity, as Jonas asserted (1959: 472), "underlie *all* (emphasis mine) social experience." This means that the sciences of society, in order to understand these relations, must first and necessarily address the problem of meaning as the *sine qua non* of social life. The processes involved in the constitution of social meaning should, as one analyst argues (Eberle, 2014: 24), "the core of the analysis of the lifeworld."

This being the case, the proper approach for understanding and explaining the structure of the social world must be a hermeneutical one. Yet, the precise dissection of the constitution and operation of meaning is an extraordinarily complex and challenging enterprise. As Eberle points out (2014: 24), among the varieties of interpretive methodologies, there is no social-scientific hermeneutics that exclusively fits the model and meets the requirements of a phenomenological analysis of the lifeworld—or, to put it more specifically, in terms of precisely delineating the extent to which, and the ways in which, social actors grasp the meanings and perceptions of others. This is, in sum, the limits that intersubjectivity, as such, imposes on the scientific observer, as the latter tries to reveal its nature at the deepest level. In this regard, there is the problem of fully grasping subjective meaning in a way that is empirically demonstrable. There will always be nuances of intersubjective meaning that will escape the grasp of empirical assessment, of "complete [analytical] adequacy." As Eberle (2014: 24) remarks in this respect, "a certain distance between the subjective meaning constructions of everyday actors and their scientific reconstruction [always] remains."

In the same vein, Habermas postulates that the principles that guide social action are identified and internalized collectively, ultimately becoming "objects of [collective] experience at the level of the understanding of symbols" (1989: 58). This means that these cultural symbols do not arise within the individual consciousness by means of introspection, but are, rather, developed in consciousness as a result of people's socialization experience—which is collectively based. In relation to this process, they come to operate at the level of intersubjectivity. Therefore, the reference to "personality" in the present discussion—that is, to the factors and processes of psychology, of individual consciousness—is not at variance with the sociological conception of this human attribute, such as articulated, for instance, by Simpson and Yinger (see Rex, 1983: 139, in this regard). This study endorses the view that "personality" is very much a product of group life, and *changes* with changes in the architecture of group life.

Chapter 4

The *Because-Motive* and the Constitution of the Self

It is axiomatic in sociology to say that the self is a product of society. Selfhood arises from the dialectical negotiation between the two elements—the Individual, on the one hand, and society on the other. Numerous scholars in sociology, psychology, anthropology, and philosophy have grappled with this most important of issues. In sociology, pride of place is given to those theorists whose work is generally considered to bridge sociology and psychology, namely, the *sociologists of everyday life*, among whom the major luminaries are, in the U.S. context, George Herbert Mead and Charles Horton Cooley. Psychologists, as might be expected, and especially those who work in in the clinical and *gestalt* fields, have always shown great concern with the explanation of the Self (Bock, 1988: 197). This is also true for the work of some literary figures, such as Proust, and philosophers, such as Bergson or McIntyre. The contributions made by these scholars toward the understanding of the self, and how they relate to the thought of Alfred Schutz in this regard, will be briefly considered in this chapter.

Schutz's contribution to the discourse on the constitution of the self is explored in this chapter in reference to the key formulation pertaining to the motivational context of social interaction, the *genuine because-motive*. This concept was examined in the previous chapter, and it entails the apprehension, by the active subject, of the relevant lived experiences from his or her past—in Schutz's words, the recovery of "the meaningful ground of [her/his] behavior" (1967: 86)—toward the explanation of present behavior. At the same time, these past experiences express the ways of the collectivity, the society's typifications—shared culture, in other words. Thus, subjectivity represents "from the outset . . . an intersubjective world of culture" (Schutz, in Ferguson, 2006: 93).

In treating social reality as a process resulting from the everyday actions of active subjects, and exploring the complex relation between subjectivity and intersubjectivity, Schutz's work, like that of the other thinkers discussed in this connection, is very much within the tradition of social psychology.

THE SELF AS SOCIAL PRODUCT

The ideas of Mead and Cooley are in basic harmony with those of Schutz regarding the conception of the self. Mead starts out by stressing its social and historical nature—that is, its genesis in social life, its embeddedness in personal history. As he puts it, the self "has a development . . . [it] arises in the process of social experience and activity, that is, develops in the given individual as a result of his relations to that process as a whole and to other individuals within that process" (1962: 135). Thus, Mead's position shows clearly how social life—culture, as such—takes on an ontological character, insofar as it becomes the very ground of selfhood, of our sense of existing as a distinct human unit among countless others. The very process of *self-inter-action,*[1] a process of abstraction which, according to Mead, the individual is constantly engaged in, whether alone or in interaction with others, and which fundamentally amounts to reflecting on the stimuli perennially flowing from other persons, situations, and so on, before deliberations are made in consciousness and a course of action is pursued—none of that would be possible without the person's developmental history in the collectivity, and the previous learning of a whole complex of cultural norms, meanings, and so on, which in turned provided the means for role-taking at the level of the *generalized other*. Role-taking, the principal Meadian mechanism in this respect, stands for the person's internalization of (via socialization), and response to, social stimuli (regarding Mead's discussion of the social foundations of thought, and therefore of the emergence of the self, see 1962: 253–260).

Cooley described the genesis of the self in terms of what he called the reflected or *looking-glass self* (1922: 184). This involves a three-dimensional process, made up of a set of interrelated impressions or imaginings, which, like the Meadian explanation, emphasizes the *social* origin of selfhood. We start with the person's participation in social life, or projection of oneself unto the social group. This leads the person, first, to imagine that she or he is making an appearance to others; then, to imagine that others are making a judgment on that appearance; and finally, on the basis of these first two phases, to develop a particular type of self-feeling—that is, a sense of what kind of person one is. Cooley categorized this self-feeling emerging from this process broadly, as "pride or mortification." Generally, this will have an effect of future courses of action for the individual involved. In other words, this generalized process of self-assessment on the basis of what is reflected on "the looking-glass" will exert a shaping force on social behavior, as we become oriented by what we imagine that others, the community as such, think of us. In presenting social behavior as being primarily determined by the psychic unity or integration of the collectivity, Cooley has been said by some authors (e.g., Swingewood, 1993: 264) to have slipped into a position of mentalism. However, what has greatest relevance in Cooley's *looking-glass self* formulation for the present analysis is the notion that the development of the self, and social action as such, are oriented by collectively shared meanings and definitions, by the workings of intersubjectivity. "Self-feeling," Cooley remarks, is "connected with the thought of other persons . . . [and] has its chief scope *within* general life, not outside of it; the special endeavor or tendency of which it is the emotional aspect finds its principal field of exercise in a world of personal forces, reflected in the mind by a world of personal impressions" (1922: 179).[2]

THE HISTORICITY ASPECT

The historical dimension of the self is not a distinct or separate aspect, but simply expresses the uninterrupted flow of experience in the person's life. As indicated in the previous chapter, Bergson addressed this continuity and indivisibility of the present, of existing within the present, in terms of the *durée*, his term for the flow of time—not mathematical or chronometric time, an artificial construct which cannot capture the true nature of human life, which is a flux, or an uninterrupted flow, which therefore can only be apprehended via "intuition"[3]— but *inner time*, which captures the "inwardness of life" (Bergson, 1998: 176). The operation of inner time means that what we refer to as the lived present is time that has already passed, or gone by; hence, it is past time, and "already far from me"; and it is toward the time-yet-to-be, or the future, that my present life is oriented. This intertwining of temporal stages is reflected in Bergson's assertion: "What I call 'my present,'" he says, "has one foot in my past and another in my future." In other words, it is toward the future that my present is tending; my present is my "impending action." In the context of the *durée*, the (indivisible) present is essentially "a perception of the immediate past and a determination of the immediate future." These are the foundational, interwoven aspects that reflect our "continuity of becoming" (1991: 137–140).

The invisible determining effect of the unconscious (vs. the conscious assertion of rational choice), as linked to past experience, in establishing the patterns of personal life and the development of the self, is clearly evinced in Proust's major work, *A La Recherche du Temps Perdu* (1987). He makes a reference to *l'edifice immense du souvenir* (the immense edifice of remembrance; 1988: 46), an idea that underlines the crucial role of memory in the constitution of the self, here in relation to what the symbolic effect of the *madeleine*. Furthermore, consciousness operates always and unavoidably in terms of this retrieval and reconstruction of the past and its integration into the present—"the prolongation of the past into the present" (Hughes, 1977: 386). The thinking self is imprisoned in the past, because the memory of past things and events comes unceasingly to mind without being consciously summoned. Thus the past becomes the present in a perpetually dynamic motion. In this respect, time is bent, and the traditional dualism of the past and present is dissolved.

Proust's attention to the existential significance of the *madeleine* attests to how, in his work as well as in that of Bergson, the main focus is placed on the memory of objects and/or events in the past that bear a particular significance for personal life and the constitution of the self. As Meyerhoff puts it, this involves "the recollection of single, unique, unrepeatable experiences . . . [treated as having] . . . a special function in the quest for the recovery of time and the self." In this respect, Proust's treatment of the past has a specific affinity with Bergson's *durée* (Hughes, 1977: 386). The following passage is instructive in this respect:

> The recollection of these single events in their original, qualitative content, the good-night kiss, the bell at the gate, the books in the library, the magic lantern, the hawthorn in bloom, the *madeleine*, the curbstone, the clatter of a fork or spoon—the recollection of these and a multitude of other events *serves to convey a meaning of selfhood* (emphasis mine) which could not be elicited from the contents of immediate experience. These recollections, together with their significant associations, set the process of creative imagination in operation and sustain it. Creative imagination is creative recall. Recollection is an activity, an operation—not the passive reproduction of habitual memory responses. To construct a work of art is to re-construct the world of experience and the self. And thus a concept of the self emerges, through the act of creative recall translated into a process of artistic creation, displaying characteristics of unity and continuity which could not be attributed to the self as given in immediate experience. (Meyerhoff, 1955: 47–48)

In the work of Mead and Cooley the social and historical nature of the self is likewise emphasized. For Mead, what we may refer to here, in a general way, as psychic equilibrium, revolves around our ability to identify and organize the mental elements of our daily experience—things, events—in terms of "the point of view of our past experiences" (1962: 135). Thus, we get our psychic, and more fundamentally, existential, equilibrium in present life through the ability to frame the things that surround us in the present—events, experiences, our *consociates* (i.e., people we interact with, who belong to our contemporary world), objects, in the larger span of our personal history. When someone or something escapes, in the person's consciousness, that person's ability to "date" the said person or object, we do not rest until we are able to retrieve this person or this object from what people in Brazil call *o baú do esquecimento* (the trunk or chest of forgetfulness)—a procedure that brings out more clearly the importance of memory in this connection. In accomplishing this, one situates, as noted, the concrete aspects of our daily lives that concern us in our personal history, at a particular point in it, and thus restore existential equilibrium. People's existential bearings thus hinge on people's command of their .personal history.

Mead's conception of the self stresses its historicity insofar as he characterizes the self as a formative process based on the person's ongoing interactions with others in society over the life cycle. Mead postulates this process in terms of a progressively developing ability of individuals *to take the role of the other*, a developmental process that lasts through the life cycle of the individual. Concerning this role-taking activity, Mead's emphasis on the historicity of the self is dramatically revealed in his formulation of the *I* and the *Me* aspects of selfhood, which are in fact the structuring elements of the self. The *Me* stands for the socialized self. It corresponds to how one sees one's self from the standpoint of every other member of society, of the attitudes of the collectivity—of the whole community as such. Thus, this is the dimension of the self as *object*. It stands for the unceasing reaction of the person's self toward its socialized manifestation, or the Me. This signifies the operation of the self as *subject*. It occurs at the mature stage of role-playing, when the individual becomes old enough (still in childhood) to take the role of the *generalized other*—that is, to objectify oneself from the standpoint of the expectations of the community. As such, the *I* acts as the potential source of personal resistance to social regulation and control. To sum up, in this viewpoint, the self is structured by these opposing forces in the context of the constant tension between the individual and society. The dialectical entanglement between these two elements is generally never fully resolved—which is not a matter of direct concern here, but it does show the historically changing and contingent nature of the self, as it develops and reaches maturity through the continual struggle between the individual and society. Ultimately, as indicated, this is a never-ending process, shaped by the impact (in consciousness) of accumulated, or historical, experience.

In both Mead and Cooley, the main distinguishing feature of the self is its ability to objectify itself. This results from—and is only possible in relation to—its emergence as a product of society, its embeddedness and constitution in collective life. It is from the perspective of others like ourselves, Mead explains—from the perspective of the *generalized self*, as he termed it—that the self of individuals is able to assess itself, to look at itself, and in this way we gain a sense of who we are. Because the self of individuals can be an object to itself, this becomes the basis, the condition of possibility, of its constitution. The self operates through this continuous reconstruction of past experience, of situations, of events, in which the person was involved.

The historical dimension is also presupposed in Cooley's view of the constitution of the self. When, in the second moment of the looking-glass self process, we imagine that others are making a particular assessment or judgment of our appearance, this presupposes a common sharedness of what Schutz called typifications. More precisely, this assumes the history of everyone in the community living and growing up together, and internalizing the complex of typified behaviors, meanings, interpretive schemes, and so on, associated with the community-at-large. The weight of the past bears down heavily on people's interpretations of the present. The familiarity of individuals in the community with the latter's general *stock of knowledge* results from a background of systematic socialization into dominant cultural definitions, expectations, and so forth. This is true for all those people to whom we imagine that we are making a presentation or appearance. Otherwise, how could we imagine that this appearance was coming across to others as having a particular meaning, and what meaning that would be?

This discussion may be amplified by considering, in rather synoptic terms, McIntyre's narrative view of the self, which places great emphasis on its historical and social embeddedness. The integration of the self is presented in the context of the (Aristotelian) sense of unitary virtue, and the parallel need for a conception of selfhood that rests on the unity of a narrative that "links birth to life to death as narrative beginning to middle to end" (McIntyre, 1984: 423). The idea of historicity in this formulation of the self should be obvious enough, and it is principally addressed via the concepts of intelligibility and accountability, which function as the very basis of personal identity. These two elements express the individual's ability to put forth an intelligible account of her or his background, past events and behaviors in which one was involved, and which, therefore, influenced one's personal development. "By recalling our personal history," he remarks, "we give ourselves a personal identity" (1984: 14). Of equal importance is the fact that this undertaking, through which personal identity is systematically extracted and developed, extends beyond the person herself or himself, to incorporate others—much like the moments or phases of self-recognition in Mead or Cooley, whereby gaining a sense of who I am involves my perception of how others see me as well as my own perception or interpretation of how I am seen by others. This is a dialectical interplay that immediately reveals the social constitution of the self, a salient aspect of McIntyre's theory of self as a narrative process.

Thus, as individuals endeavor to formulate a self-identity, they are not only responsible for this process of accountability themselves, but can also involve fellow human beings in the same experience. As McIntyre puts it, "I am part of their story, as they are part of mine. The narrative of any one life is part of an *interlocking* [emphasis mine] set of narratives" (1984: 425).

SCHUTZ'S PHENOMENOLOGY AND
THE CONSTITUTION OF THE SELF

Schutz's phenomenology dovetails with the formulations presented above, in connection with his major theoretical contribution to the understanding of the self with his idea of the divisions of the world of everyday life. The latter is composed of the *mitwelt* (or the world of contemporaries), the *vorwelt* (or the world of predecessors), and the *folgewelt* (or the world of successors). Schutz postulated that selfhood is something that depends on the integration of experiences that have occurred, that are presently occurring, and that have yet to occur. This basically corresponds to the differentiated segments of the lifeworld. The theorists considered in this regard essentially share the view of the self as a dynamic, constantly evolving entity that participates in the life-world in an integrative manner, drawing together its formative elements from the past, which then yields its constitution in the present, and its orientation toward the future. In the world of contemporaries, or the present time, social actors get involved with one another in consonance with regulatory principles laid down by their predecessors, namely, the whole *stock-of-knowledge-at-hand* and *typifications* available to the members of a given community, carried over into the present from the world of earlier generations, our ancestors, and internalized via the socialization process as the standard to live by. Our connection with the world yet to come, of course, is necessarily different. We have no knowledge of our successors, nor of the social world they will inhabit. We can only imagine or assume, as Schutz indicates (1997: 143), that the world of the future and its inhabitants will correspond ideal-typically, in terms of its structures and conditions, as well as basic patterns of social interaction, and so on, to the world in which we presently live. Thus, none of the theorists introduced here treats the self in the manner of certain strands of sociological explanation—such as, for instance, structural functionalism of the Parsonian variety[4]—as an entity emerging solely from the world of contemporaries—the ahistorical self, a product of the effect of the prevailing structural conditions and arrangements of the society.

Against the backdrop of the commonalities among the theories of the self discussed here, it may be said that subjectivity—specifically, self-conception or self-image—amounts to a process of accountability or story-telling, perpetually going on in consciousness. McIntyre's incisive analysis of this aspect is of first importance. As noted above, he frames the developmental character of the self in terms of the necessary integration of the process of accountability, or the necessary "unity of a narrative quest." Selfhood and personal identity are indistinguishable in this theoretical model, and they "are presupposed by the unity of the character which the unity of a narrative requires" (1984: 425). Of equal importance is the fact that such a unified "narrative" and the unified self that it generates do not occur in isolation, but rather in the context of society—in the context of interaction with others; in more pointedly phenomenological terms, in the context of intersubjectivity. "The narrative of any one life," says McIntyre, "is part of an interlocking set of narratives" (1984: 425). Herein lies the connection of the individual with society, and it is in this sense that we are said to be bearers of a tradition, the larger history and structural circumstances in which we have lived, and which are bequeathed to us in each society, by our predecessors. This is an extremely important point, as we proceed to examine the self in the specific social sphere of race, through the lens of Schutzian social phenomenology.

These essential properties of the self connect harmoniously with Schutz's theory of motivation, which, as explained earlier, encompasses two general types of motivating forces of human behavior, the *in-order-to motives* and *because-motives*. It is with the latter that we shall be mainly concerned, because of its being situated in the person's past experience. It involves, in Schutz's words, the retrieval of "a lived experience temporally prior to the [action being presently undertaken]," and therefore it has "the temporal character of pastness" (Schutz, 1997: 92–93). The social actor interprets and reconstructs aspects of past life that will provide the motivational context of, *and thus explain*, the behavioral project-at-hand. That is, the past is meaningful in relation to "the relevances of the present" (Barber, 2001: 100). This reconstruction also presupposes an underlying continuity and unity of the historical background involved, since the social actor will seek out the historical instances and experiences—whether personal, related to family life, cultural situations, and such like—that unite into a cohesive constellation of variables from which certain factors are identified as logically accountable for present behaviors, projects, and so on. As the social actor gains an understanding of how her or his life trajectory reveals her or his present projects, commitments, and so on are what they are, she or he is concomitantly gaining a sense of who she or he is—which means, a sense of self. The process of accountability associated with the *because-motives*, and consisting of the recovery of the past to account for or explain the present, stands at the very base of the constitution of the self. Thus conceptualized, *because-motives* are the building blocks of identity and selfhood.

Schutz's interpretation thus clearly emphasizes the social origin and the historical character of the self because it presents the *social* background of the individual as being accountable for personal behavior, and all of these social forces operate, in historically variable form, through the length of personal history. Our lives are sustained by our incorporation of *the social*, of the history of the society as manifested in its traditions, and typifications. Thus, society molds subjectivity over the life cycle of individuals. In incorporating society into our self-development, we are determined by it. All the typifications operative in the world of everyday life at different points in time— habitual practices and modes of thinking, meanings, schemes of relevance, goals, and so on—will determine the nature of subjectivity. It follows, then, that the intersubjective determination of the social construction, either positive or negative, of individuals in society, will strongly affect the individuals in question, either positively or negatively.

SOCIAL INTERACTION AND MEMORY

Schutz's account of the motivational-context-as-meaning-context of social interaction affords us an understanding of the dynamics of the individual-society dialectic. In this specific context, *social interaction* stands for Society, and *memory* for the Individual. That is to say, the Subject—subjectivity, as such—is represented by memory, inasmuch as it is formed through the process of recovering the past—through the capacity to remember, to evoke Proust's remark again. In seeking to account for her or his project-at-hand, the individual relies on memory to retrieve and select past experiences toward the determination of the appropriate meaning-structure for that project. It is through this process of retrieval, as noted above, that subjectivity, or the self, is formed.

To recapitulate the points made so far: the construction of the self is a historical process in that it derives fundamentally from the person's memory of past events, objects, experiences. The memory of the past constantly reacquaints us with experiences we have had, which have exerted, in varying degrees, a shaping influence on our psychological development, yet form a cohesive stream running up to the present. These experiences give meaning to present life, and continuously structure our sense of self. Thus, the past is a frame of reference from which we can never extricate ourselves. The present time keeps us occupied with schemes of relevance that are more immediately geared to the utilitarian concerns of daily life, to the courses of action that we embark on and justify through the *in-order-to motives.* However, the sense of selfhood is not gained *in toto* from the practical projects and concerns of everyday life, but rather from the larger context of the person's history. It is drawn from the inventory of experiences the person has lived through, from the earliest stages of life.

Moreover, the recollection of this historical material is undertaken in relation to the cultural environment in which the person has grown up, and with which he or she has been constantly and intimately involved, right down to the present time. This process stands for the dialectical encounter between the individual and society, out of which the self emerges. In Schutz, the dialectical relation between the individual and society—between subjectivity and intersubjectivity—involves the subject who relies on memory to recover materials from one's history, and integrates them into a meaningful and cohesive story, so as to make sense of present circumstances. The logical organization of this accountability process, furthermore, imparts to it the quality of intelligibility. In this respect accountability and intelligibility are coterminous and interdependent "moments" in the constitution of the self.

At the same time, the attributions of meaning to past experience is grounded in intersubjectivity—in the historically and commonly shared meanings of the society, which points to the social origin of these meanings, thus indicating their social origin. In other words, when the subject engages in these processes, it does not do so in isolation, like the Cartesian self. Obviously, then, consciousness does not operate in a social vacuum, apart from the typified structures and practices of society, but in direct dependence on them. It is in this context of a dynamic interrelation between the individual and society that McIntyre offers the idea of co-authorship, implying that one cannot extricate oneself from the social context. Schutz remarks, in reference to the establishment and interpretation of meanings, that these processes "are pragmatically determined in the intersubjective sphere" (1997: 74).

Schutz's great emphasis on the meaning-context of social experience addresses interrelated themes, such as, first of all, the pivotal importance of inner time—the *durée*—in the formation of the self. The flow of life in consciousness cannot be divided up into precise, homogeneous spatiotemporal portions, but, instead, must be articulated and understood through " 'unities' of inner duration, which are relational unities" (Schutz and Luckmann, 1973: 56). The movement of consciousness backward, as involved in the expression of the because-motive, occurs in the stream of inner time, in which case the latter becomes the condition of possibility for the validation of the actor's explanation of present actions, of the accountability process. Thus, the *durée* is what makes it cohesive, intelligible, meaningful.

Secondly, Schutz's discourse on meaning highlights the idea that social meanings and typifications in general, which make up the society's stock of knowledge, have a profound impact on the lives of individuals, as the latter engage daily in these typical patterns of acting and thinking on which social interaction rests. This is the dialectical process mentioned earlier. It is from this encounter with social meanings that a perception of the type of person we are within the collectivity will emerge. These meanings will obviously affect individuals and groups differently. However, under normal circumstances—that is to say, where members of a society function in a condition of interchangeability with everyone else in the larger community, that is, unencumbered by their social (ascribed or achieved) statuses—individuals will, for the most part, understand and use these meanings to interact with others in rather consistent and uniform patterns. Accordingly, in the degree that these various aspects of social interaction, and the activities of consciousness associated with it, are expressions of the selves of the social actors involved, these selves are being expressed in a generalized way—that is, being affected only by the "normal" things, the difficulties, challenges, aspects of daily life common to everyone in the lifeworld—notwithstanding the significant variation in the actual configuration of the self of individuals, due to the variation in these individuals' personal histories. As can be gathered, these meanings have a decisive shaping effect on the formation of the self, individually as well as collectively.

However, under certain circumstances, social meanings and typifications may exert a harmful effect on the psychological structure and development of individuals and social groups. This involves meanings that deny the basic humanity of the people toward whom they are directed, in the sense of proclaiming their essential inferiority. In the present study, these meanings are examined in the context of the interaction between dominant and nondominant racial groups. In conditions of institutionalized race-based inequality and domination, racial meanings and attributions normally unleash a number of negative consequences for the development of the self of racialized individuals, ranging from cognitive dissonance and alienation, to bitterness and self-hatred, to servility and despair—in sum, a whole array of interrelated afflictions that interfere with their social existence (this problem will be more fully examined in chapter 6).

In connection with this model of intergroup relations, subjectivity and self-development for minority-group members—that is, the racialized parts of the population—as associated with their attempt to establish a context of motivation and meaning for their present projects or action patterns by recourse to *because-motives*, their retrieval of the past will amount, fundamentally, to a retrieval of a personal history of social marginalization and oppression, involving, more specifically, a complex of typified ideas and practices in the wider society that has historically harmed them, materially and psychologically, thus adversely affecting the development of their self. Out of this dialectical encounter with society, a particular conception of themselves will emerge, expressing their daily experience of contradiction. Several well-known analysts have written about the internal hardship and turmoil associated with life in a society split apart by racial meanings, negotiating the construction of the self amid contradictory social attributions—such as, for example, their formal definition as citizens, entitled to basic constitutional rights and liberties versus the daily formal and informal negation, in a variety of ways, of this citizenship status.

THE BACKWARD GLANCE AND
THE MEANING OF THINGS

On the basis of these reflections, we may establish the following points: Schutz's treatment of the motivational context of social action, particularly his focus on the employment of *because-motives*, is of paramount importance for this discussion. These motives consist of the Subject's "attitude toward the past," specifically of how much importance is assigned by the Subject to lived-experiences from the past, which make them relevant to the circumstances of the present. The present, therefore, is accounted for by the past. The recovery of past experiences through memory is carried out in the inner stream of duration, not in the world of mathematical or chronometric time. The type of interpretive treatment that the Subject will confer to the lived experiences selected from the past is determined by the conditions of the Here-and-Now—and, more precisely still, by the "mode of attention" that the Subject directs to courses of action just completed, and concomitantly and in a broader sense, to the entirety of its experience (Schutz, 1997: 73, 96). As Schutz remarks: "It is from the point of view of the present moment that the shaft of attention is directed backward on the elapsed phases" (1997: 73). To phrase it in a different way: how the Subject (Ego) defines and establishes its attitude toward the past hinges on its attitude to life as such, its *attention à la vie*.

Schutz distinguishes between the subjective and objective meaning of things, and also identifies distinctions within each category. For the purposes of this study, the basic subjective/objective distinction, in very abbreviated form, will have to suffice. The former is the meaning provided by the social actor. As pointed out earlier, Schutzian theory holds that we normally account for our present actions either in terms of a future orientation (*the in-order-to motive*)—as in, for instance, where we pursued a particular course-of-action in order to achieve a desired outcome; or in reference to our past experiences—the *because-motive*—as in the case of our accounting for present behaviors in terms of experiences and events in our background. By appealing to the because-motive for what Schutz termed the "explanation of the deed" (1997: 91) we put forth a *particular kind* of explanation, in which the *meaning-context* of patterns of behavior, projects, and so on is always established on the basis of the backward turn of consciousness. Projects in the present are always driven—that is, motivated—by past events, by lived experiences that are temporally prior to the event in the present. In activating the *because-motive*, the actor "looks for past experiences which were relevant to [his, her] actions" (Schutz, 1997: 29). The objective meaning is determined intersubjectively, and shared by the group—they are, in other words, typifications, making up the group's stock of knowledge. The meaning we confer upon the things of the external world is commonly shared, since the external or public world "is given equally to all of us." Therefore, the meaning of things emerges and is formed "as an intersubjective phenomenon" (Schutz, 1997: 32; see also Münch, 1994: 146–147, vol. 2).

Additionally, as noted before, our subjective grasp of the meaning of our actions is a process of accounting for those actions, a process of accountability. It involves the *motivational understanding* that we have for our actions. The connection between this subjective process (i.e., the motivational understanding in the person's consciousness) and society may be seen in the fact that it starts in consciousness on the basis of an already-established *objective* meaning. This means that the motivational understanding that social actors have of their actions originates in a context of meanings that are *socially or intersubjectively produced and established*, and thus operate independently of what meanings and attributions may emerge in the individual consciousness (Schutz, 1997: 31–33).

The accountability process that is activated in relation to the *because-motive* is engaged only when the person engages in a particular type of "self-explication" (Schutz, 1997: 95), which normally does not occur, which means people are normally driven to present an *in-order-to-motive* type of explanation for their actions. But, when this self-explication is activated, the individual resorts to the backward glance, and to the selection of a specific interpretive scheme (i.e., the cohesive narrative mentioned earlier) that is relevant to the present situation.

These considerations immediately foreground the critical importance of social meanings as *shaping agents* of social action. Irrespective of whether the social actors affected by these meanings adjust to and incorporate them into their self-conception or self-image, or whether they consciously seek to fight them, the overall, group-wide negative effect of these meanings is beyond dispute. Thus, what has been said so far points, first of all, to the crucial importance of history in accounting for and determining what occurs presently. In more specific terms, we can see how the meaning of historical events and practices that have marked the relations between dominant and nondominant social groups shape the nature of their present-day relations. This is illustrated by the ill effects brought upon by racial meanings on the development of the self and the lives of racialized individuals.

As a rule, the individuals involved will resolve their dialectical relation with the society in terms of some form of accommodation. In multiethnic/multiracial contexts where racial bipolarity and the corollary society-wide segregation of the two groups are enforced by law (e.g.., the case of the twentieth-century enforcement of Jim Crow in the United States, and *apartheid* in South Africa), the accommodation is made, in the main, through conformity to second-class citizenship and all that is associated with it. When the institutional support of racial bipolarity is removed and the society moves on to full structural—though not necessarily cultural and biological—assimilation of all its members, the *idea* of the validity of society-wide racial separatism typically remains ingrained in the public mind. In U.S. society, the new (i.e., post–Jim Crow) pattern of accommodation has essentially reflected the persisting legacy of the Jim Crow period, whereby members of the groups codified as racial minorities embrace the socially construed separatist identity and everything associated with it, such as the notion of a set of essential (i.e., racially driven) cultural traits. During this post–Jim Crow era, the dominant racial segment of the society for its part encourages the overall race-based informal separatism, by affirming and celebrating minority-group difference. The latter also finds legitimation in formal sources, such as the politics of difference, or identity politics. In reality, the group differences have been the product of social forces, namely, the systematic legal enforcement, in times past, of racial separatism across all spheres of social life. In any case, with the shift to comparatively more peaceful and less discriminatory conditions of living for racial minorities, these traits have crystallized into a distinct subcultural form of group life.

Drawing together the theoretical ideas presented so far, we argue that they are acutely important for the study of race and ethnic relations. The next couple of chapters will explore in greater depth how the construction of the self of individuals is influenced by race as a regulatory principle of social relations. Chapter 5 develops this idea by tracing the parallels between the problems of daily life for members of racialized groups, and the circumstances of the Schutzian *stranger*. Chapter 6 then follows up with a discussion of the baleful consequences, such as social alienation and marginalization, brought upon minority racial groups by racism.[5]

NOTES

1. Self-interaction expresses the dialectical relation between the individual and society, conceptualized by Mead in terms of the tension in consciousness between the "I" and the "Me." In his words:

the "I" . . . in this relation of the "I" and the "me," is something that is, so to speak, responding to a social situation which is within the experience of the individual. It is the answer which the individual makes to the attitude that others take towards him when he assumes an attitude towards them. Now, the attitude he is taking towards them will contain a novel element. The "I" gives the sense of freedom, of initiative. (1962: 177)

2. Their theoretical affinities notwithstanding, Mead and Cooley may still be distinguished in reference to the fact that Cooley is conventionally regarded as being more clearly "idealist," inasmuch as he gives primacy to processes of consciousness in the constitution of the self. In his work, society is defined psychologically, as a "psychical whole," as Mead pointed out (1930: 703). Mead, on the other hand, takes a more pragmatic, behaviorally oriented approach to the explanation of the self and its relation to the social environment. For him, it is in the process of communication that one finds "a world of selves standing on the same level of reality as that of the physical world that surrounds us." In a landmark article where he acknowledges the value of Cooley's theoretical influence, Mead is nevertheless critical of Cooley's excessive emphasis on "mental processes," out of which comes a conception of society as being purely "an affair of consciousness," a conception that is "mental rather than scientific" (1930: 695–706).

3. The Bergsonian definition for this concept: a type of instinct "that has become disinterested, self-conscious, capable of reflecting upon its object and of enlarging it indefinitely" (1998: 176).

4. The central feature of Parsonian structural-functionalism, particularly in its later (post–Second World War) phase, was a markedly anti-voluntaristic orientation, which emphasized the subordination of the individual unit to the social system—specifically, it made the system the point of departure for social analysis, and stressed the alignment of the motivation of social actors with the dominant normative cultural standards of the society.

5. The race-and-ethnicity literature for the United States contains a considerable number of theoretical as well as literary treatments of this issue. Classic accounts include, inter alia, Dubois (1903/1990); Baldwin (1963); Moody (1968); Wright (1966, 2008).

Chapter 5

The Racial *Other* as Schutzian *Stranger*

Drawing, no doubt, on his own experience as an immigrant to the United States in 1940, Schutz utilizes the resources of phenomenology in his seminal article *The Stranger* (1944) to explain the sense of outsidedness, of *otherness*, that the typical newcomer goes through, as she or he starts life anew in a strange land. The concepts of his phenomenological system lend themselves admirably well to the description of this particular form of alienation, the sense of not-belonging, which emerges as the outsider tries to adjust to a new set of surroundings, a new language, a new worldview, and the way of life.

In this chapter, as noted earlier, the main attempt is, first, to identify the structural similarities between the condition of otherness of the Schutzian *stranger* in the new society and the otherness of people victimized by the operation of race (i.e., by institutionalized racism in all its forms) in their own society. Secondly, to show how living in otherness, whether caused by the lack of familiarity and adroitness toward the new sociocultural environment, in the case of the stranger, or by the systematic attribution of degrading meanings by the wider society to the members of racialized groups, has a pernicious impact on the construction of the selfhood of these individuals, leading to various forms and degrees of social alienation. Both the newcomers to a foreign land, and members of racialized groups, share this condition of otherness as a shaping factor of their subjectivity, and of their sense of who they are in the society-at-large.

In Schutz's essay, cultural differences establish several levels of *otherness*, denoting the stranger's inferiority vis-à-vis the society's native residents. For example, the Irish of the first wave of Irish migration to U.S. society in the 1840s were defined as slavish Papists, improvident idlers, disturbers of the peace, pugnacious drunkards, and such like. These dominant social meanings impacted heavily on the lives of the first-generation and second-generation Irish immigrants, both materially and symbolically. They had much to do with their severe impoverishment in the ethnic enclaves of the large U.S. urban centers where they were concentrated—for the most part, they lived "under the most deplorable of slum conditions"—and with the violence perpetrated against them by the Protestant nativists (Burkey, 1978: 288; 244– 245). They also decisively affected the construction of their identity in the new and unfamiliar social environment. (Of course, for the Irish immigrants and other *white-ethnic* incoming groups, this situation in the main endured for only a couple of generations. Where racialized populations are involved, however, as will be explained later in the chapter, it lasts indefinitely. Therein lies the fundamental difference separating the alterity of some groups versus that of other groups.)

To be a stranger may be generalized to apply to a variety of situations involving the person's lack of familiarity with, or access to, a particular (i.e., normally, the dominant) scheme of orientation in a given social environment. In Schutz's essay, the experience of being a *stranger* applies directly to the situation of those who come "from outside"—that is, the foreigners, or immigrant persons, in a new and strange land. It is suggested here that this situation is analogous to that of groups that are barred from the mainstream of national life *within their own society*, on the basis of some particular criterion, such as, in this case, racial status. In certain national contexts, entire segments of the society's population may be differentiated and marginalized culturally as a result of the operation of institutionalized biracialism. Their patterns of behavior, like those of the Schutzian *strangers*, will be generally seen as deviations from the *anonymous typified behavior*, that is, as deviations from the typical pattern of social behavior for the society in question. The racialization of social life transforms, in this way, the minority individuals into typical Schutzian *strangers*, in their own cultural habitat, which is the national community of which they are members.

Being immersed in the natural attitude, or taking the cultural way of life as a *given*, is the natural consequence of living in the collectivity. This is so because the patterns of collective living everywhere—all the cultural conventions, established arrangements and practices, ways of thinking, and so on— are the very foundation of people's existence and identity. They define who we are. Typifications—linguistic, behavioral, ideological—surround us in every way and on every level. For those well integrated into their respective sociocultural environments, these typifications furnish existential affirmation, security, reassurance, and overall comfort. Otherwise, when individuals are confronted directly and over a period time with the customary ways of living of *other* societies, this experience has the opposite effect and may provoke anxiety and insecurity, irritation, aversion, and things of this nature. This latter scenario describes the life of *the stranger*, trying to function satisfactorily in an unfamiliar social world.

In the present study the interest is to consider the problem of foreignness and alienation *vis-à-vis* the world of conventionality, but not in terms of the typical Schutzian stranger. Rather, Schutz's theoretical formulations will be applied to the sphere of race and ethnic relations, and more specifically still, to the conditions of society-wide legally enforced racial bipolarity, which were in effect in the United States when his article was written. Therefore, the frame of reference for this discussion of the condition of *being-a-stranger* will be racial status, not, strictly speaking, nationality status (nationality status being the domain identity of the immigrant group). Naturally, in social systems where racial status does not prevail as a determining factor of the person's social integration, other factors (the person's cultural ways, peculiar history, life circumstances, etc.) may still pose problems for individuals regarding their integration into the new society's general way of life, in terms of the fact that these individuals might decide to embark on certain courses of action and/or lifestyles that would not be aligned with mainstream values and expectations, with the conventional behavioral and ideological patterns of the masses. These deviations from the conventional lifestyle could have taken different forms. One could, for instance, during the first quarter of the twentieth century, maintain a critical stance against the operation of Jim Crow, be a health faddist, or, more radically, be a Trotskyan anarchist in New York City. But, this would be a deliberation to be made, by and large, by the individuals involved. This also represents a characteristic phenomenon of modern societies, where individualism as dominant cultural orientation affords everyone considerable autonomy in this regard.[1] It is not so, on the other hand, in settings where ascribed status, such as race, determines the nature of the life situation of people.

In *The Stranger* Schutz dissects the process by means of which the stranger's system of knowledge or relevances enters into contact with that of the dominant group in the new society, or the *ingroup*, and various points of congruence or lack thereof will be manifested. We have already seen how our coexistence with others in the lifeworld has this taken-for-granted quality, stemming from society-wide patterns of socialization, which normally ensure a high level of conformity, systematicity, and cohesiveness in the action and thought of the population-at-large. As a rule, we are not conscious—in the sense of having a theoretical grasp—of the fact that we have access to the subjective experiences and processes of others, and that the subjective life of others is open to our interpretation or "reading" of it (Schutz, 1944: 501; 1997: 140). In all our everyday dealings with others, we are constantly engaged in an *epoché*, or *bracketing* of the world around us, which means a suspension of all doubting and questioning regarding the people and things we come into contact with (Zaner, 1961: 87), and the way in which the behavior of these people, and the configuration of these things, are *given* to us.

This means that whatever difficulties may arise in the normal exchanges among members of a given social world should not ideally be linked to a perception of how others conduct themselves, or to speculation about what type of socialization background others might have had. In other words, if any sense of a problem in social interaction should arise among the participants, this should not have to do with their perception of a deviation, on the part of the participants in the communicative exchange, from the society's common system of meaning. Rather, it should be simply related to other things, such as, for instance, one of the interlocutors not having heard what was said to him or her, or a problem of understanding because of variation in the regional accent or regional dialect, and so on. On the other hand, such a perception is a typical characteristic of the interaction between social groups that have been kept historically apart, within the same society, by legally mandated segregation.

Since members of the minority group (the *outgroup*) are still socialized into the core elements of the dominant culture, this allows for a *general* congruence between the majority and minority systems of relevances and, therefore, for a sufficient degree of mutual intelligibility (among *all* members of the society) to make the communicative exchange possible. However, at some important levels, the interaction will still be marked by the lack of harmonization of the two meaning-contexts (in the manner expected of the interaction between members of subcultures and the general population). The behavioral responses of the culturally marginalized minority persons will be frequently perceived as deviations from "anonymous typified behavior," or the typical behavioral patterns of the dominant group. The inequality of social status and power that separates the ingroup from the outgroup also makes it incumbent upon members of the latter to make themselves understood. This effort *itself* causes the parties involved in the interaction to become aware of the crisis in meaning, that is, to develop a directly intellectual, reflective grasp of the communicative situation, which then destroys the taken-for-granted, *thinking-as-usual* character that this situation is supposed to have (Schutz, 1944: 501). In so doing, it brings to the fore the special character that social interaction often assumes under circumstances of intrasocietal cultural separatism.

Whether in the interaction of foreigners with native residents—or, by analogy, in this example of race relations in U.S. society, between members of groups in the same society who have, by virtue of racial ascription, been acculturated differently—awareness of the communicative difficulty as described above may generate feelings of frustration and irritation for all involved; and with respect to the *strangers*, feelings of inadequacy, disorientation, *outsidedness*. Communication may then, during the most critical moments of the communicative crisis, be reduced to its minimally required level of *technical* comprehension, in order to satisfy the practical or utilitarian ends of the exchange. (For instance, people with different cultural orientations within the same social system may still go through social exchanges adequately, such as in the case of purchasing merchandise from a store and cashing a check at a bank.) Likewise, with reference to the situation of racial minorities in this specific example, the experience may be especially unsettling because of its implications of inadequate social performance, with the attending power implications. An important part of this experience is the sense of less-than-perfect membership in a social system to which members of these minority groups are (at the present time, in the United States) presumed formally to have as much claim as anyone.

Schutz's analysis again suggests the need for members of the society *to be granted universal access* to the mainline cultural system, so as to reach the level of full-scale inclusion into the social system, referring to the circumstance of anonymity in social relations. Anonymity, in its different versions (Schutz and Luckmann, 1973: 252–253), suggests invisibility in the mass, in the sense of interchangeability or undifferentiation, which parallels the use of the idea of *sameness* in the present work. More to the point, in our interaction with *the Other*, the exchange is mediated by a mutual recognition of the *objective* meaning of *the other*'s behavior, whether in an "immediate social relation," such as interacting with my uncle Adalberto, or in apprehending the conduct of a social type, such as the "football referee" in the stadium. What Schutz and Luckmann designate as "fullness of content" of the social type is contingent on the extent to which it conforms to typifications, and "the more typifications an individualized type is built on, the more anonymous it is" (1973: 81). This is a crucially important consideration for this discussion of race relations and inequality, insofar as the racialization of individuals (as demonstrated in this particular context of national life), this basic condition of interchangeability and equality of individuals in the social world.

In connection with this principle, in racially bipolar societal settings, there is a clear element of *visibility* at the initial point of contact between individuals, as they apprehend each other, whether in the dyadic relation or in the contact between groups. This mutual apprehension will be effected in terms of either *sameness* or *difference*, and these two circumstances, as indicated, are conceived on the basis of the perception of whiteness or nonwhiteness. Being construed as a natural or essential condition, and as the basis of the fundamental *sameness* (anonymity, in connection with universality) or *difference* (otherness, in connection with particularity) of individuals, racial status is what regulates dominant-minority *cultural* relations. Specifically, it keeps members of the minority group from ever achieving (in the eyes of the majority population) the level of anonymity necessary for being equal to everyone else; it keeps them from ever being perceived as representing the *universal*. Rather, they are perceived as the permanent *particular* (on this issue of anonymity, see also Isaacs, 1963: 348).[2]

Schutz's study of the *stranger*, as pointed out, sensitizes us to the overriding importance of access to, and incorporation into, the society's dominant meaning system, in relation to the social functioning of individuals. By virtue of having been historically limited to less-than-complete access to the society's dominant cultural orientation, members of minority racial groups, like Schutzian *strangers*, come to experience their society essentially as an alien society, and the cultural system with which they are *formally* associated (by definition, as citizens of the society) as "a labyrinth in which [they have] lost all sense of [their] bearings." This is all the more problematic in view of the fact that, unlike the true stranger, they are in a society which is their own. It is true, of course, that alien or foreign groups in general, provided their acculturative experience is set in motion without major complications, are initially unable to transform the host society's scheme of cultural orientation by integrating it with their own—an obstacle common to the experience of most *strangers*, and a phenomenon that Schutz spoke of as the inability "to convert all the coordinates within one scheme of orientation." (This is certainly true at the *individual* level. However, at the level of the immigrant or alien group as a whole, that group may, and usually does, in the process of negotiating its inclusion into the new sociocultural milieu, leave its imprint on the host culture as well, a reciprocal association that may become increasingly significant in the degree that the host society is willing to participate in syncretic relations with the culture of the alien group.) This is a fairly typical occurrence. By the second generation, however, the alien group has generally blended into the core culture, and is no longer concerned with achieving an integration of cultural perspectives, since it now claims the national culture-as-a-whole as its own. Nevertheless, in the case of minority individuals, who are members of the same society, but who remain culturally segregated on the basis of racial status—a status construed as inalterable through the society's biracialist system—the inability to integrate the two cultural orientations is likely to persist indefinitely. Thus, the so-called minority person becomes (in Schutz's words, borrowing from Park and Stonequist) a *marginal man* indefinitely, one who cannot be thought of as being affiliated with anything other than the cultural system of their society, and yet is constantly reminded of having been granted only partial inclusion into it, "a cultural hybrid on the verge of two different patterns of group life, not knowing to which of them he belongs" (Schutz, 1944: 505–507).

This speaks to the condition of being locked into permanent *otherness*, no matter what happens. A 2018 TV documentary titled *I Am Not Your Negro*, based on James Baldwin's work and life experience in the United States, presents several instances in which Baldwin levels a frontal attack upon the aspect of *otherness*, the condition which, during the Jim Crow period, was forcibly imposed on the social status and identity of African-Americans in the United States—in fact, on the social status and identity of all those people categorized as nonwhite. His scathing criticism of the victimization of black people in U.S. society is also directed toward the notion, propagated by the liberal camp starting in the mid-to-late 1960s, that by that time significant progress and improvement had already been occurring in the lives of blacks in the United States, notwithstanding the rather slow pace at which Jim Crow arrangements were being dismantled. The Democratic candidate for president in the 1968 election, Robert Kennedy, went so far as to predict that in some forty years an African-American man could become president of the United States (one in fact did, exactly forty years later). But the problem, as Baldwin's comments on this issue suggested, was that this progress for Black Americans in their own country, achieved in the form of *structural* integration, revealed the inadequacy of the latter when it operates *in isolation* from other dimensions of social inclusion. This situation is evidenced everyday insofar as individuals who are formally or informally codified as racially nonwhite in the United States continue to symbolize *otherness* in the eyes of the larger society, notwithstanding the actual degree to which they may have risen in the social scale. Therefore, social progress in these terms amounts merely to the larger society having become more generally tolerant and flexible concerning interracial relations, to the point of accommodating what remains codified as the *otherness* of minority racial groups. In other words, the society has elevated its level of *structural* inclusion of nondominant groups—in sharp contrast to the earlier time (i.e., the Jim Crow period) when permanent exclusion from institutional life was normatively determined, but it stopped short of full inclusion of nonwhites in the post–Jim Crow period. The immigrant groups classified as white ethnics, on the other hand, never had to deal with this problem since their initial *otherness*—which had to do with *cultural* difference only—was typically overcome by the second generation.

Another analyst has remarked that "the blackness of black people in [U.S.] society has always represented the blemish, the uncleanliness, the barrier separating the individual and society" (Williams, 1991: 198). Thus, groups to which racial status is assigned in rigidly bipolar terms, as indicated, have their racial circumstances *naturalized*—that is, considered to be a product of nature, of their biological endowment—and the variations that they display from the cultural ways of the racially dominant group are therefore seen as a natural expression of their perpetual inferiority. Over time, members of *both* the dominant and minority racial segments of the population tend to internalize this idea, which sets in motion a process of identity-formation *for both groups*. The subaltern group develops a perception of itself as a foreign, alien presence—a perception of its permanent otherness—in the larger society where, concomitantly, they are constitutionally defined as full-fledged members of the society-at-large—a case of ontological separation and differentiation going on within *the same* national community.

The historical enforcement of intergroup separatism in the United States, together with biracialist social organization, has resulted, among other things, in the operation of a double standard of assimilation of alien groups, whereby, starting from the earliest phases of immigration in the U.S. territory, along a continuum of assimilation comprising structural, cultural, and biological dimensions, members of incoming groups classified as white, pushing aside the initial difficulties stemming from their cultural difference, were gradually absorbed into national life at all levels. Lingering intergroup differences and/ or animosities tended to vanish in proportion with the increase in the level of intermarriage between members of these groups and the ruling English-American population. Irish-Americans may be taken as an example of this phenomenon. By contrast, members of the groups classified as nonwhite, for the larger part of their historical experience in the United States, were significantly barred from (secondary) structural assimilation as well as biological (family life and intermarriage) assimilation, something which expectedly inhibited their *cultural* assimilation. That the destruction of de jure segregation in the late 1960s and subsequent efforts over the ensuing decades to incorporate ethnic minorities into the major institutional sectors of the society failed to include their incorporation into the informal and cultural sectors as well appears to be the main reason why members of these groups, many of whom have risen to positions of prominence in key social institutions, remain perpetually confined to minority status (as witnessed, for instance, in the frequent references to a "distinguished minority person").

Thus, the tradition of political liberalism in the U.S. social system has facilitated the operation of cultural pluralism-*cum*-assimilation, but this phenomenon has *two meanings*—or it should be understood as having these two meanings in the U.S. context. The first applies to the case of the *white-ethnic* groups (e.g., Irish Americans, Greek-Americans, Italian Americans). These are people who, starting with the second or third generation, became fully acculturated into the majority cultural community, and, as their acculturative experience progressed through succeeding generations, have been culturally allowed (despite views to the contrary [e.g., Novak, 1971]) to re-knot the threads of their cultural life with their ancestral background, and this has actually had a favorable impact on their overall standing in the larger society. Examples of this phenomenon may be seen in the Irish-American St. Patrick's Day celebration, the Swedish-American Midsummer Festival, the Dutch-American Tulip Time festivities, and so on. Most people in the society recognize this as having the most salutary and enriching effect upon the citizenship status of members of these groups, and on the society as a whole. The society is diversified and, therefore, enriched by it. Group members have an enhanced sense of belonging and self-esteem from being able to remain, in some degree, connected with the cultural universe of their ancestors, while at the same experiencing these cultural expressions as a source of benefit to their national membership—in the context of assimilation, a clear-cut situation of having your cake and eating it too.

THE HISTORICAL BACKGROUND OF THE *RACIAL STRANGER*

Where members of ethnic groups codified as nonwhite are concerned, however, a different story must be told. In the specific case of African-Americans in the U.S. social system, the biracialist administration of intergroup life, in effect from the earliest beginnings of the nation as an English-American society, drove them into the impasse of, on the one hand, being granted only partial incorporation into the majority mode of life; and on the other hand, being discouraged (or expressly forbidden, as was the case during most of the slavery period) from re-establishing the patterns of their African ancestral heritage on the new land. Partial assimilation into national life, coupled with forced dissociation from aboriginal traditions, led them to forge a subnational way of life which endures to the present day (on this aspect, see, e.g., Herskovits, 1972; Pinkney, 2000: ch. 9). A product of race-based castelike segregation, this subcultural lifestyle—or, for that matter, the attempt to preserve ancestral traditions in any degree—has had a direct impact on the lives of the individuals under consideration. It causes them to be perceived by the society-at-large in a way that is significantly different from that in which members of *white ethnics* groups will be generally perceived, should they decide to do the same thing, as noted above—that is, should they decide to maintain connections with the cultural heritage of their ancestors. Specifically, where minority racial communities are concerned, instead of solidifying and enriching their national membership, the attempt to re-establish continuity with their ancestral background feeds into a circular process of exclusion, setting in motion further majority/minority differentiation, leading to more exclusion from the mainline cultural model, and that in turn to more differentiation, more exclusion, and so on.

These individuals and their descendants have had, up to the present time, to maintain their *essentiality* as groups of restricted assimilation, as symbolized by their hyphenated identities. The racially binary administration of the society has preserved what racial ideology, together with Calvinistic Protestantism (see Camara, 1997), has construed as the purity of the white community, and the essential difference (i.e., non-whiteness) and natural inferiority of the rest of the population. In this connection, the idea of disturbing what is taken as the natural order of things has been historically regarded as an abomination, a serious affront to Reason and Revealed Truth. In the 1920s, Paulo Prado (1962: 159) remarked that people in the United States were fond of saying that "God made the white man, God made the black man, but the Devil made the mulatto," an allusion to the deep aversion characteristic of U.S. society regarding black-white miscegenation, and to the presumed deleterious effects of this process to social organization. In the same vein, the ship's captain John Codman, who visited Brazil in the mid-1800s, observed the high degree of racial mixture of the population and considered that to be the greatest scourge with which Brazilian society was afflicted—"the mixture of two bloods which the Almighty never intended to be brought together in a single stream" (1867: 176). Similar examples of this fiercely negative stance toward racial fusion abound in the travelers-accounts literature, in particular the accounts of travelers and missionaries from Protestant countries—even though in those same Protestant countries where slavery was also in operation during the eighteenth and nineteenth centuries, the biological intermingling between the members of the slaveholding and slave classes had also been occurring, in varying degrees.

The focus on which specific brand of Christianity is the major religion in the society is pertinent to the present study. Religious ideology, most notably evangelical Christianity of the Protestant variety, has indeed contributed significantly to the preservation of the structures and mental habits of racial bipolarity—and, therefore, to the crystallization of the quality of *otherness* attributed to racial nonwhiteness. As observed frequently in this chapter, this has involved framing the otherness of minority groups in ontological terms. Furthermore, in the particular context of U.S. society, there arose, in connection with this, the idea in the public imaginary that Anglo-American society was created by Divine Providence as a sui generis universe of whiteness, and as the most authentic expression of the Divine among all other human communities around the world. The great ethnic diversity generated by immigration in the United States, which reached its height in the latter part of the nineteenth century and early twentieth, failed to alter the basic thrust of this ideology, quite simply because the influx of all the various immigrant groups was automatically inserted into the binary scheme of racial classification. This basic pattern endures to this day.[3] The incoming national groups classified as white (hence, as potentially assimilable, despite their significant cultural differences from the general pattern of the receiving society), once the initial difficulties of acculturation were overcome, something that normally occurred after the first generation, were progressively absorbed into the general population through intermarriage. Consequently, the diversity of cultural traits they brought with them to the new society dissipated steadily as they became integrated into national life. The groups classified as nonwhite, also very different culturally from one another (and from the host culture), were also lumped together as a homogeneous block of nonwhites, and steered toward partial inclusion. Their respective variations in their assimilative experience in relation to one another mainly had to do with degree, and this in turn was decisively influenced by the amount of phenotypical dissimilarity they exhibited in relation to the dominant phenotypical features of the majority (i.e., English-American) population.

In slavery times, the very notion of blacks in freedom was aberrational within the social organization of Southern society, inimical to all that the latter stood for. Free blacks, as Stampp (1956: 215) reminds us, were seen as an anomaly, "a living denial 'that nature's God intended the African for the status of slavery.'" Another writer, William Goodell, put it thusly, in his important documentary study of the American slave codes: "To be a free Negro," he declared, "differs widely . . . from being a free man" (1853: 357). In time, the emancipation of the Africans came to be seen as a plausible proposition only when "connected with transportation to Africa" (1853: 364). The general sentiment to deport liberated slaves, and Africans in general (the "Back-to-Africa" movement), found material expression in the formation of the American Colonization Society in 1817, under whose auspices the West African colony of Liberia came into existence in 1822, with assistance from the U.S. federal government (Quarles, 1976: 95–96). Change in the civil status of the blacks in no way or degree changed their condition of being *perpetual strangers.*

The political inclusion of minority social groups *by itself* will not prevent politically assimilated individuals from relying on the existential connections that bind them to their *cultural moorings*—in other words, to the symbolic universe in which they grew up, namely, the minority community. If that symbolic universe defines them as racialized persons, this adds an ontological status to their social existence as racial minorities. In myriad ways, this may manifest itself in terms of their seeking internal consistency (in light of continuing societal maintenance of informal dominant/minority separatism) by pursuing courses of action, making lifestyle choices, and so on that may contradict and/or interfere with their admission into the formal spheres of society. Here, we may take the example of the overtures, since the 1990s, toward re-establishing segregated facilities for racial minorities. This reveals the crystallization of group difference—at the levels of lifestyle, identity, and so forth—construed on the basis of race, of racial otherness.

For those who are not fully integrated culturally—corresponding to Schutz's *stranger*—the taken-for-grantedness with which they relate to their world of everyday life is "thrown into question" (Psathas, 1973: 9), in the particular sense that they are constantly faced with situations and modes of thought and behavior—the typifications—of the larger way of life, which are not continuous with the *structure of acquaintedness* (Landgrebe, 1940: 49) of their home world—specifically, the familiar subcultural world in which they have grown up. This is said to throw their taken-for-grantedness into question because it is constantly objectified, inasmuch as it is constantly coming into contact, often colliding, with the national pattern of social life. Thus, the racial stranger inhabits parallels social worlds, with obviously negative repercussions. This will be addressed more specifically in the next chapter.

THE HOMECOMING *OTHER*

Schutz explores another dimension of alienation, related to that of *the stranger*, which bears on the problem of the time and space dimensions of the person's life, namely, the experience of the returning *émigré*, who has been away from the homeland for an extended period of time. He addressed this issue in his 1945 article *The Homecomer*, as related to the experience of the returning American GI during the Second World War. This experience may be said to parallel that of the newcomer to an alien society, insofar as the individual that leaves her or his home country for a significant period of time also feels a similar sense of strangeness upon returning. Being away from the home culture, from familiar ways of doing things, from familiar ways of reacting to the world, these things recede more and more in the background, and therefore, steadily elude the grasp of consciousness. This reaches a point, in cases when the absence from the homeland is sufficiently prolonged, where they become alien things themselves. The home culture becomes *terra incognita* another foreign land of sorts.

The experience of *the stranger* is characterized in Schutz's article as being substantively different from that of *the homecomer*. With respect to the aspect highlighted in the article—that is, the stranger struggles to adapt to a land and culture which were entirely unknown to her or him, the homecomer struggles to readapt to a land and culture with which she or he had intimate familiarity before. This is one particular aspect which, as noted, distinguishes between the two experiences. In a broader and more fundamental sense, however, *both* the stranger and the homecomer are dealing with the same sense of alienation toward unfamiliar territory.

In both situations, the individuals involved struggle initially with the unfamiliar, but at the end there is a restoration of the familiar. In the one case, that of the stranger, it is a foreign land that constitutes the unfamiliar, and which gradually, over time, becomes the new homeland, the new familiar territory. In the other case, that of the homecomer, it is the homeland itself that presents itself as the context of unfamiliarity, but which also, over time, transforms itself again into the homeland; that is, it returns to its original condition as familiar territory.

The main theme expressed in this essay is "coming back home," the experience that is, paradoxically, with respect to the returning soldier, enveloped in unfamiliarity and anxiety. In this connection, it is of paramount importance that, from the outset, the idea of "home" be addressed in terms of what it precisely means, and to whom. Schutz mentions a whole array of things constituting the world of familiarity that had been left behind by the *émigrés*. In basic terms, *home* stands for the world of the natural attitude, in that it comprises all the familiar typifications and schemes of relevances that we take for granted, and that guide our patterns of acting and thinking in the social world. In this world of perfect familiarity with everything around us, the world of "home," we feel that "[t]hings will in substance continue to be what they have been so far" (Schutz, 1945: 371). This stability is perceived either consciously or non-consciously as a perennial source of psychosocial comfort and security.

When this stability is disrupted, we are typically jolted into awareness of its long-standing effect. This may happen when members of a given cultural community are exposed to cultural difference, or, worse yet, when they see foreign ways infiltrating their familiar world of experience. Normally, this leads to conscious resistance against the change.

More fundamentally, Schutz's discussion leads to the idea that *coming back home* means coming back to active membership in "actual or potential *primary groups*" (1945: 371; emphasis mine), but defining these groups in the context of a culturally integrated homegroup (which is consistent with the idea of cultural integration implicit in Schutz's foundational concepts, like the stock-of-knowledge-at-hand, typification, scheme of relevances, etc.) But, this is a conception of home, as Schutz points out, that applies only to those who live in it, not to those who have left it. Therein lies the basic truth familiar to a great many of us, expressed in Thomas Wolfe's adage *You Can't Go Home Again*—and that is, quite simply, because the home one left no longer exists. In a broader context, it speaks to the philosophical awareness of historical change, which stretches all the way back to the pre-Socratics (i.e., Heraclitus), with the idea that one cannot be in the same river twice. As applied to the concrete situation of the homecomer, the loss of continuity in time and space makes for a significant rupture in the person's conception of *home*. Schutz concludes with an appropriate adage: *Partir, c'est mourir un peu* (To leave is to die a little).

In very typical fashion, those who leave the homegroup and homeland attempt, whether consciously or not, to "freeze" the world of "home" just as they left it. This is very characteristic of *émigrés* as a group. In actuality, the "home" world continues to change, uninterruptedly, during the entire period of absence—and those who have left are no longer there to relate to, and mentally register, the evolution of their "home" world on a daily basis, and to feel that things are just as they have always been. It is not the case, of course, that the home world, being experienced daily, is not changing; it is only experienced so. The perception of this stability being a property of the world of experience is accounted for solely by the living presence of those who are still in it. In fact, as Schutz points out (1945: 373), those who remained in the home world are generally aware of their changing environment, but their conscious grasp of this process is tempered by their living in this ever-evolving world, and adjusting daily to it, adapting "their interpretative system" to it.

When race is brought into the discussion of the meaning of *home*, within a specific historical and geographical context, this adds considerable complexity and thus warrants elaboration. The theoretical considerations in Schutz's essay were formulated at a time when Jim Crow laws and practices in the United States were very much in full effect, and would remain so for another quarter-century. This must be kept in mind when considering the situation of the returning black GI during the Second World War. For the black soldiers, as Baldwin accurately points out, the very idea of home (understood as the wider U.S. national community) began "to have a despairing and diabolical ring" (1964: 68), which would certainly not have been the case for their white counterparts. So, the Schutzian description of the process of homecoming must be reworked here to apply to the particular situation of the minority GIs—especially when, in addition to the aversive feeling that the idea of returning home would have awakened in them, they had never felt freer as regular persons than they had in their sojourn in the strange lands of Europe.

The experience of the African-American GIs during the Second World War was essentially identical to their counterparts in the First World War. The U.S. armed forces, like all other institutions and areas of social life, were sharply segregated, and African-American soldiers fought in all-black battalions. Black officers, for example, were eventually stripped of the leadership and authority rights that came with their rank, lest they find themselves in a situation where they would have to exercise command over white soldiers. The very presence of the black GIs in the armed forces was problematic, so some arrangement was worked out whereby black soldiers would begin to serve under French command, inasmuch as the French, like the U.S. military, were also fighting against the Germans. At the end of the war, many African-American soldiers won decorations for their bravery in battle, and received much honor and respect, in a general way, from the French, in that respect. Imbued with this new sense of self-worth as well as professional competence, they returned home to the United States with a fresh resolve to make democracy really work "at home." Their efforts and new assertiveness, however, largely fell flat (in spite of that outcome, those efforts actually came to represent the first wave of the civil rights movement), as they met with ramped-up resistance on the part of the majority population, who simply dismissed their military accomplishments, and stood firm by the conviction that no amount of achievement by the black folk in foreign lands would in any way alter their second-class citizenship back home in the United States.

THE RETURN: TIME, MEMORY, AND MEANING

In the classical situation of the returning soldier, the idea of the homecoming fits the classical mold of the ideal-typical returning warrior, from any historical period or geographical area. There is an absence from the home-country and the home-group. The return is couched in a sense of estrangement that takes over both the home group and the soldier. Both are consciously directing themselves to, or aiming to reconnect with, an image of a past which they have kept "frozen" in consciousness during the entire period of absence, but which is no longer applicable, because of the changes that have occurred, during the soldier's absence, in both the home setting and in the returning son. In the majority of cases, the transformations that took place would not have been so drastic as to prevent the perception, on both sides, of an unbroken familiarity, the familiarity that prevailed in the past (i.e., prior to the homecomer's departure). In actuality, the continuity of the past has been broken, and neither the soldier nor the homeland is the same as they were at the time of the soldier's departure.

The situation of the returning African-American GI reframes the dynamics of the homecoming process. There is much documentary material on how African-American enlisted men and women served in a segregated armed forces. As they left for the battlefields of Europe, Asia, and Africa, the longer they stayed abroad, the more the daily humiliations they had been subjected to at home in the United States, on a daily basis, became a fading memory. At the same time, the more they were impacted on by their interactions with the local people in the foreign lands. Living in the natural attitude back home meant, for the majority of the black population, pragmatic and unthinking conformity to Jim Crow conditions, as they went about their daily round of activities. In the European settings there was a switch to being treated, for the most part, like ordinary American soldiers. This contrast—that is, being treated with respect, being treated like the universal or typical American GI[4]—would not only have been refreshing and an eye-opener for them, but also placed them in a better position to objectify their experience back home. Schutz (1945: 375) invites us to consider the parallel between the situation of the black soldiers experiencing life outside their own society, and that of the mariners from Greek mythology, who tasted the lotus plant of the lotus-eating men, and no longer wished to return to Greece. The feeling of homesickness faded away, they have tasted the lotus and no longer long for the foods from back home. The analogy is very appropriate, but needs to be examined further. The lotus plant has narcotic properties, and typically made the people who ate it drowsy, leading to sleep in a peaceful indifference to their surroundings and life concerns. The black soldiers did certainly welcome "the taste of the lotus plant," but they did not succumb to its delights (i.e., a permanent life abroad), but returned home with a renewed and revitalized consciousness of the problems of living in a segregated society, and with greater determination to resist the daily oppression of Jim Crow. Much attention has been devoted to this specific aspect of the history of civil rights in the United States, in the race and ethnicity literature.

Their experience upon returning to the homeland transcends that of the typical (i.e., racially white) soldier in several ways. In abstract terms, or in the more general sense, it is much the same experience, insofar as both the soldiers had changed, and so had the conditions of the homeland, in both the black community and the society as a whole. But additional complexity is brought to this analysis by the fact that the returning African-American GIs brought home with them something that had no parallel to anything they had experienced in the home setting prior to their departure for the battlefields in foreign lands. This made the dynamics of their absence from home, and of their return, radically different from the same experience for the white soldiers. In the alien lands, black GIs had been treated, *for the most part*, as common, ordinary American soldiers; as the *universal*, rather than as the *particular*, GI type. They had, in other words, mainly received the treatment of anonymity reserved for those in the category of *sameness*, not *otherness*. They felt the exotic and tantalizing taste of representing the standard of universality—the universal (American) soldier—in their contacts abroad, rather than the category of particularity. Not for them anymore the familiar, yet bitter, tastes of home—although, to be sure, those tastes of home were, from time to time, brought back to them, in all their ugliness and repugnance, by their white comrades-in-arms, a reminder that Jim Crow had been transported by the armed forces across the ocean as well, along with the all the military equipment, apparel, provisions, and so forth.[5]

Schutz evokes the story of Odysseus to shed light on the processes of change in the consciousness of the ordinary (i.e., racially white) soldier, during the latter's absence from the home land. Although this type of soldier would normally be gripped with feelings of homesickness, the longing for the world left behind, the daily experiences outside that world would assert themselves and mar the purity of this sentiment. As the Greek epic poem went, Odysseus found himself in the island of lotus-eaters, who, rather than punishing the Greek intruders, had them eat a dish made with this exotic plant. As the Greeks tasted it, the desire to return home weakened, while the desire to stay in the island, and continue to enjoy this food, grew stronger. A very apt metaphor to describe the emotions that, *latusensu*, run through the typical traveler, away from home, and being torn, on the one hand, by the pull to return to the familiarity and comfort of the home environment, while at the same time escaping the intricacies and frustrations of life abroad; and, on the other hand, by the pull to succumb to the temptations and the excitement (despite the potential dangers) of life abroad, of "the magic fruit of strangeness" (1945: 375). This is a familiar situation of ambivalence to all who have ventured outside the home environment.

Despite the fundamental distinctions that obviously need to be made between the experience of the returning GIs that Schutz writes about (he wrote about the *typical* returning soldiers, implicitly those who would have been members of the racial majority in the United States, since he did not intentionally set out to consider the particular situation of the minority soldiers as well), and the African-American soldiers, the metaphor of the Odysseus story is very much apropos to the case of the returning black soldiers (some of its aspects particularly so). As indicated above, the basic parallelisms are there: as a rule, the soldier is away from home in a foreign and strange land, and longs to return. Upon returning, change has occurred both in the homeland and in him(her)self. There is estrangement, a diminished familiarity, on both sides. But, then, fundamental differences emerge. The home the minority soldiers longed for was not the society-as-a-whole, but the familiar, secure, comforting world of the racial subculture—the refuge from the harshness of the larger society.[6] The black soldiers felt torn as well between the feelings for that world, and the lure of the "magic fruit" of the foreign land—a lure which, for them, was all the stronger because, in sharp contrast to the way their native land dealt with them, their reception abroad was, in the main, characterized by lack of differentiation between them and their fellow American GIs. There was no real pull from the homeland *qua* entire national community. There was a pull from their particular subcultural community, but that was counterbalanced by the sweet taste of the lotus fruit. Toward the national community as a whole their feeling would have been one of aversion. It took a war and the physical departure from their native society, together with regular contact with people from other lands, to bring their plight back home into sharper focus for them. This is why the African-American homecomers had, comparatively, much greater difficulty than their white counterparts in readjusting to the society they had left behind, when they left for the battlefields of Europe and Asia. In connection with that experience, they collectively became a critical galvanizing force behind the civil rights movement, as it started to gain momentum in the post–Second World War years.

The typical homecoming is accompanied, according to Schutz (1945: 375), by "the wish to transplant into the old pattern [into the way of life of the home society] something . . . of the skills and experiences acquired abroad." This desire, on the part of the African-American homecomers, translated into a renewed determination to forge ahead with the resistance to the Jim Crow system, and to speed up its demise (which would not actually take place for another quarter-century, in the late 1960s to early 1970s). When this happened, it was a milestone in the history of race relations in U.S. society.

That the homecomer returns a changed individual should be obvious enough at this point, in light of these considerations. The homeland too would have changed in small-scale, incremental ways, during the soldier's absence. Schutz maintains that the society in question, through its "propaganda machine," ought to take cognizance of this fact, and also bring to public notice a more realistic picture of both the archetypal soldier, and of military life as such—phrased differently, the means of information and communication ought ideally to promote the truth, rather than the glorification of a "pseudo-type of the combatant's life" (1945: 376), the latter being undoubtedly very characteristic of the Hollywood war films and other mass media of the period. This recommendation is incisive and useful, and directly applicable to the situation of the returning *émigré,* under normal circumstances, whether in the U.S. or other similar societies. But it certainly runs into problems when transferred to the specific case of the returning nonwhite GI, for that historical period, in U.S. society. Against the backdrop of the full-scale operation of the Jim Crow system, the returning African-American soldiers would find what to them was more truly *home*—the African-American community—basically unchanged in its framework of security and reassurance, despite the aspects of its *general* historical evolution. They would also find the larger society unchanged, insofar as the social treatment that was accorded to them before the war had remained undisturbed—that is, it was just as oppressive and dehumanizing as ever, notwithstanding the fact that these soldiers were U.S. veterans, and a good many of them had been highly decorated for their competence and bravery in war. Their perception of their national community as a whole expressed Karr's well-known maxim, *plus ça change, plus c'est la même chose* (the more things change, the more they stay the same). The black soldiers had changed significantly, however, far more so than their returning white counterparts. Their experience abroad, as indicated, had made them aware of the possibilities of a different kind of life in society—they had tasted the lotus plant abroad—and now they felt emboldened to embark on the vigorous effort to have the same experience at home. They returned with greatly increased determination to resist Jim Crow practices and arrangements, and bring them to an end.

On the society's side, that is, the larger home group, the military experiences of the black soldiers had in no way, as indicated, altered how they were viewed by the society's racial majority, by the "white people." Their nonwhiteness made them different not only in external appearance, but different in kind, that is, at the ontological level. Therefore, this was an essential trait assigned to every person codified as nonwhite, which no amount of change in their life circumstances could ever eradicate. There were innumerable instances, during the war years, of returning black soldiers being pushed into segregated facilities as they had been before, their uniforms and military demeanor notwithstanding. On them, the uniforms, for all their intrinsic value, and symbolization of all that was decent, and brave, and honorable in the eyes of the society-at-large, *when worn by the white soldiers*, on the African-American enlisted personnel this meaning was lost completely. Blacks wearing the military uniform were a phenomenon reconstructed in the consciousness of the dominant group as something that made no sense, a travesty of the real thing, much like a costume. Otherwise, if the situation were to have been considered in the traditional context of respect for its deep social significance (as a cultural marker, like the flag, the cross, etc.), when worn by the nonwhite *others* this would have even amounted to an affront to the system. (A similar situation may be brought to the fore here: African-Americans in the 1960s South, marching and pushing to enter courthouses to register to vote, while holding and waving small American flags to symbolize their citizenship status, and having that most sacred of national symbols, the flag, being brutally taken away from them by the police. This may be interpreted, from the standpoint of the black protesters, as their attempt to legitimize their efforts to vote by drawing attention to the flag as a fundamental marker of their citizenship status, and from the standpoint of the structures of Southern power, as blatant insolence on the part of the protesters, an attempt to subvert the social order in making a travesty of the Constitution and the juridical system.)

Thus, no degree of social achievement had the generative power, under these specific social circumstances, under the definitions and attributions established by racially binary social organization, to transform the prevailing model of intersubjectivity, when it came to racial relations in the society under scrutiny. Dubois, that most dazzling of intellectuals, was seen as no different from any other black person, even from those occupying the lowliest of social occupations, or even involved in the most execrable of criminal behaviors. James Baldwin, in his unparalleled grasp of the racial dynamics in the United States, had repeatedly thrown this basic truth into relief: the common racial epithets, discriminatory institutional and interactional practices, and so on, reserved for blacks in U.S. society in pre–Second World War times, were as current and deeply entrenched in the social *mores* when the African-Americans returned as they had been before.

THE HOME-WORLD AND THE ALIEN-WORLD

Schutz's discussion of *the stranger* and *the homecomer*, while framed in different concrete circumstances, namely, on the one hand, that of the foreigner who enters a strange land and thus becomes *the stranger*, and on the other hand, that of the native son who returns home after a period of absence (*the homecomer*) and experiences estrangement from what was once totally familiar, deals with the same issue of experiencing a given social environment as something alien. The home world versus alien world dualism—the dualism of the familiar versus the unfamiliar—may be further explored by drawing from Husserlian insights on the matter. These two worlds are characterized as quite distinct, yet interrelated. They are characterized as existential spaces to be experienced phenomenologically. Therefore, the focus is not on the concrete aspects that separate them (which are also perceived and experienced differently by the social actor), but on how the exposure to one or the other world affects us at the level of consciousness—that is, of how we perceive them to be. This recalls not only the idea of the Bergsonian *durée*, but also, as an instance of the latter, the case of the Proustian *madeleine*, which was objectively something from the past coming to the present, triggering in consciousness, by means of the senses—that is, of a smell, a sound—a whole range of living experiences long gone. This process demonstrates the flow and continuity of inner time.

The dualism involving the nature of existence in one world versus the other is undeniable. Travelers typically experience the transformation, visually or concretely, and otherwise, as they move from one world to the other. They see the changes in the physical environment—in the architecture and the interior of buildings and homes, in the food generally eaten and the clothes people wear, as well as in the structure of social life. More pertinently for this discussion—and this is truly what generates the sense of discomfort and estrangement as the individual moves from one world to the other—there is a phenomenological basis for relating to one's presence in the home-world or the alien-world, and for comparing how each world can be experienced. Landgrebe (1940) writes about how the home-world can be experienced in terms of a subunit of the larger home world—for example, it may be constituted by a small village in the Austrian Alps, or by the whole of Austrian society. In this and similar cases, there is always some degree of specific (occasionally, significant) cultural dissonance between them, but structurally and phenomenologically the two contexts are basically integrated and homogeneous, and besides, the cultural dissonance is largely overridden by the predominance of the national culture. In any case, the individuals involved are living simultaneously in both contexts.

Within the home-world as such—the society in which the social actor finds himself or herself—the social actor finds that the boundaries of his or her existential horizons can be expanded significantly—and this, of course, can be more easily accomplished than if we were dealing with the shift from the home-world to an alien-world. Within the home-world or the world of familiarity, one's living experience may be limited to life in a small and remote settlement (within the larger society). But, given the common cultural ground for the entire society, it is easier for people to traverse (culturally) back and forth within this society and accommodate themselves to the shifts, large or small, in the particular ways of living of different national regions. However—and the reference here is to the interconnectedness of societies, of home-worlds connecting with and overlapping into other home-worlds, a phenomenon that is increasingly pronounced in modern times)—the social actor finds here, too, that his or her experiential horizon can be extended beyond the boundaries of his or her specific home-world. This is because, we are reminded (Landgrebe, 1940: 49), "everywhere the different social groups are tied together by countless threads." This predisposition, which presumably enables us to further the limits of our accommodation to *the world as such*, and to recognize a line of continuity between the multiplicity of "worlds" in the world-as-such, is, we are told, due to "an antecedent awareness" that we all have of alien worlds out there. It amounts to the idea of a *natural world-concept* (Husserl). This previous awareness manifests itself in terms of *varying degrees* of actual knowledge of these worlds beyond our own—that is to say, this knowledge can be very vague or very precise—but regardless of the limits of our comprehension of the nature and operation of these alien worlds, we are able (by reference to this *natural world-concept*) to understand that they all make up one and the same world "as the total horizon of possible experiences" (1940: 50).

This particular conception of the natural world-concept, this pre-philosophical understanding of the world, sets Husserl's position off from that of Schutz's—an issue that cannot be properly explored here given the purpose and scope of this study. Suffice it to say that Husserl's view of this problematic is more *cosmic*, that is, more globally oriented and set up in more abstract terms (in the sense of being informed by the formulation of a [Kantian] *a priori* originating in consciousness itself), whereas our greater interest here is in the narrower and more substantive situation of what goes on within a specific home-world involving its formative groups.

There is a consideration which actually encompasses both the Husserlian and Schutzian conceptions of human existence *in the world*, to the effect that within our world of familiarity itself, there are areas of variation in the forms of living and understanding—variations on a central theme. To phrase it in the Husserlian lexicon, the home-world "embraces many separate horizons." The reference to this is normally linked to variations in the social roles of individuals, all of which, at the same time, conform to the overarching horizon of that world (Landgrebe, 1940: 51). This study, on the other hand, reframes this variation in the context of intrasocietal divisions, with immediate cultural (and other) implications for all the people involved.

To live in the (social) world entails some universally valid implications, foremost among which is that we are bounded by its limits. More specifically, our actions and understandings of things normally conform to the prevailing horizons (of our home-world), which provide the fundamental map of orientation for our existence. Those horizons do not normally become "thematic" for us—in other words, we are not normally aware of them, since we live in the natural attitude—unless they are disturbed by an "alien world" imposing itself on our own (Landgrebe, 1940: 51). This is very much applicable to the familiar situation, mentioned repeatedly throughout this study, of how historically established intra-societal separatism eventuates in the cultural marginalization (conversely, limited cultural incorporation) of members of minority cultural communities, who, simultaneously, have to function in and be oriented by the meaning system of their subcultural community (i.e., their *home-world*, with which they have the greatest degree of familiarity), and the meaning system of the society-at-large, which is also, technically speaking, their home-world, but which separatism of long standing (particularly of the kind represented by the circumstances of the Jim Crow system in the United States) has turned into an alien world, which still remains in this capacity, *albeit* to a lesser extent than before, right down to the present time.

This has been the historical pattern, this division of the lifeworld into opposing segments, opposing spheres of meaning (and practice), with harmful psychosocial repercussions for the lives of social minorities. This persisting separation of the lifeworld into two distinct worlds, one familiar, one alien, for minority-group individuals, although having been far more intense and dramatic in the past, lingers on in the present time as the legacy of the past, notwithstanding the removal of the formal (legal) framework that, at one time, kept the majority and minority groups apart. What is called the thematization of the horizon of our world represents an intellectual objectification of this horizon, of its nature and effect—a stepping away from it, which, under normal circumstances, the natural attitude keeps us from being able to do. This applies to the classical Husserlian discourse on this issue, and to the regular intrusion, as it were, of foreign elements into our home-world, this intrusion being so dramatic at times that we cannot help but become aware of the fact that our way of living has been, in a manner of speaking, infiltrated. Immigration is certainly one such phenomenon, by means of which all manner of "alien" things come into our field of consciousness, affecting the horizons of our world, by which we orient our living.

Because of the universality of the phenomenon discussed above, social actors are not generally disturbed or disoriented drastically when their exposure to alien elements takes place. By and by, they are able to adapt, to make compromises, to incorporate them, without much psychic disarray. It is a different story, however, when a group of social actors collectively experience the exposure to problems of meaning, as they navigate the waters of daily living *within the same society*. In this case, what is involved is not just a situation of intellectual adaptation (on the part of members of a given cultural system) that is required whenever their daily cultural experience is differentiated by the introduction and inclusion of foreign elements, different styles of living, and different sets of customs and rules of conduct. This simply expresses the classic phenomenon of contact and interpenetration of cultural worlds, observed repeatedly around the world, over the centuries. When this happens, the foreign living styles may fit in with the dominant patterns of the home-world, already in place, or they may clash with them, in varying degrees. In the majority of cases, there will be mergers, syncretistic associations, between the native and the foreign lifestyle patterns, and therefore, some overall accommodation, in the home-world, and the restoration of normalcy.

What is at issue here, however, is a special case of intergroup contact, of worlds of meaning, of systemic horizons, that owes its existence solely to a conscious, power-based manipulation of group relations, within a given ethnic-pluralist society. Its impact is relentless, unyielding, and particularly dramatic, on the lives of members of subaltern communities. After all, our world—in this specific case, our home-world—"functions as the basis for every particular experience." It should not matter, therefore, in this case, that in the most general sense of human existence in the world-at-large, the social actors under scrutiny (i.e., the members of the minority groups) have this primordial sense of the multiplicity of possible worlds and their ultimate unity in the global sense (as Husserl would insist—a more abstract line of theorizing). They are being affected in a more immediate and tangible way by the conditions of their own home-world, in the context of the relations between the hegemonic and non-hegemonic racial parts of the population, with distinct effects for both groups, at the level of intersubjectivity. There is no fusion, but, rather, the unremitting tension and incompatibility between horizons. The customs, practices, and psychological attributes of the subaltern community are viewed negatively, when not held in utter contempt, by the dominant racial community. The other side of this coin applies to more recent decades, when other formal mechanisms have been set in motion in the society, causing minority cultural ways to be not only acknowledged but enthusiastically encouraged. This, however, has only had the effect of crystallizing the existence of these minority lifestyle patterns as essential, that is, racially driven, attributes of these groups, hence, as *permanent otherness*. The disadvantaged group, for its part, also engages in the racialization of majority-group ways—how majority-group members live is *being white*, which is therefore thus inimical to the living style of the minority group, something to be avoided. This clash between the majority and minority racial segments of the society hinges ultimately on the question of meaning and intersubjective relations. It sets in motion a process of reinforcement of the naturalization of the ways of the groups (i.e., they are considered to spring from racial status), leading to continuing negative evaluation of the minority group, separation of the dominant and nondominant communities, seclusion into the subcultural community for the minority element, more negative evaluation by the dominant group, and so forth: the cycle of social exclusion.

NOTES

1. Among the famous American poet Carl Sandburg's innumerable works we find one that is most directly related to this study, namely, a 1919 account of the race riots in Chicago. Sandburg would apparently have been one such person to whom integration into U.S. social life in the early years of the 1900s (i.e., social life in the United States at that time was already built on the Jim Crow system) would not have been problematic in reference to his own racial status. By that we mean that this status would not have constituted a barrier to his adjustment to prevailing social conditions. To state it differently, his racial identification would not necessarily have impeded his immersion into the natural attitude with reference to interracial relations, his taking the prevailing pattern of interracial relations for granted. Other factors, however, specifically his concern for justice, his youthful association with socialism, his commitment to racial equality, and so on would have re-directed him, in his daily encounters with Jim Crow conditions, to objectify his participation in the latter, to challenge those conditions, in his own words, to "twist the tail of conventionality" (cited in Sandburg, 2013/1919: x). In this sense, he would have been able to escape the embrace of the natural attitude, with reference to that particular sphere of social relations, that is, race relations.

2. The regulation of intergroup—in this case, dominant/minority—relations in the United States on the basis of the principle of binary race and the permanent *other-ness* of nonwhites brings to mind an account (in Wagley and Harris, 1958: 142–143) of something that happened during the Jim Crow period. Four white men in some Southern state went out fishing in a boat, and took an African-American guide with them. They mixed and communicated more freely while the fishing was going on, but when lunch time came, the white men moved to one part of the boat and laid a stick across to separate them from the African-American young man. One might say, in this respect, that *breaking bread together* establishes a condition of greater equality among the participants, and that would have been perceived as a violation of Jim Crow segregationist laws and racial etiquette. Being locked in racial *otherness* was not something that could be removed or even suspended, because it expressed a particular model of *being*, a category of existence. The immutability and inferiority of

that *otherness*, as members of the dominant group saw it, was beyond any question. Baldwin writes about this problem in a stark, brutally frank way. The society, he said in letter form to a nephew (but, ultimately, to every other member of the African-American community in the United States), had "spelled out with brutal clarity and in as many ways as possible, that you were a worthless human being" (1964: 21).

3. Bernasconi (2000: 186) attests to the all-encompassing racialization of social life in the United States—in this case, the racialization of ethnic or national origin—in reference to his own experience as a British national, who, upon arriving in the United States was automatically inserted into the *white* category, while his specific *ethnic* affiliation (i.e., British) was typically ignored. Other social statuses (e.g., socioeconomic, as in *the poor*; geographical, as in Western/non-Western; ethnic, as in *being Latin*, *ethnic* foods, *world* music, etc.) also have, in the U.S. context over the past several decades, taken on strong racial connotations. Specifically, the general public in the United States tend to see these things as having to do solely with *nonwhite* populations.

A brief note may be added here in reference to the racialization of "the Latin." In U.S. society the idea of *the Latin* has, over the past several decades, become associated with any person from "south of the border," that is, from Central or South America—which is, strictly speaking, certainly correct. However, this attribution is directed *exclusively* to people from Central and South America. Furthermore, due to the special historical circumstances of U.S. society involving its relations with its neighbors down south, the "Latin" status is applied to the Amerindian-Spanish, or *mestizo,* population from those Southern regions (particularly from Mexico), which makes up the bulk of the migrants entering the United States from the southern part of the continent. Since the Amerindian-Spanish or Native American types are classified in the United States, both officially and unofficially, as being racially nonwhite, to be "Latin" in the U.S. context is to be racially nonwhite. This principle then is generalized for all the populations found in the parts of the American continent south of the United States. Thus, the Latin derivation of someone, for instance, from Brazil or Argentina, who happened to have the phenotypical traits associated with the white population—such as, for example, being blond and blue-eyed—would be problematic and create cognitive dissonance. Nonetheless, the essentialization of the Latin racial classification would lead to the phenotypical aspects being pushed aside and the person being classified as nonwhite (unless there was no knowledge, in the first place, of the point of origin or birthplace of the person in question). In the same vein, to be European and have a Latin heritage, such as being Portuguese or Spanish—ethnic groups which are much closer historically to the Latin matrix—or even to be a direct descendant of the original Latins, such as the Italians (e.g., some second-generation native New Yorker of Italian descent), is never categorized by the U.S. general public as being Latin (!), because they are Europeans, and Europeans *qua* formal category are *always* racially white, in conformity with the prevailing definitions and understandings of race and race classification of the society.

The pervasive influence of the racial identity as the *master status* of individuals in racially bipolar societies, such as the United States, overriding nationality and citizenship status, as well as psychological status, is illustrated by the following examples. This influence is especially cogent on the lives of minority-group members. In her research on high school students, *Why Are All the Black Kids Sitting Together in the Cafeteria?*, psychologist Beverly Tatum (in Farley, 1997: 89) reported that when students were asked to complete the sentence: "I am ____," white students normally completed it by inserting psychological traits (e.g., "I am friendly," "I am shy," etc.), whereas minority students typically filled the blank with their ethnic identity or their racial identity, as in "I am Puerto Rican" or "I am black."

The aspect of nationality status being trumped as well by racial status is detected in a 1995 television report on children of African-American fathers and Japanese mothers. Some of these children had grown up in Japan, and were therefore thoroughly Japanese in their cultural makeup, yet in the African-American community of the United States they were defined as "black," and expected to assume a "black" identity and relate immediately to U.S. "black" culture.

Finally, we may consider in this respect a television documentary from the 1990s, *School Colors*, about race relations in a Berkeley, California, high school. The Program of African-American Studies of that school socialized students into a fiercely separatist ethos, which decisively conditioned their understanding of race and racial classification. Thus, they saw themselves first and foremost as *Africans*, not as *Americans*. Another related report (*Time*, April 29th, 1996: 45) describes the exchange taking place between the teacher and students, in a *black-only* grade school. She asks the students who can give her an example of an "African American" comedian. Some children offer correct examples. Then, she asks for examples of "American" comedians. One student mentions Whoopi Goldberg (an American comedienne of African extraction), to which the teacher responds: "No, an *American* comedian!" "Roseanne" (white comedienne), says another student. "Good!" says the teacher.

4. On this aspect, see, e.g., Sawer (2015), with reference to the reception of African-American GIs in England. The undifferentiated social treatment they supposedly received, for the most part, calls again to mind the Schutzian notion of anonymity. Natanson refers to its use in "general parlance," where it means "the state of being unknown, without identity, a kind of hiddenness" (1986: 23). It has been treated in the present work as the opposite of *otherness*, of particularity. Whereas the idea of anonymity typically conjures up visions of social exclusion, lack of representation, invisibility, from the standpoint of this phenomenological analysis, the quality of invisibility associated with anonymity, in terms of the present study, is suggestive of equality and freedom, with merging into universality, in the undifferentiated sea of fellow human beings like oneself. It is fitting, in connection with this, to appeal to Tannenbaum's statement in the 1940s (1969: 180), a time when Jim Crow conditions were in full operation, to the effect that the salvation for the "Negro" in the United States would come when "he ceased being a Negro and simply became another Southerner, another American."

5. Baldwin addresses in his usual compelling fashion the depth of harm that Jim Crow life in the United States brought to the lives of the nonwhite, more specifically African-American, population: this was a system, he said, that was "bottomlessly cruel" (1964: 40). He also offers evidence, and a powerful indictment, of the way Jim Crow traveled with the U.S. military to the battlefields of the Second World War, thus

keeping uninterrupted its poisonous effects on the lives of the black military personnel. As he describes it:

> You must put yourself in the skin of a man who is wearing the uniform of his country, is
> a candidate for death in its defense, [and continues to be a target of the familiar abusive
> treatment and vicious epithets] by his comrades-in-arms and his officers; who is almost
> always given the hardest, ugliest, most menial work to do; who knows that the white G.I.
> has informed the Europeans that he is subhuman . . . who does not dance at the U.S.O.
> the night white soldiers dance there, and does not drink in the same bars white soldiers
> drink in; and who watches German prisoners of war being treated by Americans with more
> human dignity than he has ever received at their hands. (1964: 68)

6. The foundation of personal life for African-Americans in the United States
during the Jim Crow period would, expectedly, have been the more comforting and
secure cultural world of the black community. This expresses the principle which
holds culture to be the primary existential frame of reference. Some three-quarter-
centuries ago, when James Baldwin was living in France, a situation which shielded
him from the whole range of rejection and abuse heaped upon nonwhites living under
the Jim Crow system, there was a point in time (according to the television documentary on his life, mentioned earlier) when he longed to return to the United States—not
necessarily because he longed to experience anew the traditional American cultural
icons—the Statue of Liberty, baseball, hot dogs, Hollywood westerns, the State
Fair—but the cultural background that had nurtured and formed him in his younger
years, specifically the (subcultural) world of the black community in Harlem, New
York, and the network of relatives, friends, and acquaintances that he had left behind.
The cultural dissociation from the overall culture of the United States, which had
failed to absorb him, and, in this connection, the stronger pull of the subcultural community are crystal clear.

Chapter 6

Racism and Social Alienation

The consideration of the damaging effects of race-based inequality and oppression for the mental life of the victimized populations foregrounds the importance of psychosocial factors in the present study. In his important analysis of the relation between psychoanalysis and social disorganization, Alexander (1937) stresses the affinity between sociology and individual psychology. Social interaction is based on the transmission of thought—ideas, values, meanings—among members of the group, something that stands, at root, for a psychosocial process. Consequently, in order to grasp the dynamics of social relations it is necessary to have, broadly speaking, a *psychological* understanding of these relations. He continues by saying that "the historical-cultural-economic understanding of social situations should be combined with the knowledge of emotional mechanisms according to which individuals react to their social situation" (1937: 781). Halbwachs (1939) supports this "idealist" interpretation of the material forms of social life, declaring that "institutions are, first and foremost, forms—stable and stabilized ways of life. Nevertheless, if we go back to the origin of these structures, we find mental states, representations, ideas, and tendencies, which, in becoming stabilized, became in some way crystallized." Halbwachs's position clarifies the way in which ideas and collective representations tend to persist over time. Even when particular mental states or aspects of intersubjectivity appear to be inoperative, they are "capable of being revived if . . . the institution can gain a new start and assume a new form" (1939: 821). From this point of view, one can better understand how certain social practices and situations (such as, for instance, intergroup cultural separatism) may be resurrected under a different guise, being driven by the same dominant system of ideas and beliefs of the society (this corresponds to what Schutz called the stock-of-knowledge-at-hand). Schutz's phenomenology expands the psychosocial orientation

151

described here, by emphasizing the operation of intersubjective meaning, as related to how social actors perceive the social world, their place in it, their access (or lack thereof) to emphasis on subjective factors the society's fund of knowledge, and so forth—all of which symbolic aspects will be probed for their connection with power relations in the wider community. It is also by reference to the mental life of individuals that such issues as being *the Other*, self-perception in relation to permanent minority status, the dualisms of particular recognition versus universal anonymity, and cultural uniformity versus separatism, will be discussed. Schutzian phenomenology will be utilized here as a "non-physicalist, non-mechanistic, non-reductionistic" (McCall, 1983: 96) explanatory framework of human behavior, to emphasize the importance of these processes of consciousness for the social functioning of individuals, which, when carried out under satisfactory circumstances, allows them to experience "the fullness of [their] humanity" (Binswanger, 1962: 20). The ability to reach this state existential fulfillment is most certainly thwarted when social actors have to contend with being in a permanent condition of otherness in the social world (see Binswanger's formulations about *dasein-analyse*, or existential psychology, in this respect; see also Laing, 1962).

We may begin this discussion by referring to an incident from the 1980s in Chicago, a sad tale of intrasocietal separatism which claimed the life of a young, distinguished African-American journalist of the *Chicago-Tribune* newspaper. The said person, feeling unable to cope with the enormous pressures and strain of having to exist and function simultaneously in two distinct cultural worlds, ended up taking her own life (cited in Feagin and Feagin, 1993: 214). This is the kind of tragic event that immediately places into relief the fact that the civil—that is, structural—integration of society's members, critically important though it may be for their incorporation into national life, is insufficient when exercised *sans* the cultural component of integration. The experience of cultural marginalization affects dimensions of social life that may prove to be of first importance for the people involved, not only in terms of feeling themselves to be on the fringe of national life, but also in terms of affecting their very process of civil-political integration itself.

The existence of two separate cultural worlds, coexisting side by side but never merging, is a circumstance of U.S. society that has proven especially injurious to the minority segments of the population. It was denounced at the turn of the twentieth century in brilliant pages, by W.E.B Dubois, whose incisive writings on black-white relations and the effect of racial prejudice and discrimination in U.S. society span some seventy years. In his writings he was already articulating a cohesive defense of sociocultural integration in direct opposition to the prevailing segregationist arrangements and mood of the time. He spoke eloquently and passionately of "the veil," his metaphor for the nature and effect of the polarization of the "white" and "nonwhite" worlds that formed American society. With the same subtlety yet utter impenetrability of the veil, the great dividing line of race in U.S. society was sufficiently transparent to afford a view of the world beyond the veil, but also impermeable enough to bar its access to outsiders. Dubois's family circumstances had placed him, from childhood, in association with white children, such as at school and at play, and this afforded him early on an opportunity to become aware of and familiar with the "veil." At first, he reacted to it with typical childish, and later, adolescent, indifference, then with a "fine contempt" toward those on the other side, most of whom were demonstrably less gifted than he was. As time passed, however, he became increasingly aware of the futility and defeatism of this withdrawal into social *otherness*, of how that was simply a natural defense mechanism on the part of those who had been denied access to what they in fact desired most ardently. The fact was he came to realize that those on the other side of the veil, and their mode of life, were the standard of reality, of validity, of excellence, toward which everyone else should strive. Hence, the only defensible course of action, it seemed to him, was that of struggling to break through the veil, however Sisyphean an enterprise that might prove. Any other reaction would have been inappropriate and unacceptable, for he came to understand that the riches yielded by the world beyond the veil were—or at least ought to have been—the property of everyone on both sides of the veil. "The worlds I longed for," Dubois remarks, "and all their dazzling opportunities were theirs, not mine. But they should not keep these prizes . . . some, all, I would wrest from them." These revelations bespeak a nascent aversion for separatism on Dubois's part, and for being faced with no option but to cultivate the *otherness* imposed on nonwhites by the larger society. He was chagrined to see, all around him, how sociocultural separatism forced his peers to shrink "into tasteless sycophancy, or into silent hatred of the pale world about them and mocking distrust of everything white; or [to have one's youth] . . . wasted itself in a bitter cry, Why did God make me an outcast and a stranger in mine own house?" (1903/1990: 8). He understood only too well how this set in motion the vicious circle of marginalization, meaninglessness, self-doubt, and despair, and how it quickly developed into a situation where those who were trapped in *otherness* straddled two worlds but were fully a part of neither. Experiencing the world beyond the veil through the interposing presence of the veil (such as, in a concrete sense, the "experiencing" of the larger society by minorities through the limitations forced upon them by the framework of legal separatism) meant that they could never reach a sense of existential completeness, in that they were neither full-fledged members of the larger society, nor fully outcasts. This was the dilemma Dubois referred to as "the contradiction of double aims," a dilemma linked to the most profound sense of estrangement and disorientation for those afflicted with it. "It is a peculiar sensation," remarks Dubois, "this double consciousness, this sense of always looking at one's self through the eyes of others, of measuring one's soul by the tape of a world that looks on in amused contempt and pity. One ever feels his two-ness--an American, a Negro; two souls, two thoughts, two unreconciled strivings; two warring ideals in one dark body, whose dogged strength alone keeps it from being torn asunder" (1903/1990: 8–9). This split identity of members of groups that are excluded—or only partially included—through ascriptively decreed social differentiation sent them often "wooing false gods and invoking false means of salvation" (1903/1990: 9–10). This may be observed in the several ways in which culturally marginalized populations may venture forth into identity-building projects that may prove problematic, insofar as they perpetuate the social disenfranchisement of these individuals. Dubois's commentary is uncannily timely today, in terms of unequivocally exposing the complex nature of a situation which has now been radically redefined, in connection with the preponderance in the United States, over the past few decades, of a race-based politics of difference. The latter signifies that the society now reacts to the pursuit, by ethnic-racial minorities, of alternative cultural affiliations and projects (i.e., in relation to the patterns of group life associated with the dominant racial community) without the negative ramifications identified by Dubois, but also sanctions and celebrates these alternative cultural projects as a natural phenomenon, while the minority groups involved passionately defend them as the rightful expression of long-suppressed native impulses and traditions.

The state of affairs described by Dubois resulted—and continues to result in the present time (see, e.g., Lacayo, 1989: 58–68)—from the operation of a divisive system of racial bipolarity in U.S. society, which has structured the world of everyday life in such a systematic and thorough manner as to have engendered the complete racialization of social existence: of social action, thought, discourse, and identity. The racialization of ethnicity, to take a salient example, makes the latter, to this day, a problematic category. Intended, *strictu sensu*, to apply to categories of people on the basis of their cultural makeup and common history, once racialized, ethnicity is reduced to *racial essence*.[1] Back in Dubois's time, as now, the direct corollary of the racially binary social structure was the dichotomous split of the population into the white and nonwhite segments.[2] A number of ramifications flow from this, with serious consequences for the groups codified as nonwhite, and thus permanently assigned to minority racial status. Foremost among these implications is the fact that the racialization of those who are incorporated into the "white world" takes on the aspect of universality and becomes the standard of *sameness*,[3] while the same process for those who fail to become absorbed into whiteness reduces them to the condition of *otherness*, which in itself—the condition of being *the other*—already signifies *inferior otherness*.

Since this condition is permanent, as concerns members of the subaltern nonwhite group their self-understanding, and the understanding of the nature of dominant-minority relations, tend to be articulated in racial terms. The otherness of the groups codified as racial minorities, construed as an essential and therefore fixed circumstance, has historically served the political purpose of facilitating the subjugation of these groups by the dominant one. In this respect, it also ensures the continuing, caste-like social distance and physical separation between the two groups. This kind of structural separatism, operating at both the institutional-formal and cultural levels of national life, has been a hallmark of intergroup relations in U.S. society from the late 1600s until about half a century ago, which is to say, it endured for virtually all of the society's history. The *formal* boundary lines of this separatism have largely disappeared since the late 1960s, when Jim Crow segregation was demolished, but the cultural lines still persist.

In recent years, the cultural forces that nourish this separatism have been gaining momentum, after having been dormant during the decade immediately following the breakdown of institutionalized segregation, when the order of the day in U.S. race relations was integration. This shift has taken on a formal character, over the last decade, with the implementation of the *politics of difference*. In a more general way, it has been manifested in the resurgence of separatist tendencies in the social and cultural sphere. For example, since the 1990s the relative increase in the black presence in TV shows has translated mainly into all-black casts, watched primarily by black audiences. Blacks have also been turning recently to separatist social clubs and organizations, in the effort to preserve the "black" or subnational identity.[4] This has inevitably impacted on formal-institutional settings as well, such as, for instance, in terms of fostering the implementation of racially segregated and gender-segregated elementary-school instruction;[5] or, segregated housing on university campuses.[6] Expectedly, this upsurge in society-wide formal and informal separatism affects members of the dominant and nondominant groups alike, in ways that are mutually reinforcing. More specifically, the increased societal emphasis on group difference—that is, on the recognition and preservation of this difference—ends up driving minority segments into greater isolation, self-sufficiency, and distinctiveness, and heightens their sense of identity as minority communities. This in turn strengthens the separatist ethos of the larger society all the more, generating more minority-group isolationism, and so on, and in this way the circle of segregation is completed.

The aspect of the minority-group identity is crucial. This identity and the fervor with which minority-group members embrace it are, first and foremost, a function of the biracialist division of the society in which this takes place, and of the resulting crystallization of the dichotomous racial categories. This model of ethnic stratification leads inevitably to the enforcement of

socialization mechanisms that stimulate the development of a minority consciousness among members of the subordinate groups. Like everyone else in
the society, these individuals internalize the definitions and stipulations of
biracialism, with a twofold effect. On the one hand, they assume the separatist
identity *with a vengeance*, keeping their distance from the majority population, and refusing to identify with and participate in general patterns of living
that would cause them to be perceived in their communities as "acting white"
(on this aspect, see, e.g., Gregory, 1992: 44–46). In this sense, the minority
consciousness exercises a sort of monitoring or "policing" function, leading
to an alertness on the part of these individuals toward transgressions of the
biracial code of conduct, whether by their peers or anyone else in the society.
(Developing this level of attachment to the minority identity has been, among
other things, a coping mechanism which the subaltern group relies on in its
struggle against ongoing discrimination and prejudice; hence, this identity
serves important psychosocial and political functions.[7]) This code comprises
such aspects as the treatment of race and racial divisions *as a given*, the
observance of endogamy, and the equation of the minority group's cultural
ways with its racial status. On the other hand, the incomplete assimilation of
these segments into national life has also historically produced an impulse of
over-immersion or over-identification on their part towards dominant cultural
norms and meanings, to the point of their becoming *plus royalistes que le roi*.
This phenomenon was foregrounded, for instance, in Gunnar Myrdal's magisterial 1940s study of the black experience in U.S. society, and in Clark and
Clark's psychological studies of the 1950s.[8] In the final analysis, members of
the minority racial part of the population may recognize that their racial status
and identity, as defined and imposed on them by the larger society, are the
source of their social deprivation and oppression, but, the dynamics of intergroup relations work in such a manner that the very historical circumstances
of segregation and oppression that produced this identity led them to adopt it
as a necessary medium of their social emancipation.

As discussed above, the dismantling of de jure segregation in the late
1960s occurred in the face of continuing segregation in the social and cultural
spheres of national life. In other words, the formal changes in the relationship
between "blacks" and "whites" did not necessarily translate into a re-structur-
ation of the cultural dimension of this relationship, toward increased cultural
exchange and syncretism, nor did it lead to a substantial rise in the rate of
black-white intermarriage, both of which factors would have diminished
the difference between the two groups. As a result, by the time the Reagan
administration took effect in 1980, barely a decade after the end of legally
upheld segregation, the integrationist impulse that had spurred the efforts of
Civil Rights activists in the 1950s and 1960s had begun to wane noticeably,
while concrete manifestations of separatism (by then no longer grounded in

the law, but separatism all the same), drawing new strength from the old separatist ways of thinking, began to reappear ever more frequently and openly.

The racially binary administration of social life, with its totalizing reach over collective life and consciousness, has clearly had a markedly unfavorable effect on the lives of minority-group members, materially as well as symbolically. The main concern here is with the problems it creates for social functioning[9] and the development of identity,[10] which may eventuate in a pervasive feeling of alienation and anomie, and overall psychological stress. In connection with this, our main task in this chapter is that of diagnosing pathologies of intergroup life, in terms of identifying and explaining dysfunctional aspects of the dominant-minority interaction, and of minority-group assimilation, with special focus on their manifestation at the level of intersubjectivity.

SOME NOTES ON BIRACIALITY

The central theme of this chapter is the way in which biraciality affects intergroup relations at the nonmaterial level, and ultimately at the material level as well. The focus may be said to have been placed on the social psychology of the problem, and the implications therefrom for the structural assimilation of minority groups. In this chapter, Schutz's phenomenological principles are used to support the idea that the biracialist administration of a multiethnic society lends an ontological character to the racial status of individuals, which then brings about negative psychological consequences for members of minority racial groups. This in turn exerts a disruptive impact on their social mobility and integration. Specifically, the biracial organization of the society, achieved through the legal system and through custom, naturalizes and thus perpetuates the separation and differentiation of the dominant and subaltern groups, the sense of minority existence for the latter, its cultural and social marginalization, and, finally, its structural marginalization. This is therefore a factor of the greatest importance both in the explanation of the processes of consciousness of minority-group members, and, more broadly, of the dynamics of intergroup life, whether within a single society or in comparative context. The focus on ontology will allow us to get around and overcome the limitations of traditional methodologies used in the study of race and ethnicity because it reveals intergroup relations as they *really* appear in society, and persons in the collectivity as they *really* are.

The binary system of racial organization as operative in, and represented by, U.S. society is a separatist model where the idea of race is construed in terms of a rigid dichotomy of whiteness/non-whiteness, based on ancestry or descent. The key organizing principle of this system is the rule of hypodescent, or *one-drop rule*, according to which *any degree* of genetic connection with the minority racial community results in the automatic classification of the individual as a member of this group, independently of physical appearance or social standing. The extreme reached by this process is clearly and comically illustrated in the following story. In the 1920s musical *Showboat*, a white young man whose actress girlfriend was of mixed parentage (hence, black) was accused by a Mississippi sheriff of violating the state's Jim Crow law against miscegenation. The young man quickly pricks the finger of his beloved with a knife, swallows a drop of the blood, and then declares his new racial status to the sheriff—that is, he was no longer a "white" man—since "Negro" blood now coursed through his veins. The sheriff is taken aback for a moment by the novelty of the situation, but eventually bends to the logic of racial classification operative in the state—according to which the action of the young man had radically reconstructed the situation, thus calling for a new interpretation—and lets the couple go (Adams, 2005). The comical and far-fetched character of this story notwithstanding, it effectively reveals the depth and inflexibility with which the principle of biracialism and its corollary assumptions (such as the purity or discrete nature of the racial categories, in this case) have structured intergroup life in the Anglo-American context.

Furthermore, where this particular framework of racial organization is in operation, the society naturalizes the dichotomous racial division of the population, as being a condition naturally determined by biology. It is impossible, therefore, for the several intermediary categories between the ends of whiteness/nonwhiteness to be properly recognized, as would be the case in multiracial social systems, where these taxonomic variations are determined phenotypically. The binary treatment of *mestiçagem* simply presents this condition as a variation on the theme of nonwhiteness, versus being a separate, autonomous condition. In recent times, as an effect of the politics of difference, each particular group version of nonwhiteness, as presented by the group in question, is acknowledged and celebrated in its distinctiveness by the society-at-large. In any event, the overall effect of the society's racially binary structure tends to override all other considerations, and particular forms or versions of nonwhiteness (e.g., the nonwhiteness of East Indians, or that of the Australian Aborigines) become indistinct from nonwhiteness as such—that is to say, from what has been referred to in the discourse of race and ethnicity, at some points in time and in various contexts, as *négritude*). In the end, it all returns to the basic dichotomization of the categories.[11]

In social systems built on the principle of racial bipolarity, race structures social life in an absolute and complete way. Institutional processes, interpersonal relations, social discourse—in short, all that represents culture—are regulated, seen as being determined, by the principle of race. To the latter will be reduced the remaining attributes of people, whether formal (i.e., ethnicity, culture, nationality, class, citizenship) or informal (e.g., personality traits). This has been addressed earlier, and it shows the operation of race as the *master status* of individuals (Hughes, 1945), their principal *scheme of reference* (Schutz, 1944: 502) for relating to the world of experience, defining who they are, interacting with others. The social construction of race as *essence*, therefore, naturalizes and reifies all of its social manifestations.

Formally and informally structured racial bipolarity in the social world impart, in this way, an ontological status to people's racial condition, inasmuch as "being white" or "being nonwhite" is treated as a particular mode of existence, one that is fixed and hierarchized. A change in the individual's racial status becomes, therefore, an impossibility, because it implies a transformation of one's very existential status—it implies a superimposition of ontological categories. Consequently, each category—that is, that of whiteness or nonwhiteness—becomes all-encompassing and impenetrable. Those codified as nonwhite will never be socially absorbed to the point of dissolving into the anonymity of the mass, which is the true mark of complete integration into national life. Social anonymity, as has been suggested before, is manifested as invisibility, and equates with equality, within national life. In other words, it signifies a point at which individuals are capable of representing *the universal*, rather than *the particular*, in national life.

Given that whiteness is the dominant standard of social existence, it might be said that its absolute impenetrability, the intransigence with which what people can/cannot be biologically and culturally is determined, amounts to a strict denial of admission to the majority standard of social life to the nonwhites—undeniably, a process of ontological domination. In U.S. society, the internalization of the separatist identity, therefore, leads to the perception of members of the society's dominant racial echelon as simply *American*, an identity that symbolizes full integration and membership in the white community, while the rest of the population is categorized as the hyphenated Americans (e.g., Chinese-Americans, African-Americans), a compound identity distinct from the dominant one, which is simple and unified. This may be seen in the fact that, for instance, nonwhites are always categorized as *minorities*, quite independently of their actual socioeconomic standing, or level of social advancement, education, and so on. Success in some professional area merely causes the nonwhite person to be seen as a distinguished minority person. Obviously, in this case, people's identity and their level of incorporation into the social mainstream are aspects conditioned and determined by their *racial* classification, not by class, professional achievement, or personality traits.

It is widely known that about a half-century ago the *Jim Crow* system of legally upheld racial segregation and discrimination in the United States came to an end. This was a period during which American society was effectively split into two great racial castes—the *whites* and the *nonwhites*—kept rigidly apart, yet co-existing in the same national space, on the basis of extreme socioeconomic and political inequality. Segregationist and discriminatory practices and arrangements were in effect everywhere: in the job market, education, public places and transportation, interpersonal life. The social and political subordination of the minority caste was repeatedly and systematically reflected in the physical structure of daily life. Thus, when a member of the subaltern caste sat in the back of a bus, or drank from a "Colored" drinking fountain, this process reproduced for that individual—whether within his or her conscious grasp or not—the social inferiority of the minority identity; and for the community-at-large, the moral worth of the system. When this social order was disturbed, physical violence was often resorted to so as to restore integrity to the system. It is worth citing, in this regard, the late 1800s account of Cuban patriot José Martí about social life in the United States (1975: 212), pointing specifically to an incident in Oak Ridge, Tennessee, where several black people had been lynched when it became known in the community that a black man had been living with a white woman there.

The dismantling of Jim Crow in the late 1960s and the concomitant official efforts to integrate nonwhites into the mainstream of national life stopped short of radically transforming the spheres of culture and informal interaction involving the two racial segments of the population, as can be witnessed in the persistence of informal segregation in U.S. social life. As the 1980s wore on, the integrationist impulse cultivated by the civil rights movement began to wane, while separatist tendencies gained strength.

THE QUESTION OF ONTOLOGY

The cultural life and common existence of people cannot be distinguished. Therefore, the discussion of ontology involves a *social* ontology, and culture, at its most inclusive and fundamental level, is its principal manifestation. That said, it must be argued that, if, in principle, the mode of cultural life of people is their ontological foundation—their main creative and driving force—it follows that in social systems where culture is permanently fragmented on the basis of people's ascribed status—race, in this case—this rupture amounts to a rupture in the very existential space of these people. That being the case, the cultural way of being of individuals is also their basis of social and psychic integration. It is, furthermore, a dynamic condition and in constant flux, a point that is clearly applicable to the experience of people both in the overall culture and in the subcultural community, inasmuch as both of these contexts operate as self-contained, total universes.

On the other hand, in societies regulated by the principle of racial bipolarity, the lifestyle of the group—comprising affectivity, family life, leisure, entertainment, language, modes of understanding, formal activity, and so on—loses this dynamic, historically variable quality. It takes on the stability or fixedness of a metaphysical condition. Thus, *being white*, or *being non-white*, is invoked not only as a racial signifier, but as an ontological signifier as well. As a result, the majority and minority living patterns, reflecting their origin in opposing racial essences, become polarized and irreconcilable, notwithstanding their coexistence in the same social system. At first glance, this might not seem problematic, as it might only denote internal pluralism in the society-at-large. However, this is not about the type of sociocultural pluralism commonly seen in polyethnic societies where the groups involved coexist under a basic civic-political equality—the so-called *corporative pluralism*, such as operative in Switzerland or Canada (see, e.g., Marger, 1991), nor is this a defense of the model of unilateral imperialist assimilation imposed by the larger society on its minority ethnic communities. What is at stake here is the fragmentation of the society's cultural system, brought about by binary social organization based on ascribed status—race, in this case. This promotes the reification of racial status, and of the form of collective life associated with this status, and, ultimately, the permanent division of the lifeworld where the groups in question are found. The social inclusion or exclusion of individuals will be carried out with reference to racial status. The condition of whiteness will express the existence of the hegemonic group, the standard of universality, the fundamental criterion of equality, and interchangeability of persons. The condition of nonwhiteness, representing the existence of the non-dominant group, is equally basic, except that it stands for difference, particularity, non-exchangeability. The creed of biraciality defines the distance between the two conditions as insurmountable, inasmuch as in being racially differentiated, the two groups are differentiated dichotomously and ontologically, thus creating problems for the admission of the nonwhites into the majority category—or even their autonomous existence in intermediary spaces, such as, for instance, the mulatto category. In this connection, members of minority racial groups are not *culturally* allowed, for example, to ignore or be indifferent toward their racial identity, toward their standing as minority groups within the larger society. Only members of the racial majority are allowed to do so, that is, not to be aware of *race* as such or of belonging to one, or of their structural position as the historically dominant racial segment of the population (vide, e.g., Waters, 1996). Cultural rules also discourage minority-group members from adopting an identity contrary to the society's biracialist system,[12] and from engaging in ways of behaving and/or thinking associated with the dominant group. Moreover, the enforcement of these norms of intergroup life is carried out by both the dominant and subaltern groups. The end result is the permanent representation of otherness by the subaltern group, and of *non-otherness* by the dominant group. The condition of *being the Other* implies inferiority *a priori*, and this problem is further aggravated in the context of biraciality because of immutability of racial condition and status. From this perspective, one can better understand the persistence of intergroup inequalities, divisions, differences, exclusions, and antagonisms. In a deeper sense, it is also clear how, as noted earlier, this situation amounts to a process of control and domination at the level of existence.

THE DOMINANT SOCIAL CONSCIOUSNESS

This section examines the posture of the dominant social consciousness toward minority difference, which concerns the manner in which minority difference is construed, experienced, and related to at the symbolic level by the dominant group, in integrationist versus separatist social systems.

In the separatist context of intergroup relations, the dominant social consciousness has essentially reacted, as mentioned earlier in the chapter, in twofold fashion toward the difference of alien cultural communities: it engages in total absorption or total rejection of this difference, and therefore neither approach represents an experiential or cognitive "openness" (i.e., a receptiveness to interchange) toward minority difference. We will analyze this problem ideal-typically, by presenting the dominant social consciousness as being centrally distinguished by the authoritarian impulse to control and absorb the world of experience. More technically put, this impulse involves the conceptual appropriation, demarcation, and classification of external objects, without a deliberate attempt to exercise reciprocity and reversibility toward them. In basic terms, this consciousness appropriates in a predatory fashion all that which is outside itself, or not-itself. When this pattern of response is concretely identified in the social world, it takes the form of a distinct model of assimilation, in which intergroup relations are marked by the rigid imposition of regulatory and classificatory schemes, as well as exclusionary practices. Minority cultural communities are straitjacketed into conceptual ghettoes, which become emblematic of their inferior social standing, and are prevented from breaking through the lines that separate them from the mainstream population, and from entering processes of large-scale interchange and fusion with this population.

Under these circumstances, the presence of the Other—that is, the presence of the alien cultural group—as difference is construed as contradiction. "Whatever differs in quality," Adorno maintains (1979: 5), "comes to be designated as contradiction." As such, the Other's difference is apprehended as "dissonant," "negative," and unfit for interchangeability, that is, ineligible for equal treatment. A dominant-minority relation will, of course, be established, but on the basis of inequality. These tendencies are most clearly evidenced in settings of caste-like social organization and stratification, where the segregation of groups is strictly enforced by law and by custom. This type of social domination evolves from the construction of the subjectivity of members of subaltern ethnic groups by the dominant population, manifested in the permanent placement of these individuals in the category of otherness; in other words, they are construed as an alien element that deviates from the hegemonic standard, thus being permanently inferior and unassimilable. In the concrete context of interethnic and interracial relations, this dominant-minority relationship is established early on, becoming the basis for a separatism that will reach across the entire spectrum of intergroup life: informal relations, kinship formation, institutional practices and arrangements, the arts, language, and so forth.

The dualistic posture of the dominant social consciousness toward minority ethnic-cultural difference may be restated as follows. There is, on the one hand, the imperialistic appropriation and transformation of this difference when the latter is perceived to be only cultural (but not physical). In the context of interethnic relations, and in the specific national context of U.S. society, this relates to the cultural difference of groups designated in the United States as *white ethnics*, and to the Anglo-conformity model of assimilation (Gordon, 1964). The idiosyncratic nature of the otherness of the minority group is simply cast aside here, while the group's swift and uncompromising adoption of the dominant cultural model is assumed and enforced as the *desideratum*. There is no stimulation of syncretic processes here, but only unilateral appropriation of the minority-group traits judged assimilable; hence, there is little chance for these traits to survive on their own terms. The Americanization crusade of the early 1900s represents the culmination of this tendency, and it was manifested in several ways. One was the practice, common among entertainment figures in the United States at one time, particularly among those of Eastern European extraction, of modifying their original names, or simply replacing them with names that sounded more Anglo-Saxon, a procedure that was relied upon as a technique of cultural survival.

The other side of the dominant social consciousness's voracious consumption of minority difference deemed assimilable is the emphatic repudiation and exclusion of difference deemed unassimilable. This occurs when the group remains categorized as a minority group on the basis of race. The dominant social consciousness then establishes and maintains an unbridgeable gap between itself and the minority difference. This phenomenon may be identified in the castelike separatism regulating black-white relations in American society especially during the Jim Crow period. This separatism was also the chief force behind the emergence of an indigenous cultural lifestyle among the subaltern ethnic communities, which resulted (in the particular case of African-Americans in U.S. society) from their having been barred from denied full admission to, and incorporation into, the national mode of life, while at the same time being discouraged from maintaining continuities with their aboriginal (i.e., African) cultural heritage. This twofold process of oppression of the minority group represents the negation of its very existential condition, a form of ontological domination expressed in the hierarchization of the ontological domains of the dominant and minority populations, respectively. This effect obtains both in terms of the negation of the original status of the minority-group members (i.e., that of "alien," of newcomers) at the initial stage of intergroup contact, through the suppression of their native cultural ways and identity; and in terms of the negation of their present circumstance as, one might say, cultural apprentices; in other words, in terms of the negation of their potential as *equal participants* in the formation of the larger sociocultural system. This creates an existential dilemma for the members of the minority group, a deep sense of inferiority, *anomie*, and alienation, which then generates their dual pattern of response, already addressed, entailing tendencies of over identification with the dominant mode of life, on the one hand, and rejection of the same, on the other.

By contrast, the ideal type of sociocultural integration affects intergroup (i.e., interethnic, interracial) relations very differently. The dominant social consciousness in this case exhibits more clear tendencies of reciprocity and interchangeability toward the minority cultural traditions—or, in reference to the concrete situation of *the stranger* discussed in the preceding chapter, toward the ways of the newcomers. These dominant-minority patterns of interaction might be viewed in the context of what Adorno, in a discussion of the operation of consciousness being ruled by the principle of identity, referred to as nestling or adhering as closely as possible to otherness—in this case, to cultural difference—without however absorbing it in predatory fashion (1979: 13, 191). In other words, the dominant social consciousness does not seal itself from minority-group difference in complete self-enclosure, but resists at the same time the impulse toward parasitic annexation of it. It acknowledges the original character of this difference by allowing itself to coexist with it dialectically, now in tension and equilibrium, now exercising a non-possessive openness and attraction toward it, in a manner that eventually brings about the "reconciled condition." Thus, it is not governed by a concern for preserving what it sees as its own conceptual unity, nor for rejecting and isolating itself from everything that it sees as a threat to this unity. In the realm of interethnic relations, this concern would be attached to the situation of non-syncretistic cultural systems, where intergroup arrangements and relations are strictly governed by ascriptive (i.e., racial, in this case) considerations, and where the dominant group would endeavor to protect and preserve its perceived cultural and/or racial purity, and to keep at a distance all elements regarded as potentially threatening to this purity. In contradistinction, the integrationist version of dominant consciousness operates in a complex and dynamic process of cross-fertilization, which reveals the workings of cultural syncretism. Bastide (1971) discusses this matter in reference to the phenomenon of dual identity for individuals, something he accounts for by means of his *principle of dissociation*. Another illuminating example in this connection may be drawn from early Brazilian colonial history. Early chroniclers inform us that when the Jesuits there embarked on the educational and religious assimilation of the young Tupinambá Indians (the *culumins*), they began by first learning and adopting their language, songs, and dances--the *culumins* were, in this respect, at once "the disciples and masters" (Freyre, 1956: 168)— thus setting in motion an intense and long-term process of cultural reciprocity that was to endure over the ensuing centuries, down to present times, and which may be witnessed especially in the Northernmost regions of the country, where the Amerindian cultural impact on religious and secular life has been significant. This impact has been felt in terms of a syncretized Luso-Brazilian Catholicism, but also in the national language, in the poetry and music, in children's games and pastimes, in the diet (Freyre, 1956: chapter II). On the basis of the foregoing, this analysis might be summed up, ideal-typically, by saying that in the integrative model of sociocultural organization, the interaction between the dominant social consciousness and the difference of the minority element is informed by a more significant level of intersubjective equality, insofar as intergroup life hinges on relations of cultural exchange and syncretism, whereas the separatist model of intergroup life is more clearly marked by intersubjective inequality, manifested concretely as relations of cultural separatism.

THE FOREIGNNESS OF THE MINORITY IDENTITY

The exaltation and, indeed, hypostatization, of the minority identity for particular groups, such as encouraged by the politics of identity and its matrix, the multiculturalist movement of the 1980s and 1990s, rather than signifying a fundamental change in the pattern of intergroup relations, simply add paradox and ambiguity to a situation which, though of long standing, was not ambiguous in former times. To clarify this further: the situation in question here is that of the structural inequality separating the dominant and minority ethnic communities upon which the Jim Crow system was built. Within this system, the permanently inferior status of .minority groups was legitimized and enforced by law and by custom, and these sources of legitimation in turn

were maintained by a full-blown popular ideology of racism that raised the
sanction of these arrangements of inequality to the level of sanctification.
Thus, the foreignness, the inferior otherness, of the minority group(s) was
a foregone conclusion and an article of faith for the mainstream population.
There was no ambiguity or discomfort in the legal system or in the public
mind at that time regarding the reality of a society divided biracially. Now,
however, with the destruction of the legal supports of ethnic-racial inequality, together with the shift toward affirming the minority difference for its
own sake, what has emerged is a paradoxical situation whereby the minority consciousness gains renewed awareness of itself as otherness in relation
to the dominant cultural model, followed by showing itself in this capacity
to the public at large, and even to flaunt this difference, hoping by this to
achieve what seem to be essentially incompatible outcomes: on the one hand,
the recognition of its individuality and distinctiveness in terms of permanent
differentiation from the national mode of existence; and, on the other hand,
the disappearance of this difference, through its gradual absorption into the
mass of undifferentiated humanity that makes up national life. This premise
rests on a fundamental misconception. It is possible, to be sure, as noted in
the preceding chapter, for non dominant groups *classified as white* to draw
the society's attention to whatever cultural distinctiveness they may have
retained, without this detracting from their favorable standing in the wider
society. The persistence of their native ways would naturally be more pronounced during the group's early acculturative phase, and typically diminish
with succeeding generations. The eventual full incorporation of these groups
into the society's cultural life would not necessarily prevent their continuing
attachment to ancestral customs and traditions. A case in point: the German-
American *Oktoberfest*, or the Irish-American St. Patrick's Day Festival. In
historical perspective, the tendency of these groups to maintain a degree of
continuity with their ancestral cultural heritage may slow down the assimilative process, but it also helps this process along insofar as it affords members
of these groups the psychological comfort and stamina necessary to get them
through the worst spots along their journey to full social incorporation. This
represents a dynamic conception of being, the condition of *being-as-becom-
ing*, which is grounded in the promise of change to occur in a future time.
Members of these groups assume the identity of "foreigner" upon arrival, but
this is an identity in flux, in that it lasts for the initial period (usually, the first
generation of the immigrant group in question) as a source of existential and
psychological support, then gradually recedes into the background, and the
void is proportionately filled by ever-increasing identification with the way
of the life of the host society, and by an increasingly automatic adoption of
the national identity. Thus, the outstanding characteristic of the "difference"
of all the groups categorized as white is its temporary nature, or the fact that

it is only a "moment" in their broader acculturative experience. But, where the permanently distinct ethnic-racial communities are concerned, matters are quite different indeed. Their simultaneous attachment to two different cultural traditions is a fundamentally different circumstance from when it is experienced by the *white ethnics*. In the latter case it is a more dynamic situation because it does not preclude the possibility of change in the future: members of the *white-ethnic* communities participate simultaneously in two cultural worlds, that which they left behind and that of the host society, but only temporarily. Immigrant groups in general have this experience, but it typically comes to an end as the assimilative process is completed. In the case of the permanent ethnic-racial minorities, the simultaneous involvement with two cultures is not so much a product of free choice—that is, the members of these groups did not start out with the collective decision to remain a permanent subcultural presence in the larger society—as it is, in social systems that operate on the basis of ascriptively determined intergroup separatism, the only option available to them. This represents a more static state of affairs. It rules out the possibility of the freedom that is found in the anonymity, undifferentiation, and interchangeability afforded individuals as they undergo full inclusion into the mainstream. The minority identity is thus doomed to perpetual visibility and operation as *otherness*, to the perpetual need to call attention to its difference, and what is most important, to function exclusively in a way that has been established as the "minority way." This rigidly imposed social duty effectively and necessarily impedes its dissociation from *otherness* and its absorption into *non-otherness*, that is, into the sameness of the mainstream. The glorification of its foreignness by a social system that is, concomitantly, the context of its genesis, development, and current existence only serves to harden the biracial lines of ethnic division, and to reinforce ideas in the public mind about the presumed inherent difference and inferiority of minority ethnic-racial groups. As such, an outcome that was once guaranteed through formal mechanisms is now being facilitated through cultural ones. Seen in this light, the preservation ad infinitum of the minority status becomes the very source of imprisonment for the minority community, an aspect emphasized in the following statement by Franklin (1997: 18): "The ethnic grouping that was a way-station, a temporary resting place for Europeans as they became American, proved to be a terminal point for blacks who found it virtually impossible to become Americans in any real sense."

THE TOTALIZING POWER OF THE RACIAL IDENTITY

The bifurcation of identity in U.S. society has been shown to be a function of the racial dichotomization of intergroup life. The latter, as might be gathered, has a distinctly totalizing effect on how individuals apprehend social reality. In this connection, it should be important to consider here that, at the most fundamental level—the level of meaning and subjectivity—people in American society resist the idea that the essence of "American life" could (or ought to) be expressed through something like Walt Whitman's suggestive image of a "teeming Nation of nations," a collection of many diverse and intertwining ethnic, racial, and cultural strains that have melded to produce this cohesive and unique model of collective existence, however much this image may have been inculcated in them through their formal socialization experience. The majority population in the United States has historically reacted with considerable ambiguity toward the international multitudes streaming into the country from various regions, over the past couple of centuries. By and large, people have not always known, do not always know, what to make of this constantly increasing ethnic diversity in their midst. Despite declarations in more formal vehicles, such as in the following excerpt from the popular press, hailing America as "the endless and fascinating profusion of peoples, cultures, languages, and attitudes that make up the great national pool" (*Time, Special Issue*, Fall, 1993: 3), in their heart of hearts a majority of Americans may still find it difficult to imagine the idea of authentic Americanhood as flowing from, and being represented by, such a hybridizing intermixture, particularly when the implications of "nonwhite" cultures forming an integral part of this mixture are taken into account. Naturally, it has been widely understood, for a long time, that the national population includes a number of different ethnic groups that stand out for their nonwhiteness and cultural diversity, but these people are "the other America"; they are not the real America. For all the new influx of "nonwhite" contingents (Asians, Middle-Easterners, Hispanics) into the society over the past few decades, individuals from these groups still have varying degrees of difficulty in truly fitting in, and, even after having been here for two or three generations, they are still regarded (though no longer formally so) by the majority population as "quasi-Americans." For example, a second- or third-generation American of Asian descent, who has become thoroughly acculturated into the dominant mode of life, linguistically and otherwise, and far removed from his or her ancestral cultural tradition other than through the memories of older relatives, but who still bears distinguishing physical characteristics associated with "Orientals," may reasonably expect questions about whether or not she or he has an interest in her or his Asian heritage, or about where she or he is from (Answer: "Los Angeles"; —Response: "No, *really?*" or: "Yes, but where are you from?" as in "What is really your country of origin?"), whereas an American citizen of Swedish or German descent will not get such a query. A more dramatic illustration of the denial of full citizenship status to racial minorities, at both the formal and symbolic levels, was the internment of some 110,000

Japanese-Americans during the Second World War, a measure defended by the U.S. government on the basis of ensuring national security. That incident reveals, first of all, the enormous discrepancy between democratic ideal and social practice that prevailed until the 1960s in U.S. society (as evidenced in the enforcement of Jim Crow arrangements and norms). The flagrant violation of the democratic rights and privileges of Japanese-American citizens suggests how the society had failed until that time to reconcile its conception of full citizenship and social egalitarianism with the "nonwhite" segment of the citizenry. The Japanese were an easy target for discrimination during that time, given their high visibility as a group, which was precisely a function of the workings of the Jim Crow system, through which they were categorically barred from intermarriage with members of the majority population, which in turn preserved their physical distinction as an ethnic-racial minority. As it turned out, not one single case of espionage or sabotage against the United States on the part of Japanese-American citizens was ever recorded. In the meantime, discriminatory institutional measures were never taken against German-Americans and Italian-Americans, despite the fact that the United States was also at war against Germany and Italy, a fact that is rather consistent with, and mirrors, the intense ideological racism undergirding governmental policy and public sentiment at that time.

It might be said in this respect that the socially prescribed minority racial identity exercises a tyrannizing influence over the individuals on whom it is imposed, in that these individuals are unable to escape its relentless grip, and to assert the primacy of their national identity by simply stating it. By the same token, as discussed earlier, members of the majority population who may have full or partial ancestry in some "nonwhite" group, but have, by virtue of their physical appearance and socialization experience, managed to escape the minority classification, arc discouraged [not formally, but by cultural forces] from publicly claiming, flaunting, or even just referring to, their minority status.

The reason for this pattern is that the acceptance of full interchangeability or reversibility as a condition applicable to all citizens of the republic, irrespective of their ethnic or racial background—a condition which would in effect be the hallmark of social equality—is something that runs directly counter to the more deeply internalized conception of the American social order as one that is, first and foremost, biracially structured and administered. In other words, to express, and therefore implicitly endorse, the idea of ethnic, racial, and cultural diversity as the foundation and true expression of American social life amounts to compromising the basic dualistic split of the population assumed in the principle of racial bipolarity, and the racial determinism and reductionism built into this principle, which function as organizing categories of the collective consciousness. Thus it happens that, when people in American society are confronted, for example, with the need to recognize the general similarity between the United States and other multi-ethnic societies, in terms of the fact that the United States and these societies exhibit varying degrees of ethnic and cultural variation as well as mixture and fusion, they may fail to grasp this similarity right away, and may even experience some cognitive dissonance, particularly regarding the aspect of mixture and fusion of the various ethnic and cultural strains. This is because, for people in general, the image of mainstream America that springs most readily to mind is not so much one that conforms to the melting-pot imagery, but one that flows from the principle of biraciality: a society that is essentially homogeneous from a racial and cultural standpoint, but which happens to have some peripheral segments in its population, which are racially and cul-turally unassimilable (at least, not in the fullest sense), and which must, there-fore, retain this quality of "outsidedness." The biological integration of the *white ethnics* into U.S. society would not have marred the (presumed) racial purity of the majority population, nor would their cultural assimilation have compromised, to any appreciable extent, the society's Anglo-Saxon cultural makeup, because of the thoroughness with which these groups have been culturally "Americanized." This homogeneous mainstream America thus stands distinguished from the other, equally homogeneous, non-mainstream America, composed of a variety of "nonwhite" minority communities, which, for all their cultural and physical diversity, have been rendered uniform in the public mind through the generalizing, reductionist effect of the nonwhite condition. These two segments of the society coexist side by side, but do not, or are ever expected to, fully interpenetrate. This matter was put succinctly and unambiguously by the racist sheriff of the small town in Mississippi, in the 1989 film *Mississippi Burning*, as he truculently attempted to tell the Northern FBI agent to leave them alone to run their own internal (i.e., inter-racial) affairs: "We have two cultures here, a white one and a black one!" alluding to the laws of biraciality undergirding the handling of social affairs, and intimating that that was the natural order of things, something not to be tampered with. He could just as well have been articulating the viewpoint of most of the population about the nation as a whole, especially during the historical period in question—the 1960s—a time when the Jim Crow system was still in operation (though nearing its end).

Leaving aside for the moment the fact that full racial uniformity is only an analytical construct, a theoretical possibility, and never an empirical feature of world societies, we could still say that people in the United States would have had greater justification in asserting the pronounced racial uniformity of their society back in the late eighteenth century, because at that time (1790) the "white" groups still constituted as much as 92.4% of the total popula-tion (Feagin, 1993: 65). The ratio of white to nonwhite in the population, however, has declined drastically over the past two centuries. That fact notwithstanding, official and unofficial classification, being fundamentally governed by the law of hypodescent or "one-drop rule," dismisses the ethnic variability injected into the general population by the major wave of immigration of the 1800s, and the ongoing influx of different strains through the twentieth century, and largely continues to enforce the dichotomic (i.e., white/nonwhite) framework of classification. (Some changes have been introduced in the formal schemes of race classification in the United States over the past quarter-century or so, but the general public has to this day remained largely unaffected by this.) Ethnic and cultural diversity is misconstrued as racial difference, that is, as racially determined group difference. An example of how this is done may be found in the way in which the ethnic and cultural differences that distinguish immigrants from Central and South America (minus Brazil and the Guianas) are disregarded and forcibly dissolved, at both the bureaucratic and informal levels, by lumping these individuals together under the rubric "Hispanic." The latter has come to mean, for the U.S. public at large, not simply a designation for groups whose cultural heritage is traced to Spain, but also a totalizing minority category, formed on the basis of the presumed racial uniformity of the group(s) involved, thus representing one among several other "nonwhite" ethnic segments. It has come to be understood, therefore, principally as a racial classification, although in reality it is an ethnic label, which should not be taken to be denotative of racial uniformity, but, in fact, embraces a striking genotypical and phenotypical variety across the different world societies colonized by Spain. However, because the label was originally used in reference to the first two major Hispanic groups in U.S. society, namely, the Mexicans and the Puerto Ricans, groups that are largely mixed in their "racial" background, and secondly, because the operation of the hypodescent rule in the United States precludes the recognition and admission of any intermediary racial categories,[13] the word "Hispanic" has become a catch-all term that forces all groups of Hispanic origin (in addition to the Mexicans and the Puerto Ricans, the Hispanic population in the United States has recently included people from Cuba, El Salvador, the Dominican Republic, Colombia, and Venezuela), regardless of their ethnic and racial background, under the racial designation of "nonwhite."

The dominant effect of the ascriptively (i.e., racially) generated minority identity in the society, as the chief cognitive and existential frame of reference, causes it to muddle up and transform the meaning of other, unrelated conceptual categories. The following may be considered. It seems, for instance, that the meaning of the concepts "middle class" and "Western," the one denoting a particular socioeconomic echelon in the stratification system, the other, a geographical and/or cultural condition (i.e., the use of "Western" to refer to a cultural aspect concerns the broader cultural complex conventionally understood as Occidental civilization), has been recast in racial terms, particularly under the auspices of the multiculturalist movement in the United States, starting in the 1980s, to the effect that these concepts may be used, at least implicitly, as designations pertaining to the "white" population. Similarly, the concept "European," which is indicative of a general sociocultural pattern of living (on the basis of which it can be distinguished from other similarly general conceptual models, such as the "African" or the "Asian"), is used to a large extent in American society as a racial badge, a badge of undifferentiated "whiteness," which members of the majority population rely on as a representation of their background. Yet another instance of this trend may be seen in terms like "the poor" or "the people," clearly notions of political economy, the one referring generally to the "have-nots," the other, to the masses, with the latter concept usually connoting asymmetry of wealth and power in relation to the upper echelons of the population.

The reductionism and inevitable distortion of meaning associated with this tendency are such that one may run, for instance, into references in the popular press drawing a contrast between Latin American cultures (e.g., Mexico, Colombia) and the Western way of life; or even between the cultural mode of life of an ethnic racial subculture in American society like, for instance, the African-American community, and the "Western" lifestyle of the majority population(!). If Latin American societies are not Western, that is, neo-European, in their ethos and cultural orientation, what else can they possibly be? And, as far as the African-American group in the United States is concerned, despite the fact that the larger situation of sociocultural separatism, formal and informal, prevented their full acculturation into the majority way of life, and led to their development of, and adherence to, subnational forms of behavior and thought, they must still be seen as participants in a neo-European cultural complex, as people who have fashioned their basic cultural orientation and identity in the historical context of absorption of English-American ways of life. Therefore, it seems ludicrous to characterize their cultural expressions as anything other than "Western"—unless, of course, there are other considerations and assumptions lurking behind the use of this designation. It is true that their African ancestors, upon arriving on American soil as slaves, did bring with them a non-Western cultural background. However, succeeding generations of African-Americans, notwithstanding their less than full inclusion into the sociocultural mainstream, have not been anything but Western from a cultural standpoint—that is, "American," in the sense of being the product of a combination of many European and non-European cultural forms into a distinctive, cohesive type of Euro-American civilization.

As for the placement of Latin American social systems in the non-Western category, this classificatory tendency appears to result from the widespread perception of Central and South American societies as being racially and culturally mixed, hence, "nonwhite" and, as such, ineligible for the "Western" classification. In this connection, the "Latin" designation, which is in actuality an ethnic-cultural referent, has been reconstructed in the United States over the past couple of decades, so as to signify nonwhite status, as linked specifically to the minority Spanish-American groups. The idea of Latin America, therefore, that springs to mind (the minds of a great number of people, of the "person in the street") is not a cultural one, denoting a group of nations which, like American societies in general, have a European background, but differ from their Northern neighbors in terms of their common Iberian cultural heritage. Rather, it is a racial idea, this undifferentiated land of "Latins" (i.e., Spanish-speaking nonwhites), a totalizing category that does not leave out any national group south of the Rio Grande, including Portuguese-speaking Brazil. The greatest irony with regard to the Latin classification is that the Italians and the French are not really thought of as Latins, mainly because they happen to be classified as white, an irony which fairly jumps out at the observer with respect to the Italians, the ethnic group that should have the strongest and most legitimate claim to the Latin identity. It does not take much for one to see that these classificatory judgments are not at all being oriented by cultural criteria, but by racial ones, and that what is really at work here, even if implicitly, is the greater organizing and regulative influence of the principle of biracialism, cutting across and overriding all other forms of social differentiation.

ALIENATION IN THE LIFEWORLD

The problem of alienation is a *malaise* of modern life, in the broader sense, but in this study it is addressed in more specific reference to the problems affecting the assimilative experience of members of minority racial segments of multiethnic societies—and even more specifically, the assimilative experience of racial minorities in multiethnic societies of the present time, such as the United States, where racial hierarchizations and separatism, oriented by racial bipolarity, were institutionalized and legally enforced for a very large part of the society's history.

Alienation or estrangement from the normal course of social relations in the everyday world may be seen as a primary manifestation of *anomie*, in that it represents an anomic form of living brought about by the separatist pattern and circumstances of interracial life. In the classic Durkheimian discourse on *anomie*, as is known, the explanation of this condition is that is associated with major structural shifts in social structure, or in the general circumstances of social life, generated by modernization. The possibility of *anomie* and other related aspects affecting the life of members of subaltern racial groups may be considered here in reference to the larger question of meaning. Since these individuals find themselves having to perform simultaneously in the society's central system of meanings as well as in their subcultural one, they end up treating *both* as valid and legitimate, notwithstanding the differences, and even contradictions, between them with respect to certain critical aspects. Hence, they feel that both systems demand their attention and commitment *in the same degree*. We thus have the simultaneous operation of two distinct sets of social stimuli, with which minority persons have to contend every day in the lifeworld, exerting demands and pressure at the level of subjectivity. The Bergsonian formulation of *attention-to-life*, discussed earlier, is directly relevant in this respect, in that it pertains to what we select as the principal focus of our attention and interest, that which orients us, cognitively and emotionally, in our daily exchanges with the social world. Lapoujade states in this regard that attention-to-life "is the operation through which we adapt ourselves to the exigencies of the outer world, through a kind of equilibrium" (2005: 1146). : However, in order for this orientation to work properly, it is of cardinal importance that the aspects which absorb our attention in the world of everyday life also be internally consistent, inasmuch as everything revolves around "the cohesion of these elements in the normal operation of the mind" (Bergson, 1970: 226). This is the kind of psychic equilibrium that must be reached. In situations of race-based intergroup separatism, codified in the law and social practices, with its physical and cultural manifestations, this psychic equilibrium, internal consistency, that Bergson writes about, simply do not exist, as concerns members of the minority racial community. These people inevitably come to feel that they are being pulled by opposing forces, every single day. Any psychological disturbances resulting from this, there-fore, would have to do with difficulties in the process of integration of the ele-ments in the social world that are linked to the operation of attention to life.

The relevance of Schutz's formulations for the analysis of this problem is twofold. First, and principally, his version of phenomenology, as has been repeatedly stressed, gives primacy to the *social* constitution of reality and consciousness, rather than to how social reality might be constructed in con-sciousness. Schutz's objectivist conception of the world of daily life lends a strongly sociological character to the analysis, which is essential. Secondly, his descriptions of the everyday world and of the dynamics of intersubjective life provide an effective context for examining and clarifying the problem of alienation from the standpoint of the social-existential situation of the person.

There are, furthermore, two interrelated aspects in the Schutzian project, addressed earlier, that are pivotally important to the present work. The first is his conception of social reality as a product of the daily collective engage-ment of individuals in a common process of meaningful interaction—their engagement in the *lifeworld*. The second is his emphasis on the foundational and constitutive role of meaning and processes of consciousness in human collective life. Social relations are structured and carried out on the basis of shared meanings, manifested as typifications. As has been indicated, universal, full-range access to the society's majority system of typifications is afforded through the internalizing mechanisms of socialization, by means of which they form the taken-for-granted world of everyday life. This internalization process is also the sine qua non of social integration, in that it not only structures the interaction of members of the community-at-large, but also provides everyone with admission to a sphere of equality and interchangeability among similarly socialized social actors. This common circumstance, to wit, the *sameness* of members of a given sociocultural system, makes possible their mutual recognition of meaning, and the ability of each member of the society to predict and respond appropriately to the actions of others. The stock of cultural knowledge involved here is mainly represented by a common system of relevances, and the latter acquires such cardinal importance in organizing social behavior that it constitutes "a principle of structurization of the lifeworld itself" (Zaner, in Schutz, 1970c: xx).

We have dealt earlier with Schutz's refinement of the concept of lifeworld in terms of four interrelated levels, of which the most pertinent for our purposes is the *sozialemitwelt*, or the social world of contemporaries. This is the world we live in presently, which is temporally and spatially bound. This social domain is further differentiated or segmented into two dimensions: that of *directly experienced* social reality (*umwelt*), made up of relationships among individuals who are immediate companions or *consociates* to one another, fellow human beings in direct experience; and that of the social world more broadly conceived, inhabited by people who, though contemporaries to one another, do not experience one another directly—that is, they do not experience one another in terms of one another's subjective experiences—but only in terms of typifications. The two other realms incorporated into the concept of lifeworld, as we have seen, which affect how we relate to the present, are the social world of our predecessors (*vorwelt*) and the social world of our successors (*folgewelt*) (1997: 142–143; see also Munch, 1994: 146, vol. 2). We are primarily interested here in the *mitwelt* level, since it expresses the *lived social world*, the world of experience in which we live and function every day, encompassing the larger social structure and community of actors. This is precisely the context to which the idea of typification applies most directly (Munch, 1994: 146), which means that it is the sphere of social activity where the determining effect of culture is most evident.

The social world has been shown to be a world of meaning, "the constituted texture of *meaningfully interlocking* activities of actors on the social scene" (emphasis mine), the essence of which, for Schutz, was its quality of *sharedness* (Zaner, 1961: 71). In this connection, collective life must be understood as consisting primarily of a network of interlocking processes of consciousness. Intersubjective relations, expressed though they may be in physical terms—that is to say, as behavior, in accordance with the mundane exigencies of daily life—are in fact, in their *modus essendi* (or in the ontological sense), manifestations of the activities of the mind. They are "psychical," as such. Consequently, these relations are grounded in the understanding of meaning (*sinnverstehen*), as "the condition of all sociality" (Jonas,1959: 472). These ideas are central to understanding the importance of people's integration into, and their sense of being integrated into, the society's majority system of meaning, when it comes to their psychological well-being.

A distinction is intended here between the communicative-symbolic plane of social existence and that of strictly formal-institutional relations, and, furthermore, between the degree of influence of each plane in the constitution of social life. This analysis assumes the overriding importance of this world of sociality, or the communicative environment, in determining the nature of collective life in general. Also, with regard to the substantive focus of the present study on the situation of minority-group members and their incomplete incorporation into national life, aspects of intersubjectivity are treated here as a critical yardstick and determining factor of their material and psychological welfare. As Schutz contends, all phenomena and aspects of the social world (hence, anything that pertains to intergroup relations) are fundamentally related to and influenced by "this primordial sphere of our *lived world*"; therefore, it is not only feasible but also desirable that *all forms* of the social world be investigated "within the framework of the constitutive investigation of the lived-world" (Tymieniecka, 1962: 106–107). The life-world structures collective behavior and thought under conditions of stability as well as change. When change occurs in the wider social environment, which requires assessment and reconstruction of existing modes of thought and action, it is still the prevailing lifeworld stock of knowledge that remains the primary basis of orientation and conditioning force of social behavior, the element that "exerts its structuring effect on any new construction of social knowledge" (Munch, 1994: 147, vol. 2). If this be granted, then it should be clear that to unveil the truth of any type of social situation—interethnic or otherwise—one cannot rely solely on concrete indicators, and draw inferences about the nature of the situation being investigated solely from that which is immediately given or observable. Schutz insists on the need to focus on the world of intersubjectivity—on how individuals construct their social reality—and to treat the intersubjective world as an *objective dimension* of social existence, since it represents a complex of interpretations and meanings produced by the group, a complex of collective representations, available to all within the group. These representations and meanings have their origin in a multiplicity of individual subjectivities, and in this sense they are idiosyncratic. However, they are synthesized and systematized in their common *inter*-subjective state, *and thus universalized* in the lifeworld as distinct, objectively identifiable, enforceable set of normative guidelines for collective action.

Thus, to revisit some fundamental considerations made in chapter 3, it is important to emphasize again that this objectivist conception of the lifeworld establishes the latter's importance as the ground of normativity in collective life, as well as the main unit of analysis. The existing culture of the lifeworld constrains and determines the character of individuals and their subjectively motivated patterns of thought and action (Schutz, 1997: 33, 132–136; Munch, 1994: 148, vol. 2). This communicative environment in turn is made possible through "the primordial experience of the we-relation" (Schutz, quoted in Jonas, 1959: 474), a concept which, as discussed earlier, concerns the multiple face-to-face exchanges that we engage in everyday with one another. These exchanges organize social life as a whole, and also afford us access to the lifeworld in its constitutive aspects, namely, the different contexts of temporality delineated by Schutz, which are all integrated, forming a "reciprocal interlocking of time dimensions" in the daily interactions of individuals. All of this also expresses a complex of meaning (Schutz, in Natanson, 1977: 119), to which social actors are supposed to have access, as part of their membership in the society. More to the point here, the interlocking of the time dimensions of the lifeworld consists of a reciprocal interlocking of "perspectives, motives, and behavior" (Zaner 1961: 75, 87–89). When applied to the present analysis of the interethnic problem, this principle becomes especially relevant because of its implications for admission to, and participation in, the mainstream meaning system of the society.

In the We-relationship actor A confronts actor B and assumes the latter's attribute of sameness, a circumstance common to both, which was discussed earlier as the typical interchangeability of society's members on the basis of a common socialization experience. This sameness may be said to operate at the level of existence. It enables the participant in the interactional encounter to form a "face-to-face *Other*-orientation toward the partner." Actor A directly experiences Actor B as a "fellow man," and this is what constitutes the *Thou-orientation.* This mutual experiencing between social participants is only a concept, a formal construct. In real life, these encounters are filled with content (Schutz, 1997: 163–164).

In connection with this, under conditions of institutionally sanctioned and mandated interethnic/interracial separatism, members of the dominant group *will not* experience members of the subaltern group as "fellow men"; they will not experience these individuals as being the same, or equal to, themselves. Thus, in this case, they will not be able to assume the possibility of the reciprocal Thou-orientation upon which the network of We-relationships is based. This outcome is ruled out beforehand, because the systematic separation of the two groups keeps them differentiated culturally, and this difference—this difference *in the way of being*—is understood by all to be a natural, hence fixed, condition. The encounter begins with the foundational framework, which is the physical encounter of the parties—the groups in question—ready to establish a face-to-face *Other*-orientation with each other. But the successful completion of this relation, construed here as mutual understanding grounded in shared meaning, is thwarted by the background, or past experiences, of each group of actors. Thus, members of both the dominant and non-dominant groups will view each other as being *essentially* (i.e., ontologically) different. The physical separateness and the emergence of separate cultural modes of life for these social segments means that they will rely on two different systems of typifications or relevances, as they interact with each other. Even if members of the minority group display *at first glance* the same modes of behavior and thought used by members of the majority group; many of their differences will be subtle in nature, others not so subtle. Yet, it is necessary (says Schutz, 1997: 170), if the kind of primordial face-to-face encounter of the We-relationship is to be effectively realized, that the actors involved share the same (social and cultural) "environment."

Several decades after the abolition of the formal structures of intergroup separatism in U.S. social life, the problem of meaning continues to plague dominant-minority relations. The objective and subjective dimensions of this problem are intertwined. Subjective meanings both form and are formed by the intersubjective meaning complex of the society. Intersubjective meanings amount to cultural meanings, and they are objective in the sense that they represent an "already constituted," total complex of meaning (Schutz, 1997: 134). That is to say, even though they originate in individual consciousness, when integrated and transformed into the collective structure of meaning they cease to be idiosyncratic—meaning, they are no longer applicable to the reality of the individual alone—now being embedded in sharedness, in the culture as a whole. At this point, these meanings begin to function as the universe of significations to which society's members normally have access, and on which they naturally rely at all times. In any case, social interaction, whether formal or informal, takes place mainly on the basis of the communicative difficulties that may arise hinge on this element. The example may be offered here of the train conductor who makes an announcement, but, because of (the conductor's) subcultural speech variation, it may not be fully understood by the passengers. This suggests an instance of incomplete assimilation into the mainline system of linguistic typifications, involving semantic variation regarding the use of particular cues or signs, key linguistic signifiers, intonation, and so on. Still, the message would have been organized on a sufficient number of linguistic typifications, of the *technical* kind, in order to make its meaning accessible to the passengers. Some of the information missed will be inferred from the part of the message that was intelligible. This is because, as will be indicated later, people grasp the meaning of things in terms of the unity of this meaning. Now, in this specific example—as in any kind of similar situation involving secondary relations—there is no real need for the people involved to know the subjective meaning behind the conductor's message, which is to say, to go beyond the purely objective or technical meaning of the message, so as to get to the meaning-context or motivational forces that operated in the mind of the conductor when the announcement was made. There would have been no need, to put it in Schutz's terms, for the passengers to know "'the project which the speaker must have had in mind'" (1997: 127). The objective level of meaning affords each participant in the communicative exchange the ability to understand the meaning of the action of others *in the social context*, or in the context within which this meaning is universally accessible, accessible to all who experience it in terms of society-wide definitions. This meaning "is grasped as an objectification endowed with 'universal meaning'" (Schutz, 1997: 135). There is no reference, therefore, to its strictly subjective origins or connections.

As noted earlier, the objective and subjective meaning of things are intertwined. This may be demonstrated in the fact that knowledge of the objective meaning of behaviors, as expressed through typifications, *also* enables individuals to have the predictive ability to know the *motivational orientation* of the other, and thus to know what course of action will be taken. In other words, while mastery of the hegemonic system of typifications allows individuals to understand those with whom they interact, in reference to the pragmatic reasons for their actions (i.e., in terms of these actions representing typical patterns of behavior), it also makes it possible for them to understand their behavior as symbolic indexes of the subjective forces working behind the production of the behavior, since each person's subjectivity is *ordinarily* externalized in ways that are objectively available to the community at large, or, that are in accordance with prevailing cultural definitions and standards. Again, the essential prerequisite here is the sharing of a common cultural environment.

This discussion is primarily anchored to the problem of relevance. The action and thought of individuals in the collectivity are grounded in and oriented by a system of relevances, which conditions the way in which these individuals see themselves and the world around them. The idea of *interest* is germane in this respect, and refers to the particular context of relevance that grounds interindividual life in the lifeworld. More specifically, the interest situation is constituted by "the set of motivational relevances which guide the selective activity of [the] mind" (Schutz, 1970c: 64–67). The operation of interest is what determines the system of topical relevances, or that "by virtue of which something is constituted as problematic in the midst of the unstructuralized field of unproblematic familiarity—and therewith the field into *theme* and *horizon*" (1970c: 26). These topical relevances, selected from the world-taken-for-granted (i.e., from the lifeworld, as such), establish the main focus for individuals as they go through the daily round of activities: it establishes their *field of consciousness* (1970c: 3–5), in relation to which behavior and thought are directed, the contours and limits of this social action and thought are established, and the type and amount of knowledge required for social actors to deal successfully with the situation or problem at hand are specified.

THE PSYCHOSOCIAL IMPACT OF RACISM

In considering the function of race as the main axis of social life, the hallmark of racially binary social systems, much has been said already that shows how this model of intergroup life sets up a system of interpretational relevances, with its specific functional and technical utility for the society-as-a-whole. This means that under circumstances of intrasocietal biracialism, race powerfully influences the emergence and operation of particular concerns, definitions, and determinations in the consciousness of the social actors making up each of the racial halves of the population, regarding the choice of specific courses of action. As such, it exerts a strongly regulative effect on intergroup relations, effectively determining the outcome of these relations. In reference to this, it not only provides a blueprint for intergroup relations at the practical level, but also sets the basis for the construction of identity. The socially assigned racial status of individuals becomes the overriding frame of reference for self-definition, for *who they are*—an ontological dimension of race that is, as discussed before, an outstanding characteristic of racially binary social systems. This leads us back to the domain concern in the present work, which is to demonstrate how social existence is constitutively affected by schemes of perception and understanding, processes of consciousness, or, to phrase it differently, by aspects of culture. The ability of individuals to correctly apprehend the nature of objects in the world, the nature of the behavior of others, and the nature of social situations in general, and to respond appropriately to the diversity of social stimuli depends on their recognition of the typicality of these things. Their degree of access to the prevailing schemes of relevance (grounded in the stock of knowledge) of the society and, more importantly still, their ability to experience the society's meaning system as being internally consistent will determine their level of success in the process of being socially integrated. Ascriptively based, legally enforced intergroup separatism violates this principle, as it hampers the full absorption of certain groups in the population into the cultural sphere, thus creating schizogenic conditions in the area of social meaning, and problems for the psychosocial welfare of the members of culturally marginalized groups.

Racism in all its forms invariably produces an alienating effect on the lives of members of dominant and nondominant groups, and this effect is extraordinarily enhanced with respect to the lives of members of the latter group, a process that reaches an extreme in racially binary social systems. The racial reductionism derived from this model of social organization does not affect the population uniformly. Members of the racially dominant group (i.e., those who are racialized as members of the "white" community) can afford to engage in their daily social performance without being directly conscious of race. They are able to shake off the mantle of race, and function unimpeded by racial considerations, to lose awareness of this group trait—that is, racial status—and navigate the waters of *non-difference*, of universal sameness. This is one of the benefits of living in the dominant existential category, that of non-difference.

Members of the minority racial communities, on the other hand, remain locked in racial otherness, and all that this condition entails, independently of the amount of change and improvement that they may have brought to their social circumstances and positions.[14] These individuals exteriorize themselves daily as official members of the national community, as they engage in the process of constructing the society. In U.S. society in recent times, they benefit from the formal legacy of political liberalism of the society of which they are a part, which means that they are not distinguished *formally* anymore (as would have been the case during the Jim Crow period) from the mass of citizens, as regards their capacity to exercise and enjoy formal rights and privileges without being hindered in this process by ascriptive status, namely, race. Nevertheless, in contradistinction to dominant-group members, they are not correctly *represented* in the larger community. The way in which they are reflected in the social world does not fully correspond to what the society's civil and legal structure grants to them as citizens, nor to what the process of *formal* socialization prepared them to be—save for the *official* representation, which is the only viable form of *full-scale* recognition or social incorporation under the continuing operation of biraciality. The societal model that they have to deal with is a contradictory model of social existence, which daily negates the official attributions conferred them by civil society since the 1970s (the end of the Jim Crow system). In other words, in their social exteriorization, they must deal with the social presence and performance of a dissonant and contradictory *I*—not the idealized *I* in its liberal-democratic construction, but the *not-I*, the image of oneself as *difference*, as *the Other*, as *the stranger*. This is the most salient aspect of the performance of these individuals in the world of daily life, thus creating a division and permanent tension between their *I* and *not-I*. As a corollary of this basic bifurcation of the *I* of these individuals, existential alienation is likely to result, in varying degrees.

I wish here mainly to focus on the psychosocial implications of this phenomenon, particularly when manifested as existential alienation. As indicated in the previous chapter, race-based cultural marginalization turns members of ethnic-racial minorities into typical Schutzian *strangers*, except that their problem is more severe than that of the typical "foreigner" or immigrant, because their strangeness, their *otherness*, occurs in relation to their existence *in their own native societal milieu.* The separatist societal context in which they live fails to affirm their existence in twofold fashion, thus creating schizogenic conditions for the development of identity. First, it denies them full-scale integration into the social mainstream, which forces them to seek refuge in *otherness*, that is, to construct themselves on the *outside.* Then, it denies formal legitimacy to their subnational mode of life, since, after all, they are under the jurisdiction of the larger society-that is, they are a part of the larger civil-political community, and do not *truly* exist outside of it.

Thus, these individuals can neither enjoy *in full measure* the safety and stability of the dominant identity and way of life—their claim to the latter is qualified; the hyphenated identities they use are but one critical and irrefutable indicator of their problematic membership in national life—nor can they seek refuge in the minority identity and way of life *completely*, to the exclusion of any attachment to the larger society because of their civil connection with the latter. It is a cumbersome, stressful, and absurd situation, one that has caused those in its grip to experience varying degrees of difficulty in adjusting to the daily round of social existence, and being in harmony with themselves.

The problem of alienation associated with the interracial situation may be correlated with the model of alienation in the workplace, as described by Marx. In the Marxian context working persons externalize themselves into the lifeworld through their labor activity and the products of that activity, and have these personal attributes taken away from them by others, and then coming to confront them as alien objects. As a result, they do not find themselves represented in that into which they have externalized themselves; *all they find is their negation.* Thus is established a relation of permanent tension between themselves and the world of *work.* The latter becomes the source of their permanent self-alienation. In parallel fashion, members of groups codified as ethnic-racial minorities (as determined by biracialist social administration) externalize themselves daily as formally categorized members of the national community into the construction of this community. These individuals are heirs to the formal legacy of political liberalism of the society of which they are part, which means that they are ideally to be rendered indistinguishable in the mass of citizens regarding their ability to exercise rights and privileges, and also to be able to function among their consociates unimpeded by ascriptive barriers. Yet, unlike the case of dominant-group members, they do not find themselves accurately or fully represented in that community. What they see reflected in it *is not* what the legal-civil structure of the society, and their *formal socialization* experience, have prepared them to be. It is not this formal, idealized social construction of themselves as Americans, with all its attending symbolic and material implications, that they find, but rather, a contradictory model of social existence which daily negates all the formal conceptions of themselves as citizens that have been bestowed upon them by the larger society. In their everyday social externalization, they are confronted with the operation not of their *self*, but of their *not-self*, an image of themselves as *difference*, as *the Other*, as *strangers*. Such is the product of their externalization, which denies their formal existence as "Americans," thus creating a permanent division and tension between the *self* of these individuals and their *not-self*. Alienation ensues, in varying degrees and ways, from this basic bifurcation of the self—alienation at the level of Being, or ontological alienation.

During the *Jim Crow* era, when the separation between the dominant whites and the nonwhite minorities reached its peak, both concretely and otherwise, there also occurred the greatest discrepancy between, on the one hand, the model of citizenship and identity which minority-group members were encouraged to adopt, as dictated, first, the national ideology of universal liberty, justice, and equality, and secondly, by the idea of national unity (*e pluribus unum*) as articulated in the analogy of ethnic fusion (i.e., the melting-pot analogy); and on the other hand, the actual social treatment they received. For example, during the Second World War, more than one million African-American men and women in the United States served in the armed forces, half of whom served overseas. Yet, as they returned from the European or Asian battlefields, many with a distinguished record of combat duty, they continued to be subjected to the same segregationist humiliations and indignities of the prewar period. We are told (Pinkney, 2000: 27) that "one of the more humiliating practices for black servicemen was that of restaurant owners' serving German prisoners of war in places of public accommodation in the United States while denying similar service to black servicemen." The negation of the ideal social self for African-Americans during that period was concretely and clearly expressed, throughout the entire spectrum of social life. Moreover, as the wider society embarked on the gradual *structural* (i.e., economic, political) integration of the racial minorities after the end of *Jim Crow* in the late 1960s, this transformation did not completely eradicate separatist mechanisms and tendencies, which remained "deeply ingrained in the *mores*" (Pinkney, 2000: 20). This made for continuing inconsistency in the social life of these individuals. The underlying stratum of *American-ness* continues to press on their collective consciousness via their formal membership and participation in the larger community, but this is constantly undermined by their actual social experience. The effects of the politics of difference, set in motion about a half-century ago, have strengthened the separatist minority consciousness, or the consciousness of existing as a *particular* type of American, through the validation and celebration of subnational distinctiveness (i.e., of minority-group *otherness*), while at the same time advocating ever-greater representation and inclusion of the minority segments into national life.[15]

By the 1980s the multiculturalist movement in U.S. society had started in earnest, and thrived through the 1990s and into the early years of the twenty-first century. It involved a considerable amount of social activity as well as discourse geared toward the implementation of multiculturalist ideals. These ideals were obviously strongly conditioned by the circumstances of inter-group politics of the specific society—in this case, the United States (on this issue, see, e.g., Ceaser, 1998), with group separateness being pursued for its own sake, both formally and informally, and the dividing lines between the majority and minority groups being drawn ever more sharply. It seems scarcely necessary to stress at this point that the main effect of all this was that of *inhibiting*, not encouraging, minority-group inclusion and the larger process of national consolidation, at all levels. When it is taken into account that the politics of difference, one of the chief offshoots of multiculturalism, has been fueled in the U.S. context primarily by racial considerations, it should surprise no one that this has had, to the present time, a most salutary effect on the society's biracialist structure. Given the endurance of these tendencies of social division and compartmentalization, it is reasonable to expect continuing tension between the conception that minority-group members have of themselves, and what is actually reflected in their daily existence in the society. The gap is not likely to be bridged as long as the factor that created it—the binary organization of interracial life—remains in place. This means that the potential for the kind of minority-group psychic estrangement explored here is likely to persist.

EXISTENTIAL DUALISM AND THE PROBLEM OF MEANING

The connection between racism and the self/not-self aspect of alienation will now be more fully investigated. The existential dualism and quandary that this conceptual formulation is meant to address may also be found to relate to the insights of existential analysis, as represented by the work of Ludwig

Binswanger (1968).[16] At the outset, it should be noted that the inquiry into the question of alienation in the context of the clinical study and treatment of psychic disorganization has been a widely favored approach. Minkowski (cited in Ramos, 1933: 114) has invoked the psychological concept of alienation to say "that schizophrenia is not *one*, but *the* mental malady." In the language of existential analysis, the psychic mechanisms of alienation are examined in reference to the strain produced by a fundamental split or rupture of the individual's experience in the everyday world. This entails the person's inability, as Binswanger put it, to simply "let things be," meaning, to adjust serenely to or come to terms with the prevailing circumstances of one's life, to deal successfully with "the inconsistency and disorder of [his/her] experience" over which one feels a lack of control. The sense of powerlessness and despair persists and increases in the degree that the individual continues to pursue what he or she perceives to be the way the world should be. This is the prelude to the "splitting-off of experiential consistency" into alternatives that cannot be reconciled, a schizophrenic form of life in which the person's *Dasein*—that is, the person's existence in its most general and fundamental conception—"can come to rest on neither side of the alternative, and is driven from one to the other" (Binswanger, 1968: 252–257).

Human existence is assuredly characterized by a series of oppositions or antinomies which we are, for the most part, able to deal with and overcome—at least to the degree necessary for maintaining psychic equilibrium and order, and, therefore, existential integration. The domains of psychiatry and psychoanalysis, literature (e.g., Goethe) and philosophy (e.g., Nietzsche), have long drawn attention to this fact, that the human psyche is not fundamentally disrupted or disorganized as individuals deal with these basic antinomies of social existence, what Jung characterized as the "problem of the contrary" (*Gegensatzproblem*); rather, it synthesizes them, and in this way psychic life remains in a state of stability. The art of living, from this standpoint, consists therefore in what Arthur Ramos, following Goethe, spoke of as "the rhythmic and harmonious succession" of the opposing or contrary movements of life, which express the "problem of the contrary" (1933: 114–115). This is in accordance with Schutz's idea, underlined earlier, to the effect that we function simultaneously in multiple realities, in the social world. However, the kind of existential rupture described here *transcends the boundaries of normality*, or, stated in different terms, it is not the sort of existential dilemma with which individuals would be normally confronted.

This is a point of utmost importance. It is the reason why psychic disorganization may result from it. In the particular context of the relations between ethnic and racial groups in ethnically pluralist societies, such a degree of psychic turmoil may result when individuals find themselves caught between the boundary lines that divide the social world—in this case, the boundary lines of ethnic and racial separatism, manifested through physical and cultural segregation. These boundary lines represent the significant cleavages brought about within these societies, either by legal means or by the impact of postmodern conceptions of intergroup life, such as represented by identity politics.[17] While these types of cultural rifts, as a rule, leave the lives of members of the majority population essentially undisturbed, they tend to create serious problems, of both a practical and psychosocial nature, for members of subaltern segments of the population. This was dramatically exemplified in the story of the Chicago journalist in the beginning of this chapter. That tragic event underscores the connection between the problem of meaning, which phenomenology grapples with as its primary concern, and social alienation.

The inflexible social divisions lead to corresponding divisions in personal lives, which may ultimately be accompanied by serious disruptions of mental life. It ushers in a problematic ("deficient") mode of life, one that is not expressive of social integration, of "*belonging* or being-with in commerce or intercourse with others" (Binswanger, 1968: 257). When existential equilibrium and integration slip from our grip in this manner, this is the time when "our life synthesis begins to weaken" (Minkowski, 1958: 134).

The synthetic ability that we all have to reconcile opposing alternatives and thus maintain psychic integration and equilibrium, and the kind of crisis experienced when this ability is lost, may be examined in reference to the question of meaning, when individuals experience a breakdown in the interpretation of (social) meaning. Schutz reminds us in this connection that we shift our attention frequently across situations and problems that are presented to us in everyday life, deeming new situations to be topically relevant and worthy of our attention, while "releasing our grip" on the old ones. These adjustments are handled as a matter of course, by virtue of the "counterpointal structure of our mind," in relation to which the constant shifts, interruptions, and so on, in the sphere of meaning which we face every day, and the schizophrenic quality that is assumed by our consciousness in our everyday dealings, as part of "the normal course of affairs" (1970c: 12, 120–121). Now, it is undoubtedly true that the meaning schemes that we rely on in the world of work may not apply to the world of leisure, or to the world of the family, and soon—but there is a fundamental coherence regarding the relevances involved in these different settings which integrates them, and *makes them into a unity*. This is, in fact, what constitutes our stock-of-knowledge-at-hand. It is a different case, however, with respect to the kind of rupture of social meaning produced by biracialist social administration. The white/nonwhite dichotomization of the society, kept alive historically through various kinds of mechanisms (i.e., formal laws, public policy, custom, ideology), gives rise to a bifurcation of the society's core meaning system, whereby *neither province of meaning*, the dominant or the subsocietal one (as pointed out before), is treated by nonwhites as being marginal, although they may be clearly dissimilar and even contrary to each other in some fundamental ways. The guidance available to us through the psychic property Bergson denominated as *attention à la vie*, although it makes provision for the various spheres of relevance that we devote our attention to, and integrate, in going through the daily round of activities, playing different roles and so forth, still requires that all the elements constituting the substance of our primary cognitive-emotional focus in daily life be *internally consistent.* Otherwise, this guidance will not operate effectively. Psychological tension and disorder, such as that stemming from the sense of existential rupture, would accordingly be related to problems of "attention to life," or, to put in Schutzian terms, to the way in which the Ego lives and functions "on the level of consciousness of the space-time world" (1997: 47).

As has been mentioned, the majority and minority ethnic-racial communities in the United States have been historically separated and differentiated in the aspects of political economy, family life and intermarriage, and (more to the point here) cultural life. Cultural separatism in this specific historico-spatial context of intergroup life has specifically meant the absence of a significant degree of syncretism or reconciliation between African-American and Anglo-American custom. More importantly, if it be granted that, *at the most basic level,* we *are* what we are *culturally*, individuals and groups who are different from one another in their cultural ways are ultimately different from one another at the level of existence itself, the level of Being. This is as true of the cultural distinctions *across* national groups, as it is in relation to cultural distinctions *within* national groups. To be sure, within the boundaries of each cultural system individuals will not be affected by, nor do they have to be much concerned with, *crossnational* variations in modes of living. But, in the case of *intrasocietal* cultural differentiation enforced on the basis of ascriptive factors, certain segments of the population will most certainly be adversely affected by this, in terms of their reduced access to the mainstream way of life.

Biracial social organization construes race as the foundational aspect of the Being of social beings, which means that it grants ontological status to it. By implication, the cultural way of life and identity of individuals, both of which are presumed to flow directly from racial status, acquire ontological status as well. Thus, considerations of race and culture in this model of social organization come to affect people's lives at the deepest level, the level of existence, of being-in-the-world. It follows from this that in such a context questions of selfhood and identity are intimately tied to the interplay of these two elements—race and culture—and that the resulting institutional and cultural divisions, double standards, exclusionary practices, and so forth generate sufficient cognitive dissonance and problems of identity-building (as related, in this analysis, to the self/not-self contradiction) and its connection to the question of meaning in the social world, to bring damaging consequences to minority persons at the level of consciousness.

The focus on the split of the self here connects with the question of meaning and with the crucial requirement that individuals be able to apprehend their world of experience in terms of its unity, or its *gestalt*. According to Schutz, this concept consists of "the habitual possession of meaning-contexts which supply the indivisible unit of the phenomenal configurations in which we apprehend the objects of the outer world" (Schutz, 1970c: 93). This mode of perception was referred to by Bergson as the "cinematographic function of the mind" (1971: 101–112, 227). But, in order for us to be able to grasp the world of everyday life as it presents itself to us, that is, as a unity, it is imperative that we immerse ourselves in it, and keep from being fragmented by internal divisions within it. This means that it is necessary, from this perspective, for us to function in a world of meaning which is internally consistent.[18] As noted above, members of dominant groups in racially binary societies may remain untouched by these internal divisions, since they are in any case fully integrated into the hegemonic symbolic system, and therefore do not need to be particularly concerned with the presence or effect of peripheral (i.e., subnational) cultural communities. This does not happen this way, however, with minority-group members, whose racial classification perennially frustrates their intent to be fully functioning participants in national life, yet they must function in it all the same—and even more so since the demise of the Jim Crow system in the late 1960s, inasmuch as they are now supposed to fulfill the promise of full-scale civil-political enfranchisement heralded by the destruction of legal segregation. This means that they are formally expected to exercise first-class citizenship in the larger society, made possible through change in the law, while remaining attached to, and functioning, in their respective minority communities.

Taking into consideration the constitutive influence of meaning in people's lives, and the fragmentation of social meaning which these minority persons have to contend with on a daily basis, it is only natural that they should endeavor to establish a satisfactory measure of semantic integration, and with that, integration of personal life and identity. However, in this particular case, this amounts to a continuous effort to reconcile elements that are essentially irreconcilable,[19] in parallel fashion to the refusal to simply "let things be," mentioned above, an effort that is ordinarily fraught with much frustration and distress. For some of the individuals involved, the struggle to maintain cognitive and psychic equilibrium and integration under these circumstances may become intolerably stressful. Such was the plight of the journalist whose sad story opened this chapter. Like any other member of her (minority) community, she had to respond every day to *two* contexts of everyday life, *two* worlds of full-awakeness (as Schutz put it; 1970: 116), both of which were foundational to her social existence. From the standpoint of meaning, we would say that the complex of topical relevances which she relied on for orienting herself in the everyday world was perpetually cleft by oppositions and inconsistencies. Thus, she did not exist within a unity, but in a world that was divided materially and symbolically, each half of which operating independently and in tension with each other, yet exerting equally powerful pulls on her attention, loyalties, and identification. Clearly, this created intractable problems of identity, making it impossible for her to relate to her existence as a cohesive whole, in terms of its unity. For her, the *feeling of harmony with life* (Minkowski, [1923] in May 1958) was sorely lacking. The psychic strain eventually took its toll, causing her to end her life.

This examination of racism and alienation has indicated—and the account of the Chicago journalist has powerfully underscored—the fact that in societies organized on the basis of racial bipolarity, structural assimilation by itself, as manifested in the material (i.e., civil-political and economic) betterment of people's lives, fails to erase the normative effect of race in intergroup relations (i.e., the racialization of social life and intersubjectivity) and therefore it cannot be counted on to guarantee the complete integration of individuals into national life. This compromises their psychosocial security, stability, and well-being. In connection with this, it must be pointed out here, if only in the briefest of terms, that what is being proposed here is not assimilatory cultural imperialism on the part of the majority culture toward its minority segments[20] (an overall national tendency toward syncretistic associations between majority and minority cultural strains is more effective toward the goal of national consolidation). In any case, it seems clear that full-scale access to the mainline meaning system and mode of cultural life must ideally be granted to all of society's members, and that all ascriptive barriers in this regard must be eliminated.

NOTES

1. To illustrate: living in a racially bipolar social structure enables members of U.S. society to react to European surnames of U.S. citizens *of any European origin* (i.e., Russian, Polish, Greek, French, Dutch, Italian) as belonging to people who are simply "American." The reason for this is that these are the people who have come to be categorized as *white ethnics*, a status which automatically inducts them into the great common mass of Americanness, and allows them to have (the option to claim) no ethnicity (see, e.g., Waters, 1996: 444–454). From this perspective, the society and its way of life appear to be perceived, by members of the dominant racial segment, as having neither historical nor spatial antecedents. Rather, it is as if it simply materialized, at some imprecise point in time, through the work of Divine

Providence, as a community of whiteness—which is its essential condition. We see here a metaphysical conception of the social community, understood as racial essence, which has reigned supreme over all other conditions of collective life. Over time—in a more concrete historical sense—additions to this community took place (through immigration) involving human populations deemed assimilable, and others deemed unassimilable. In both cases, aspects of ethnicity, culture, and nationality of these groups were dissolved. The unassimilable groups, given their membership in the category of nonwhiteness, were incorporated mainly as excrescences, that is, not as full-fledged members of national life. This phenomenon may be witnessed in the experience of, for instance, Americans of Chinese and Japanese extraction. These are individuals who (like the white ethnics) may be in the third of fourth generation of the group, being therefore fully acculturated into the dominant mode of life, and far removed from their ancestral cultural heritage, other than through the memories of some older relatives. Yet, because they bear distinguishing physical traits associated with "Orientals," they may reasonably expect questions about where (in Asia) they are from, whether or not they have an interested in their Asian heritage, and so on, whereas an American of Swedish or German descent will not get such a query. In times past, their distinctiveness made them targets of more openly and violently exclusionary and discriminatory practices, such as the internment of some 110,000 Americans of Japanese descent during the Second World War. The hyphenated identity of members of these groups remains, to this day, the mark of their qualified admission into the larger, national community.

2. This type of social division derives from the application of the anthropological rule of hypodescent, which has been addressed in various works (see, e.g., Harris, 1974, 1997: 320). This rule establishes the automatic affiliation of the offspring of intercaste (i.e., white/nonwhite) unions with the subordinate, rather than the superordinate, group. This serves the political purpose of avoiding the categorical complications and ambiguities stemming from the recognition of an intermediary identity. It also favors the interests of the dominant racial group inasmuch as majority-group rule normally operates more effectively when the majority and minority groups are placed into dichotomous categories.

3. The idea of sameness has been introduced in a phenomenological sense at various points in this work as a signifier for equality and universality, in the sense of not being in otherness, or being like everyone else. From this standpoint, it pertains to the general circumstances within which we apprehend the subjectivity of others—specifically, involving how *the Other* is perceived as a fellow human being like ourselves, sharing the same sociocultural world, unconsciously sharing the same stream of consciousness, and so on.

4. *Time*, July 2, 2001, p. 53.

5. *Time*, May 21, 1990, p. 83.

6. A report for the early 1990s (Shea, 1993: A26–A27) registers the establishment of segregated housing ("program houses") on the Cornell University campus, and indicated that other campuses were following suit.

7. As long as *race* continues to function as the linchpin of social organization in a given multiethnic society, the issues and problems of individuals associated

with their racial status are likely to persist accordingly. In modern democratic states, bureaucratic mechanisms are relied upon for dealing with this situation, in much the same way that this is the approach used for addressing, for example, the problem of poverty in the society. In this connection, the separatist identity serves important functions, *given the prevailing circumstances*, in much the same way that psychological/counseling services are needed for helping individuals cope with various aspects of social injustice. In other words, it serves a palliative, remedial function, an important one though it may be, and it *ought ideally to represent only a transitional phase* (i.e., toward the elimination of the larger problem). Phrased in more specific terms, the psychosocial benefits of this identity for minority-group members are that it is foundational to their existence, in defining for these individuals who they are in the larger society. In this way, it serves as a refuge from the tribulations of daily living in a divided society, a source of solace and self-esteem, a means of connecting with others who "are in the same boat." In bureaucratic terms, it provides them with a badge of formal identification and classification, thus facilitating their formal representation and incorporation in the society. In more recent years, it serves to identify the groups who have been historically victimized by institutionalized oppression, and thus to facilitate the process of societal reparation for injuries perpetrated against them in the past. This would pertain to compensatory efforts currently in effect in liberal democratic societies, geared to the economic and political incorporation of minority-group members (e.g., Affirmative Action).

8. Regarding their psychosocial aspect of *role over-immersion*, Myrdal observed in the 1940s that there seemed to be a pattern in the African-American community of that time, to the effect that a certain percentage of that community appeared as having been oversocialized into the cultural ways and elements of the dominant (i.e., white) population. "The negro," he remarked, "was not only generally akin to other Americans, but also displayed peculiarities of behavior that could even be categorized as 'exaggerations of American traits' " (1962: 928).

9. Some of the social functions of individuals foreground the adverse effects that race-based structural separatism has on both community-group members, and the social system as a whole. As regards the latter, there are multiple aspects that demonstrate this. Generally speaking, the network of public services (hence, the people using these services) in the society will suffer if a segment of the workers who dispense these services have been denied, as a group, full access to the kinds of knowledge and ideological orientations required for the proper discharge of their functions and responsibilities. This parallels Bourdieu and Passeron's discussion of *cultural capital* (1985).

10. Bogardus's 1920s research on Mexican-Americans takes a close look at the restricted pattern of assimilation of the groups codified as racial minorities, and the problems of identity and social performance caused by this. He reports (1929: 283) that second-generation, and even third-generation, Mexican-Americans, despite having been acculturated into the U.S. national culture and identifying with it, were still viewed as "foreigners." In his study Bogardus also observed how the cognitive dissonance caused by this experience placed the personalities of the individuals affected "in great danger of becoming disorganized" (see also Donahue, 1995; Depp, 2002).

Another analyst (Stonequist, 1935: 1–12) explores this problem in the context of the interracial situation in Hawaii, by relying on the concept of *marginal man.*

The same pattern of separatism and its psychological implications for minority-group members has been registered more recently with respect to the situation of Asian-Americans. For the latter (as for anyone born and raised in U.S. society), the United States is home, but they "sometimes feel treated as outlanders with unproven loyalties," people whose presence in American society is "too often perceived as too alien to be appreciated as anything other than caricature" (Chua-Eoan, 2000: 40). For example, during the 1996 Olympic Games a television station announced in this way the victory of the American skater Tara Lipinski, of Polish descent, over her fellow countrywoman Michelle Kwan, of Chinese descent: "The American Defeats Kwan" (in Schaefer, 2001: 17).

11. Richard Rodriguez (2003) dissects the complexity of ethnic identity, rejecting the rigidity of the black/white dualism and the artificial nature of ethnic taxonomic compartments in the United States—"gringo contrivances"—while advocating for the fluidity and integrationist character of the *brown* identity; see also Depp (2002).

12. It is worth mentioning in this regard that during slavery times in the United States a major requirement for the maintenance and protection of Southern society's biracialist division and arrangements was for the dominant group to discourage, or formally prohibit, the slaves from learning and using proper English. The premise of the racial conditioning of the group's cultural ways, together with the assumption of the essential racial inferiority of the slaves, their speaking English like members of the dominant class would have constituted a subversion of the natural order (Genovese, 1976: 434).

13. This phenomenon is displayed by the ruling and minority racial communities alike, because members of the latter, in having internalized the separatist ethos of the larger society and the normative legitimacy of its corresponding arrangements and practices, become invested in the cultivation of their minority identity. This in turn normally leads to their rejection of the idea of an intermediary racial category wedging itself in between the white and nonwhite groups, blurring the dividing line between them, and thus dissolving the separateness which, under conditions of intergroup separatism, members of both groups relate to as the source of collective identity, and for the nonwhite group additionally, as a mainspring of political mobilization. There are, therefore, clear reasons why the blurring of the racial boundary line is seen as ontologically "illegal" in sociocultural systems marked by racial bipolarity.

14. At various points in these chapters this fundamental separatism has been thrown into relief. The minority person's racial condition, construed as ontologically inferior, is impermeable to change that may occurred to her or his other social statuses. Accordingly, black educational achievement, from the end of slavery through the Jim Crow period, was treated as inconsequential and as an anomaly, given the assumed essential inferiority of the black person. During the 1930s, a distinguished observer (Johnson, cited in Chafe et al., 2001: 207) remarked: "Literacy is not an asset in the plantation economy, and it was not only discouraged but usually forbidden. The belief that education spoiled the slave carried over with but little modification for many years into the belief that education spoils the field hand."

15. The idea of separateness-*cum*-equality is not something new. More than a century ago, a time when social conditions in the Southern states of the United States were marching decisively toward the official installation of the Jim Crow system, Booker T. Washington issued his famous and much-debated exhortation, at the 1895 Atlanta Exposition, for bettering the social condition of the African-American population via industrial education, while preserving the larger, deep-seated separatism of U.S. society. Washington phrased this in highly conciliatory (and, therefore, popular) terms: "In all things purely social," he said, "we can be as separate as the five fingers and yet one as the hand, in all things essential to mutual progress" (cited in Dubois, 1990: 37). Dubois took the opposite position, with his integrationist vision of what the ideal pattern of interethnic/interracial life in the United States should be. As he put it, "Work, culture, liberty, all these we need, not singly, but together." The ways of life of African-Americans, he continued, ought not to be kept separate from those of the larger society. Rather, the two ought to come together, "in order that some day on American soil the two world-races may give each to each those characteristics both so sadly lack" (1990: 14, orig. 1903).

16. The notion of *Dasein* is borrowed directly from Heidegger (1965). Binswanger's *daseinanalyse* consists of a creative synthetic reconstruction of psychoanalytic, phenomenological, and existentialist ideas, drawing especially on the work of Heidegger, Kant, and Husserl (see, e.g., May et al., 1958).

17. As early as the late 1970s to early 1980s, when the multiculturalist program began to operate on an ever larger scale at the institutional level in the United States, it immediately revealed its vigorous advocacy of "cultural pluralism," meaning, of intergroup cultural difference and compartmentalization. This may be seen in official documents, such as, for instance, the manual *Multicultural Teacher Education* (1980), where it is stated that the movement valued "cultural pluralism," and that efforts should be undertaken "to preserve and enhance" [it] (1980: iii)

18. The problems of other provinces of meaning, such as, for example, the realm of dreams, are reinterpreted in terms of the interpretative schemes of the world of everyday life ("the world of full-awakeness," Schutz, 1970c: 116), so there is no real split of consciousness, because at the point where we begin to think about, to analyze, the dream, we have "released it from our grip" (Husserl). We have reconstructed the dream in terms of a "transformed set of relevances," that is, that of the concrete world of daily life.

19. This aspect of incompatibility is not due so much to the fact that diverse cultural orientations and modes of living, as they come into contact with one another, are inherently averse to a *rapprochement*, harmonization of their features, fusions, and so on. After all, syncretistic associations and mergers between dissimilar cultural strains have been occurring for centuries in societies everywhere. Roman England yields an interesting example. Following the Roman occupation and the ensuing contact between the religious culture of the Romans and those of the local Celts, there began a syncretistic association between them involving the goddess Minerva of the conquerors and the Celtic deity Sulis. The Romans perceived a syncretic correspondence between the two, which then paved the way to their integration into a single deity, Sulis-Minerva, for whom a temple was erected at Bath. The remnants of this

bath complex can still be seen in that city. The decoration of this temple exemplifies the religious syncretism in its "Roman-British" combination of a classical Gorgon head, the attribute of Minerva, with an emotional intensity shown on the face—"a fierce vigor, a savage violence" (Collingwood, 1969: 114–115)—which was never found in classical (Roman) art, but which clearly originates in the Celtic background. Another, more recent, instantiation of this phenomenon is seen in the history of American societies like Cuba or Brazil, where syncretism between Christian and traditional African religious patterns has been widespread, and shows its dynamic presence even today.

The fact remains that where the biracialist administration of intergroup relations is in effect, each group's cultural traits are going to be treated as manifestations of racial essence, hence, as something that cannot be transformed, and therefore, united, with other such manifestations. This, of course, precludes the melding of modes of living of groups held to be racially dissimilar. At best, it allows for a coexistence based on mutual separateness.

Regarding syncretistic or separatist cultural relations involving different ethnic heritages, one may also consider the example of jazz music. Considered *outside of the United States* to be the most quintessential of American musical forms, *inside* the United States jazz music has met with a different reception. Historically, it has been largely viewed as a property of the African-American (sub)cultural community. During the entire Jim Crow period, and especially during the period prior to the First World War, this music and its associations of unbridled sexuality were widely spurned by the general public as "an abomination" (Collier, 1978: 127), a threatening and corrupting expression of *black* culture, not *American* culture. The latter was still wedded to the more "respectable" European-American musical forms (e.g., the fox-trot, the waltz). Henry Ford, the legendary industrialist, supposedly abhorred jazz music, and decided to fund and sponsor a folk dance crusade, where such "proper" dance styles as square dancing, the Virginia reel, and so on were cultivated. As one writer informs us, the general notion at that time was that jazz, "the music of the jungle, was a form of retrogression that was returning American society to an age of barbarism" (Leonard, 1970: 39).

The dissociation in the public mind of jazz from the mainstream of American cultural life endured as the century wore on. Peretti (1997: 92) writes about how, during the Second World War, the renowned white jazz musician Gil Evans "brought V-disks of his favorite players, especially Louis Armstrong, with him in Europe, and white GIs almost assaulted him for carrying 'colored music.'" In time, some white musicians gradually incorporated elements of jazz into their own playing style, producing a kind of music that blended those elements with European syncopation. These syncretized musical forms became hugely popular nationwide—for example, Big Band music and swing music of the 1930s and 1940s. Still, as jazz music found its way into the recording industry, and jazz records began to be produced and sold on a large scale (e.g., Bessie Smith's blues recordings), the white/black cultural dualism engendered by the society's racially binary structure prevailed, and the music came to be known as *race records* (!). A jazz writer (cited in DeLerma, 1970: 44) tells us that in the early 1920s mainstream record shops in downtown Manhattan did not stock "Negro jazz." Bessie Smith, considered by most analysts to have been the greatest of all the classic blues singers, became highly successful in the 1920s with her recordings, but her records "were never sold in white stores."

20. On this issue see, e.g., Gordon (1964), for a discussion of the Americanization movement of the early twentieth century, and the idea of *Anglo-conformity*; see also Novak (1971).

Chapter 7

Phenomenology and the Discourse of Power

At this point in this phenomenological exploration of race relations, the central importance of meaning in directing the development of the self and, in the larger sense, shaping the nature of intergroup relations in the wider society, should have become abundantly clear. This has been presented here as the cornerstone of Schutz's contribution toward the phenomenological explanation of social life, and more pertinently for this study, of the problem of race-based equality/inequality.

In Schutz's theory of social action, it will be recalled, Max Weber's treatment of meaning undergoes further refinement and clarification. For our purposes, the focus in the present analysis has been placed on the role of meaning-contexts as motivational-contexts of social action, particularly in reference to the function of because-motives as explanatory frameworks of our lived experiences. The importance of because-motives is accentuated in that they provide a particular theoretical frame by means of which the influence of society (of the social *meaning*) on human action can be revealed and clarified. In this connection, our interest in exploring the heuristic utility of Schutz's social phenomenology has to do with understanding how patterns of political (power) inequality are established among interacting groups, with race—racial meanings—as the mediating factor. Racial meanings are part of the complex of inherited typifications of the society.

It becomes essential, in this connection, that particular attention be focused on the social determination of behavior if the potential of a Schutzian social phenomenology for a critique of domination is to be fulfilled. Social actors may be generally autonomous in their pursuit of future-oriented projects, as Campbell remarks (1981: 205)—that is, their subjective experience in engaging in this process of determining their life projects occurs in freedom, a freedom exercised on the basis of the whole complex of past experiences which "the individual can use as a springboard for [his/her] own activities." At the same time, the subjectivity of individuals is treated, in Schutz's work, as the expression of the intersubjective world, not of the transcendental consciousness. The implication that flows immediately from this is that our choice of projects, our adoption of interests, and our determination of relevances are already conditioned, at the personal and collective levels, by our historical experience in a particular sociocultural environment. It is in reference to the past, as has been repeatedly indicated in these pages, that this process is brought to the fore.

In this chapter the political implications of processes of intersubjectivity involving the interaction between dominant and subordinate social groups are brought into relief. It was asserted in earlier chapters that the operation of race as a regulatory principle of social life is harmful to racialized groups in virtually every respect. More precisely, the application of racial meanings impacts directly on the construction of subjectivity for members of targeted groups, leading to a host of ill effects, both structural and psychosocial. The political aspect in this connection is revealed in the way these meanings, operative throughout the social system, perpetuate inequality of power within the social system, between the dominant and subaltern racial segments of the population.

That a phenomenological frame of analysis should be selected for elucidating the mysteries of intergroup relations, antagonisms, inequality, domination, and the like would have seemed incongruous until just a few decades ago, particularly in the U.S. academic world. We are informed of how, in the post–Second World War period through the 1960s, phenomenology as a whole was essentially viewed as a "microsociological curiosity" (Martindale, 1981: xiii). When confronted with the esoteric Husserlian or Bergsonian cogitations on the life of the mind, the more quantitatively oriented camps might simply repudiate it as some sort of academic *preciosité*. In the British philosophical world, where the influence of logical positivism still runs deep to this day, the common practice even in current times, according to one analyst (Ferguson, 2006: 1), is to "dismiss [phenomenological research] as 'continental philosophy,'" the implication being that this is a line of inquiry whose legitimacy is not quite up to par with the rigor and accuracy of British analytical philosophy. As concerns the issue of race-based oppression being investigated here, phenomenology—even a Schutzian social phenomenology, with its greater sensitivity to the substantive problems of the social world—may still be regarded in the same light, that is, as something that does not quite fit in with a social-scientific, critical discourse on domination. Actually, while the phenomenological approach may not be entirely congenial with the conventional model of a social-scientific (empirically oriented, or *positivist*) sociology, it does share territory with "an interpretive sociology and a hermeneutic approach to the social world," as Eberle (2010: 134) reminds us.

Also, the insights generated by phenomenology, in particular a social phenomenology, into the intersubjective aspects of intergroup life, afford us a sense of how those aspects are linked to the operation of political inequality between ruling and subordinate social groups.

Finally, the mutually beneficial relation between sociology and philosophy should be kept in mind here, in which respect it is fitting to consider the point made by Ferguson (2006: 1) to the effect that not only is sociology enriched by philosophical "description and reflection," but also the historic project of philosophy has much to gain from the substantive insights of sociology.

In any event, although the primary task of phenomenology is understood as the description of "general forms of human experience" (Eberle, 2010: 135), this, as we have seen, has not kept a considerable number of scholars, whether of philosophical or sociological persuasion, from pursuing the phenomenological approach in their analyses of social (race-based or gender-based) domination. This trend started about three decades ago and has not abated. Several of these scholars have drawn attention to the limitations of Schutz's phenomenological system in addressing problems of social inequality and oppression and accordingly pushed some of his central ideas beyond their descriptive function by showing how they are connected with systems of domination. Lengermann and Niebrugge, for example (1995: 25), reveal a concern with the less than forthright recognition in Schutz's work with the harsh realities of social domination, and comment that his work "is striking in its lack of any extended consideration of power." Working from a feminist perspective, these writers have stressed the need to "rework and expand [Schutz's theories of consciousness and intersubjectivity] if they are to be part of the feminist project—the critique of domination" (1995: 35). Barber (2018) likewise draws attention to the "typical dispassion" (hence, apolitical stance) with which Schutz addresses the problem of inequality between social groups in his well-known essays *The Well-Informed Citizen* (1946/1964) and *Equality and the Meaning Structure of the World* (1957/1964). The arguments arrayed in these essays present the idea of equality as being essentially relative to the group in question; in other words, equality is said to be dependent on "the domain of relevances to which it pertains [which could be linked to any number of criteria, such as race, economic standing, and so on] and on the in-group or out-group utilizing it."[1]

Notwithstanding these limitations, cultural factors construed broadly so as to encompass factors of consciousness—such as those dealt with here in terms of the influence of social meanings on social action—may still be harvested profitably, affording fresh insight into the workings of social domination.

We find in cultural anthropology perspectives that underscore the broader generative effect of culture on social action, as well as the intrinsic political thrust of cultural structures. Additionally, these perspectives construe the patterns of action by individuals and groups as human "projects." Velho and Becker, for example, speak of "empirical agents" (i.e., the Schutzian social actors) who engage in action patterns and decision-making processes with "predetermined objectives," that is, with intentionality, thus creating a proj-ect. These human projects are not "purely internal, subjective phenomen[a]" because they are manifested communicatively, by means of the society's linguistic code (1992: 14). As such, they are *cultural* structures, insofar as they are in every case "a symbolic expression . . . implying relations of power [which in turn makes them] always political" (1992: 19). The argument that the political aspect inheres in cultural structures (and therefore renders these structures political) shows a basic convergence with the idea, defended here, regarding Schutz's theoretical system containing the potential for being *extended into* social criticism. Hitzler and Eberle (2004: 68) have noted in a similar vein that, notwithstanding the fact that "the mundane phenomenology of Schutz and his followers . . . [is mainly] interested in the *epistemological explanation of the foundation of the lifeworld*," it provides a foundation for research on substantive problems of society, which are, after all, generated by "the actions of people." Human action, in turn, insofar as it is not manifested atomistically (self-interest operates always in terms of being-in-the-world), or, more concretely, in a social vacuum (people act in the context of their membership in social groups with competing interests), is always political.

THE CULTURAL AND NATURAL
ROOTS OF THE POLITICAL

Srubar (1999) elaborates an incisive analysis of the genesis of the political in social life, in the context of Schutz's theoretical system, with more spe-cific reference to the structure of the lifeworld in the capacity of a *cultural* world. It is said that the cultural features of the lifeworld—the widely vary-ing dimensions and conceptions of time, motivational contexts, schemes of relevance, action projects of social actors—issues from the pragmatic human interest in the world of experience and are in fact even more deeply rooted in human nature—in what is termed in Schutz's work the *conditio humana*—more specifically, they are rooted in the primordial aspects of consciousness, of our physical selves in nature, and of life-with-others (sociality) (Srubar, 1999: 37).

Then, the discussion continues to the effect that the separations and dis-tinctions, inclusions and exclusions, in the lifeworld emerge on the basis of "zones of familiarity/unfamiliarity," which essentially recalls the entire Schutzian description of the alignment, or lack of alignment, of social actors with typifications, the way in which this process occurs, and the resulting emergence of *ingroups* and *outgroups*. Groups are then socially included or excluded depending on the extent to which they are embedded in these zones of familiarity or unfamiliarity. In addition, regardless of the cultural variation involving ingroups and outgroups (the latter are "hetero-typified *Others*"), some "borders" of separation keeping these two groups apart are enforced even when the outgroup displays schemes of typifications (in their conduct, beliefs, etc.) that do not diverge from those of the dominant group (the ingroup). This may be empirically demonstrated in actual cases of dominant/minority relations whereby members of subaltern groups are still locked in otherness, symbolically as well as concretely, notwithstanding their *basic* internalization of the dominant culture.

This problem is then further explored in connection with Schutz's formulation of the *reciprocity of perspectives*, which, as we saw earlier in this study, pertains to the common sharing of perceptions and understandings, of typified ways of acting and thinking, among social actors. Schutz's account is then interpreted in a way that reveals its functionalist overtones, in terms of establishing that in order for the normal process of social interaction or communication (at the level of society, or the web of intergroup relations) to go on; and *in the absence of reciprocity of perspectives*, it becomes necessary for the otherness of the outgroup to be constructed as something inherent to that group. It seems clear, from this standpoint, that social inequality (i.e., the inferiority) of the outgroup must be considered as a necessary piece of the societal puzzle if systemic balance is to be maintained. Schutz addresses this problem, as Srubar informs us (1999: 38), "in a more neutral fashion"; in fact, in a more relativizing fashion, insofar as he considers ingroup/outgroup inequality and antagonism in terms of each group's particular set of typifications in relation to the other group.

The present work, as indicated, moves beyond the descriptive account of ingroup/outgroup relations, by focusing more directly on social meanings (in the context of race) and their intimate association with the relations of power between dominant and nondominant social groups. The presence of power becomes evident in the confrontation between these groups, leading possibly to shifts in the power structure of intergroup life, with a redefinition or reorientation of the dominant, group-based, scheme of interpretation. This calls for political reform or reconstruction which is driven, in Srubar's words (1999: 42), "on insight into the constructed character of social relations"—which essentially amounts, in my view, to what I have stressed consistently here, namely, that Schutz's schemes of interpretations and relevances do not

take place in a social vacuum, but, rather, reflect the character of power relations between social groups.

SCHUTZ'S THEORY AS SOCIAL CRITIQUE

In applying Schutzian ideas to the analysis of race relations and inequality,
it is necessary to recast the central concepts of his theoretical system—the
stock-of-knowledge-at-hand, typifications, fields of consciousness, themes
and horizons, and so on—all of which turn on the question of meaning, in
terms of demonstrating their heuristic usefulness in reference to intergroup
power relations; and more precisely here, to their association with the interests and activities of the society's dominant racial community. The greater
social power of this community enables its members to have their interests
become generalized for the society as a whole, and thus to naturalize the
society's entire complex of arrangements, practices, and ways of thinking.
    The point on which I wish to insist is that the political potential of Schutz's
system may be rescued by reference to his emphasis on the pivotal role of
meaning in the architecture of the social world. We may begin with his social
psychology, at the level of the constitution of the self. It was stated earlier
that in Schutz's work the self is not treated as an isolated entity, independent
of experience, but rather emerges within the world of intersubjectivity; that
is, it is born within and from the operation of a system. By implication, in the
degree that the world of intersubjectivity is built on the sedimentation of the
different types and forms of historical experiences of the collectivity (Schutz,
1997: 78–83), so too people's selves exhibit properties imparted to them by
the structure and history of the social world. Phrased differently, our sense
of self is gained in reference to personal biography, but the latter evolves
through time in the broader context of intergroup life. Again, as observed
earlier, this does not involve a situation of unilateral determinism of the
economicist or culturalist (Parsonian) variety, but rather a dynamic interplay
between subjectivity and society. As concerns society, we can see its formative influence on consciousness in Schutz's description of how the subjectivity of the Other is apprehended, and how this process is oriented by *objective*
meaning—which has to do with how the self of others is grasped in terms of
anonymous ideal types. The meaning, therefore, that arises in the consciousness of the actor in interacting with others is objective, insofar as it expresses
"universal meaning" (1997: 135). In other words, it is not particularized or
construed solely in reference to some particular Other. In Schutz's words, it
is meaning that is "already constituted and established, abstracted from every
subjective flow of experience and every subjective meaning-context that
could exist in such a flow."[2] So, to take a concrete example, if I interact with

Mr. Stapleton, the mail carrier, I will assume typicality on his part regarding basic patterns of behavior and communication, and his subjective meaning-context, all of which pertain to mail-carriers as social types; that is, they are typifications applicable to those who function in that professional category. On this basis of generality, our knowledge of others—the meanings involved in our perception of the social world and our fellow creatures—are rooted in the *social* world, in the "multiform structure" of that world (1997: 135, 139; 186–194).

Thus, it may be generally asserted that under normal circumstances everyone is determined by society; everyone's self is therefore determined by society, by the complex of social meanings in operation in the society-at-large at any given point in time. These meanings may be aggrandizing or demeaning and will affect the targeted individuals accordingly. By normal circumstances we mean the regular circumstances of social living in societies of the *modern time*, applicable to people in general, whereby they live in basic equality with everyone else—in the particular sense that, for the most part, their lives are unencumbered by the restrictions of ascriptive attributions (those of gender, race, etc.) over which they have no control. These are, of course, ideal-typical considerations. It is widely recognized that social life everywhere operates on the basis of distinctions, including those (such as the particular societally sanctioned models of race or gender) over which the person has little or no control, with direct consequences of concrete inequality for people's lives. However, generally speaking, it could be said that in the modern industrialized world people are expected to be sorted out strictly on the basis of achieved, not ascribed, status. Under such ideal-typical conditions, individuals may be said to be determined by the social environment in roughly equal fashion. Not only will their standing in society be differentiated according to their level of achievement, but their selves too will develop in this condition of basic equality.

On the other hand, when race enters the equation a unique situation is created—a situation that is uniquely detrimental to the constitution of the self of racialized persons. Race, particularly as operative in racially bipolar social systems, works in a similar fashion to a *deep structure* of language,[3] for its primordial nature as well as generative and generalizing (totalizing) effects. This is germane to the tradition of cognitive psychology, insofar as race and racial meanings establish a template for patterns of perception, understanding, and categorization, which in turn find their material expression in social structures and social behavior. In biracialist societies, the general expectations are that the two ("white"/"nonwhite") racial segments of the population will be *essentially* distinct from each other, meaning they will be different from each other on the basis of each group's racial essence. The analysis of deep structures, says one writer (Hammel, cited in Myers, 1987: 73), directs our attention to an underlying "set of rules or system . . . that affords diagnosis of the features of empirical phenomena." Race as a deep structure evinces precisely such a system.

The all-encompassing deterministic effect of race *qua* deep structure is evidenced in the way it rides roughshod over a number of different (i.e., non-racial) spheres of social life, and permeates every aspect of social interaction, from the broader patterns to the "micro-practices" (Staudigl, 2012: 36). In this respect, the different social statuses and identities of individuals are submerged under the imperious racial identity, as racial meaning is transposed onto them, a classical symptom of the racialization of social life in polyethnic societies where race is the linchpin of social organization.

Under these circumstances, how racialized persons perceive themselves to be—in other words, the construction of the self of these individuals—becomes a process that is already rigged, in that it is already predetermined and vitiated by the infusion of racial meanings into everyday life, where these meanings become embedded as society-wide typifications. Members of the society as a group then internalize these meanings and relate to them in the nonreflective, taken-for-granted fashion of the natural attitude. Furthermore, because racial meanings are typically normally degrading and expressive of the inherent inferiority (inherent *otherness*) of those to whom they are directed, members of minority racial communities are, as a rule, led to develop a negative self-image as a reflection of these internalized meanings (for a dramatic personal account of this phenomenon, see, e.g., Rodriguez, 1983: 123–127). To put this in the theoretical context employed earlier concerning the development of the self as a process of accountability, we would say here that members of minority racial communities, in their daily interactions with others in the wider community (and in some cases with those in their own communities), will typically *account for* who they are and for their commitment to particular action projects in the present time from the standpoint of those negative attributions historically imposed on them by the society-at-large. At the level of the social functioning of these individuals, this phenomenon, as has been shown, eventuates in varying levels and forms of social marginalization and alienation.

The appropriation of the minority identity or subjectivity by the majority racial group is a clear-cut case of colonization of consciousness, which is politically advantageous to this group, and thus enhances the larger process of social domination. It harms the racialized segments of the population in both formal and informal ways. Schutz provides an instructive example in this regard, with reference to the operation of the judicial system of the United States (1964: 260). In examining the *Plessy vs. Ferguson* Supreme Court decision that ushered in the separate-but-equal doctrine and the Jim Crow system, he noticed that the legal language imputed to the plaintiffs something that was already built into the law, namely, a stereotyped conception of the affected group as *otherness* (this was implicit in the legal terminology), and then—*as a corollary of the implicit idea of the group as otherness*—the assignment of some particular trait to the group, that justified the enforcement of the legal measure and its discriminatory effects. The presumption of equality (on the part of the legislators) in the installation of a two-tier society, where neither distinction of color nor social separation and hierarchies would be abolished, is obviously the most untenable of positions. Yet, the rationale for this legislation was that inferiority of social position for the African-Americans should not be inferred from the legal language, but only from the particular "racial instincts" of the "colored race [which] chooses to put that construction upon it," not only a blatant example of legal sophistry but also of a self-serving attitude anchored to racial ideology as a basis of legitimation for institutional discrimination. For our purposes, it reveals an indisputable case of social domination at the level of intersubjectivity, whereby political power enables the judicial system, which was entirely (at the time) under the control of the hegemonic racial group, to appropriate the subjectivity of the affected (subordinate) group, and to replace it with a "fictitious scheme of relevances" (Schutz, 1964: 260), through the imposition of a dominant-group typification. The typified element here was, specifically, the construction of the "colored race" as being instinctually driven to see themselves as inferior, and to spontaneously desire to steer clear of the "commingling of the races."

This shows how the workings of intersubjectivity, conditioned by the long-standing operation of racial meanings in the system-at-large, and manifested through prejudice and stereotypes, infiltrated and interfered with the proper and just application of the law, resulting in legal manipulation and much harm to nondominant social groups. In more recent times in U.S. society, notwithstanding the many and important changes that have occurred in the formal and informal aspects of race relations, dominant-group constructions of the subjectivity of the minority element (i.e., the application of racial meanings on the racialized) continue to influence, although to a lesser extent, legal and otherwise formal relations between the white and nonwhite parts of the population, with the same adverse effects for the latter.

The colonization of consciousness or subjectivity, therefore, has suffered no abatement as a classical feature of dominant/minority relations in ethnically pluralist societies everywhere, as evidenced in the way minority-group members are normally led to internalize the subjective constructions imposed on them by the ruling racial group. This is especially true of societies regulated by racial bipolarity, where long-established, wide-ranging white/nonwhite separatism has a number of ramifications,[4] a chief one among which being the adoption of the minority identity by the racialized segments of society. This aspect has been widely debated (see, e.g., Barber, 2001, concerning the anamnestic recovery of the subjective experience of minority-group members). It is a matter of general agreement in sociological circles, particularly in reference to functionalist analysis, that the minority identity serves positive purposes for both the minority communities and the society as a whole. For the former, it brings psychosocial and political benefits, serving as a basis of identity as well as political representation in the larger society. For the latter, it integrates the reified minority community into the system's racial hierarchy, which would tend to lessen the potential for intergroup tension and conflict. Reflecting the larger purpose of this study, attention is shifted here to the more problematic aspects of the minority identity, in the sense that its maintenance for its own sake (rather than as a transitional stage on the way to full social inclusion) exerts a reinforcing and preserving effect on race-based inequality. A number of negative implications derive from this. One that has already been mentioned is the widespread rejection of the majority culture manifested in the development, within certain parts of the minority one, of an ethos of non-achievement. The latter is pursued as a form of contradiction or negation of the ways of "white people." It is a no-win situation for minority-group members, as it sets in motion a vicious circle of social exclusion.

Members of the wider U.S. social community typically naturalize (even in current times, a half-century after the demise of Jim Crow) the racial bifurcation of social life, and the attending cultural differentiation of the nonwhite segments, as a foundational aspect of their world-taken-for-granted, of their life in the natural attitude. This involves, among other things, the bifurcation of the society's core meaning system into two separate, distinct finite *provinces of meaning* (as defined in chapter 3). Minority individuals (members of the African-American community probably more so than members of other "nonwhite" groups) engage in a constant negotiation between the two realms of social meaning, a corollary of not being *fully* attached to either one. Not surprisingly, this tends to generate much cognitive dissonance, distress, and the like, an issue touched on in chapter 6. We may recall Dubois's concern with and dismay over the incongruence of the "double aims" that bedeviled the existence of African-Americans in the United States under Jim Crow, something that parallels the experience of the Schutzian *stranger*. The difference is that the condition of being a *stranger*, denoting the situation of the typical immigrant, can be generally overcome within a certain period of time, certainly within a couple of generations, but that is not the case of the *permanent* stranger. It shifts to a situation where this stranger is eventually incorporated *formally* into the alien land, which then becomes her or his official *home-world* (meaning, the former stranger is now part of the community of citizens), but remains her or his de facto alien world by virtue of less-than-complete incorporation into the national community, hence, permanent existence in otherness. This qualified inclusion, as noted, operates at both the levels of social relations and intersubjectivity, and is reinforced every day. At the intersubjective level it constitutes, for the minority group, a rupture at the level of Being, an experience of social domination at the ontological level.

Permanent minority status also remains accountable for the continuing and more concrete hardships of racialized groups, such as in ensuring that members of these groups remain as targets of unequal treatment, notwithstanding the fact that the official structures of segregation and discrimination have long been gone. It interferes with the acquisition of cultural capital and, therefore, with the social advancement of these individuals because, even when they manage to rise to the top of the social ladder, the attribution of otherness does not disappear.

Much of the discussion, in chapter 3, of Schutz's foundational principles and his meticulous dissection of the dynamics of interpersonal relationships suggests, directly and indirectly, the functional importance of the society's meaning system, and the need for society's members as a group to have universal access to this system. I have also tried to convey the importance of cultural integration in the wider social system throughout most of this work (the first couple of chapters do not deal with this issue). The fact is that cultural separatism of the kind systematically engendered by biracialist social organization leads to a communicative gap between the dominant and minority groups which frequently evolves into serious problems of communication and understanding between the two groups. The Ferguson riots, which continued intermittently for several months, are a paradigmatic example. All too often confrontational encounters between minority individuals and police forces are vitiated by the fact that minority-group members, overwhelmingly non-white, and police officers, overwhelmingly white, draw on different systems of typifications in order to grasp the other group's motives and intentions, and thus end up misinterpreting the other group's language (in the Saussurean sense of *parole*, not *langue*), gestures, and so forth, with disastrous results all around. Conflict in intergroup relations is invariably stoked by factors of consciousness, and this is particularly true in settings where intrasocietal cultural divisions rest on ascriptive criteria, as in the case of racially binary social systems. As Schutz (1964: 237) reminds us, it is necessary that there be "a congruency between the typified scheme used by the actor [or by the groups—involved in the communicative relation] as a scheme of orientation, and by his fellow-men as a scheme of interpretation." This remark brings back to center stage the important principle mentioned above to the effect that interpersonal relations—such as in the establishment of the face-to-face relation as described by Schutz—require that the participants share the same set of typified behaviors, language, assumptions, understandings, and so on. For the proper communicative exchange among social actors to occur, all participants must have access to the society's cultural structure and history—to its stock of knowledge. This is what will enable them to successfully identify the intentionality of the Other, and to recognize the nature of the situation in which they are involved—as one writer put it, "to recognize a situation as being of a certain kind" (Campbell, 1981: 203).

THE UNINFORMED CITIZEN

The discussion of the development of the self in relation to social meanings is now broadened into the larger context of group-based equality/inequality. In *The Well-Informed Citizen* (1946/1964) Schutz addresses the problem of equality in reference to the "meaning structure of the social world." He embarks on a description of the several levels of interpretation of the "world-taken-for-granted" in order to turn the focus on equality (or its absence) directly to the realm of intersubjectivity, in the specific terms of the "structure of relevances" of the group(s) under consideration. These levels of interpretation encompass, first, how the ingroup, that is, the hegemonic group, interprets its own understanding of that world ("self-interpretation"), a process for which the rationale may be grounded in religion or the laws of nature. Secondly, how the outgroup, or nonhegemonic group, considers the ingroup's interpretation of that world. It has been mentioned rather consistently in the present analysis that the schemes of interpretation or meanings systems of the society's dominant and subordinate groups, respectively, do not normally coincide, and this reality typically rises to the surface when these groups interact. However, this lack of mutual correspondence of meaning systems will ultimately impact the subordinate group far more so than the dominant group. The ways of understanding of the latter, as has been repeatedly stressed, will be codified as *otherness*, deemed inferior, and an essential property of the racial *others*. As Schutz explains: "As long as a formula of transformation cannot be found which permits the translation of the system of relevances and typifications prevailing in the group under consideration into that of the home-group, the ways of the former remain incomprehensible; but frequently they are *considered to be of minor value and inferior*" (1964: 246, emphasis mine). This relates to the classical situation of intergroup inequality, whereby it is incumbent upon the minority group to emulate and reproduce the attributes of the dominant group—that is, to move toward the standard of normality, of universality—so as to be recognized as sameness, rather than otherness.

Sumner's categories of ingroup and outgroup are normally applied to *general cases* of intergroup relations and inequality. This would be the vast majority of such cases, such as in the example given by Schutz of Jewish immigrants from Iraq migrating back to Israel. In such a case, the expected clashes of meaning systems, the attributions of normality by ingroups to their own system of typifications and relevances, and abnormality to that of the outgroups, the reciprocal feelings of misunderstanding and unintelligibility—ultimately, feelings of avoidance, animosity, hatred, and so on, between the two groups—will all occur. In the present study, however, the main concern is with the *special* case of ascriptively enforced inequality based on racial status, a situation in which all these processes of consciousness express the operation of power and domination that are materially manifested in the actual social relations between the ruling and subaltern racial groups.. Thus, the "vicious circle" that Schutz writes about (1964: 247), although it is set in motion in all cases of ingroup/outgroup relations, loses its quality of neutrality in the interaction between social groups that are highly unequal in political, economic, and social terms on account of belonging to different *racial* categories. That is, the operation of intersubjectivity in this case will still allow for mutual feelings of hostility and contempt; the outgroup will still perceive its own scheme of relevances as valid, and that of the ingroup as invalid, or even "highly detestable," but in their actual coexistence in the larger society only the subjective constructions and judgments of the dominant group will be manifested and hold sway in social life.

In this article Schutz's substantive treatment of equality and inequality consists of reducing it to the social distribution of knowledge. This approach does not take into account the operation of social inequality and oppression as generally understood and theorized, that is to say, it does not devote immediate or sufficient attention to the idea of groups controlling economic and political resources at the expense of others, but his approach does touch on a dimension of inequality—that is, the control of social knowledge—that ultimately has a decisive impact on the relations between social groups. In any event, his approach is consistent with his overall phenomenological system and the premises on which it rests. He begins by emphasizing the cardinal importance of "integrated" knowledge for the life of individuals in the modern world, and the fact that people in general are not in command of this type of knowledge, although this does not stop them, in their day-to-day existence in the social world, from engaging in a manifold of situations without the specific theoretical grasp of each of these situations, trusting that things will take place in the way that they always have. It is clear, in practical terms, that the access to expert or specialized knowledge that people have is very much restricted to narrow areas of social performance. At issue here, as already indicated, is the social distribution of knowledge as a particular context of meaning. Schutz ends his introductory remarks with a consideration of a foundational principle of his overall system, that being the idea of the natural attitude, which is the psychosocial base of our existence in the lifeworld. He probes further into this aspect of life of social actors—how they relate to the reality of the everyday world as a given, as something unchallengeable and unquestionable—and asks why individuals in modern life are driven "to accept unquestioningly some parts of the relatively natural concept of the world handed down to them, and to subject other parts to question" (1964: 122).

Schutz postulates that there are three ideal types of knowledge and users of knowledge, which he characterized as "the expert, the man on the street, and the well-informed citizen" (1964: 122). These different types of knowledge constitute different contexts of meaning, and unequal amounts of social power are conferred by the society upon those who have access to and control over one or the other type of knowledge, or meaning-context.

We propose to categorize these, alternatively, as *scientific* knowledge and its exponents, *pragmatic* knowledge and its exponents, and *general* knowledge and its exponents. The first category of knowledge stands for knowledge based on a strict level of scientific precision and accuracy about the world, rather than on information produced *via* hasty generalizations, hearsay, and so on. This model of knowledge-utilization, based on scientific evidence though it may be, exhibits the same basic type of rigidity and exclusivism shown by the model of knowledge gained from hearsay. That is, it assumes its universal validity and applicability, its function as the source of *all* the information necessary to comprehend the problems of the world. As Schutz says it, the scientific expert adopts the principles of rationality and the relevances of his or her field of expertise as "the only intrinsic relevances of his acting and thinking" (1964: 122). The second category is the realm of the ordinary person, who provides the type of pragmatic, technically specific knowledge and skills designed to meet utilitarian ends. This kind of *how-to* knowledge involves specific "recipes" for accomplishing some practical tasks, generally, the tasks of immediacy; in Schutz's words, this involves "how to bring forth in typical situations typical results by typical means" (1964: 122). This knowledge type is definitely not characterized by, nor does it necessarily require, an integration of the various strands of practical-instrumental knowledge on the part of its exponent, the person on the street. To state it differently, there is no deep theoretical grasp of this kind of knowledge or expertise, by its exponent. There is no transcendental overcoming of its immediate concrete boundaries, nor does one witness its placement in the larger theoretical context. Admittedly, for the purposes of the technical operation of social life as a whole, there is no need for this type of knowledge to be grasped (and implemented) at the theoretical level, as long as the technical expertise and skills are forthcoming. Beyond the realm of pure practical action and utilization of knowledge, that is, as pertains to the larger and more complex processes and issues of the social world, the user of this knowledge type is swayed, unknowingly, by "his sentiments and passions as guides" (1964: 122). In many such cases, it is true, the judgments of this individual about the larger social issues bearing on people's lives are intended as substantial statements, carrying the weight of scientific rationality. In actuality, however, more often than not they amount to oversimplifications, revealing the absence of solid analysis and evidence. This brings to the fore the familiar sociological discussion of *common-sense knowledge*, the type of knowledge of the ordinary person, typically driven by hearsay and unsubstantiated ideas about reality. Finally, the exponent of the third category of social knowledge, the well-informed citizen, displays and operates on the basis of the kind of knowledge which, while not pretending to be the purest expression of scientific knowledge, avoids the technical reductionism and exclusivism of the other two knowledge spheres, relying instead on "reasonably founded opinions" about a diversity of social issues.

From the outset of the analysis, Schutz betrays a relativistic tendency in his treatment of social inequality. The compartmentalization of knowledge and expertise in society (with direct implications for the division of labor) is the manifestation of the particular pattern of its social distribution. In this connection, the problems of a sociology of knowledge and, more substantively, a sociology of professions, with implications for differential access to prestige, authority or power, and general advantage, as attached to the various professional functions we discharge in society, are reduced to the particular pattern of distribution of social knowledge. That, in turn, bears on the existence and operation of the realms of relevance in the lifeworld.[5]

Schutz moves the analysis in the direction of "interest" in connection with the operation of these "zones" or "regions" of relevance in a given sociocultural world, and this is an overture to the discussion of the operation of social power, but the analysis does not go far enough in that direction. He writes of "our interest at hand" (1964: 124), which conditions and determines all of social action and thought. But, what particular action processes give rise to this interest? What social effects, positive or negative, will it have, once formed? What are the larger implications for intergroup life? These connections need to be made, lest we be left with a mere description of the structural relations among the constitutive elements involved in the production and distribution of knowledge.

Schutz orders social knowledge hierarchically into four regions of relevance, on the basis of the importance and necessity of this knowledge for accomplishing goals—its importance "to master a situation" (1964: 124). The group's system of relevances determines their interests, and those interests dictate the pragmatic ins-and-outs of the situation under consideration and, therefore, the type of knowledge required. But, as Schutz reminds us (1964: 125), the person's or the group's "system of interests" changes across time and across the shifting circumstances of people's lives, such as, for instance, in reference the difference social roles we play. He is saying, essentially, that decisions made by the group regarding the problem of inequality will hinge on the specific area of interest, or domain of relevance (linked to the social roles we play), that it selects for grappling with this problem. This decision, according to Schutz, is made freely and spontaneously. The interest chosen has a corresponding set of relevances "intrinsic to it." Group members may decide to change things, by choosing another interest, therefore, another set of relevances (1964: 126). These changes in the system of relevances at work may have to do with these relevances being of the *imposed* type, or, pertaining to situations and events that people do not normally have any control over, but which force them to adopt another set of relevances. Interestingly enough, the situations and events mentioned by Schutz are things that may occur at random and to anyone, without reference to social status, such as, for instance, a natural disaster.

In any event, it should be clear that what is in effect here is a descriptive discourse, clarifying the structural relations between a number of different elements that make up the architecture of some social situation, but not the historical genesis of this particular architectural arrangement—that is, why it has taken the form that it did, and not some other form. For example, things in the world are, *generally speaking*, within the reach of people and those that are within the *potential* reach of Group A are within the *actual* reach of Group B, and Group A would have the *actual* reach of those things if it were in the position of Group B. This reveals the obvious structural relations concerning access to things, but not why those relations should be what they are.

The asymmetrical relation distinguishing the differential (unequal) access that individuals and/or groups in society may have to the sector of the world within their "actual reach" is, again, described as it is given. This asymmetry is simply addressed in reference to the fact that part of the freely chosen "system of intrinsic relevances" of each individual or group is not "shared by the Other" (1964: 128). Not only is it not shared, but what actually happens, as Schutz notes, is a case of "imposed relevances," that is, the imposition of Group A's interests on Group B. Schutz does point out that this clash of interests (whether individual or group-based) does not necessarily mean that the group on which the other group's interests have been imposed has accepted this situation. That should be needless to say, indeed. Let us take the analysis further and characterize this as a clear-cut case of group domination, and that the imposition of one group's interests on the other occurs, quite simply, because of the greater *power* of one group over the other. Thus, we can appeal to the level of subjectivity—intersubjectivity—in order to disclose an important manifestation of the exercise of social power.

"The man-on-the-street" is ensconced in his or her own small, circumscribed world of intrinsic relevances. He/She takes one day at a time, and remains unconcerned that things may happen that will press on his or her attention, and force him or her to reorganize his or her concerns and priorities (interests). For instance, the outbreak of a civil war, the impending nature of which might have already been in the consciousness of the two other types— that is, the *expert* and the *well-informed citizen*—is not within the range of concerns of the *man on the street* regarding possible future events. Typically, according to Schutz, users of this knowledge sphere would take the stance of "I will deal with that when the time comes."

"The [scientific] expert" inhabits a narrowly circumscribed field of intrinsic relevances. As pointed out above, this social type—for instance, the expert in engineering—feels that his or her model of knowledge is associated with problems that have an overriding importance not only within the boundaries of a particular field of specialization but also reaches beyond those boundaries and becomes critically important for practical life as a whole. Therefore, for this social type this is the only epistemological frame of reference needed for dealing effectively with the manifold challenges of daily life. This clearly reveals a narrow outlook on life, expressed through the monolithic predominance of a single point of view, and the inability to see beyond it.

"The well-informed citizen" represents the paragon of rationality, the type of person who is best endowed with the ability to decide on the appropriate frames of references for dealing with situations as they arise and to be mindful of the possibility of shifting priorities, which often lead to the revision of previous decisions. This *modus operandi* separates the well-informed citizen from the other two ideal types. He or she seeks to logically secure reliable, factual information about events and things so that a reasonable opinion about them can be formed. This information, Schutz notes (1964: 131), has to be gleaned from "socially derived knowledge." More importantly still, this knowledge gains in social legitimacy in the degree that it is *socially approved*. In Schutz's words, "The power of socially approved knowledge is so extended that what the whole in-group approves—ways of thinking and acting, such as mores, folkways, habits—is simply taken for granted; it becomes an element of the relatively natural concept of the world, although the source of such knowledge remains entirely hidden in its anonymity" (1964: 133). This language and the tenor of the discourse are critically important. Schutz borrows Sumner's concept of the ingroup to refer to the socially hegemonic group. The socially subaltern group would therefore be the outgroup. What is taken for granted by ingroups is what the whole society takes for granted, and the prevailing interests of ingroups also become standards to satisfy, to strive for, and so on, by society's members as a whole. The implications of power inequality should be immediately evident.

This argument still maintains the well-informed citizen in the natural attitude, for it is from the social stock of knowledge that she or he, like everyone else, derives the material to develop understandings about the world. The natural attitude, we are reminded, is "the zone of things taken for granted . . . from which all inquiry starts. This cannot possibly be any other way because our ability to make judgements about social reality and to use those judgments to orient courses of action is grounded in "the sediment of previous acts of experiencing" (Schutz, 1964: 133–134). Still, according to Schutz, there *are* differences across the three spheres of knowledge regarding the readiness of the individuals in each sphere to take social reality for granted. This is a very important point because it qualifies the natural attitude, in terms of the fact that it does not operate uniformly across the board. The well-informed citizen engages in this universal practice, as would be expected of someone who has been socialized in some sociocultural system but does so in the most judicious fashion, letting reason orient her or him in weighing all the considerations before making decisions. This suggests possibilities for the eventual development of critical consciousness.

One may rightly wonder about the heuristic fruitfulness of the epistemological discourse on the dynamics of social differentiation and stratification. The point, however, as I have repeatedly stressed, is that the descriptive account of social reality—in this case, of the organization and dissemination of social knowledge—must be carried further, toward the examination of the social genesis of knowledge. While the focus on the operation of subjectivity is of first importance in the phenomenological investigation, our present purposes dictate that this investigation proceeds to the illumination of the *social* basis of subjectivity. It has been remarked, in this regard, that "human beings typically refer back to *socio-historically* [emphasis mine] valid meaning-schemata and concepts of action in the process of orientation in their own world" (Hitzler and Eberle, 2004: 70).

The well-informed citizen wears this mantle in Schutz's classificatory scheme precisely because this is a social type that is most adept at drawing from the society's stock of socially approved knowledge so as to able to navigate the waters of daily life. On the other hand, the minority person— concretely represented in this study by the African-American person, who has membership in the part of the population categorized as racially nonwhite— has been subjected to varying degrees of sociocultural exclusion over time. Racial status has kept these individuals from being granted full-scale admission into the sociocultural mainstream, as a result of which their social lives are linked simultaneously to two distinct worlds of meaning (implying two distinct stocks of social knowledge), the meaning system of the larger society and that of their own subcultural community. As concerns this racially nonwhite part of the society, these considerations would apply not only to the slavery period, the structural circumstances of which would have obviously barred the inclusion of the Africans into national life, but also to the unique circumstance of life under the Jim Crow system.[6]

Since the well-informed citizen represents social privilege, derived from the rational, enlightened utilization of the society's fund of socially approved knowledge, and since the access to the latter for racial minorities has been hindered by the legacy of intergroup separatism, the minority person, from the standpoint of Schutz's typology, may be said to function as the *uninformed* citizen—someone who, by virtue of his or her particular background, and life situation in the larger society, is unable to utilize the available stock of socially approved knowledge freely, rationally, and to its fullest advantage, and thus to reap its multiple benefits. (We are reminded again here of the social effects of the class-based possession of the *habitus*, as formulated by Bourdieu and Passeron [1985].) Growing up in a society whose members are differentiated by racial status, these individuals have had to rely *concomitantly*, in *unequal* measure, upon two funds of social knowledge—that of the society-at-large, which they could not possibly have avoided, being de facto members of the society; and, that which has historically been the most immediate and familiar to them, namely, that of their subcultural community. Being the *uninformed citizen*, as I have called it here, is not unlike the condition of being the Schutzian *stranger*. However well informed one may be in one's native community—the *homeland*—with full access to and command of its stock of socially approved knowledge, its typifications and relevances—this does not, for all intents and purposes, carry much weight and currency in the *alien land*. The idea here, explored in detail in chapter 5, is that members of a society whose access to the majority system of meaning and knowledge is limited by that society's history of intergroup separatism are pushed into a situation where the society-at-large may appear to them as an *alien land*, This may reach a point where these individuals experience the same sense of outsidedness associated with the typical foreign person in a new and strange society.

This situation should not simply suggest a cognitive rift but something that has a much deeper impact at the level of existence and social existence. This problem has been brought into focus at different points in this study in relation to the pattern of racial and ethnic relations in the United States. It was denounced more than a hundred years ago by W.E.B. Dubois. It had much to do with the unfortunate demise of the journalist recounted in the preceding chapter. It has much to do, in the present time, with the persisting tension and animosities that flare up from time to time between the segments of the U.S. population codified, respectively, as racial whites and racial nonwhites. The broader social impact of intergroup cultural divisions, maintained through formal and informal means throughout U.S. history, was recognized as far back as the late colonial period. In the first quarter of the nineteenth century, Tocqueville (1945) saw the problem inherent in having the dominant and minority racial parts of the U.S. population coexist as "two

foreign communities"—communities which, although having become progressively equalized in recent decades in the civil aspect, remain culturally
distinct. To the extent that this historical aspect has endured, and members of
the subaltern group continue to participate in two separate, and often opposing, streams of knowledge, these individuals function as *uninformed citizens*,
rather than well-informed ones,[7] thus being at a disadvantage in many aspects
of their social existence. In reference to this, inequality at the epistemological
level translates into disadvantage and domination at the sociopolitical level.

PREPREDICATIVE THINKING AND THE
CONCEPTION OF INEQUALITY

The descriptive nature of phenomenological analysis and its corollary effect
of relativization are well recognized and also implied in the title of this section. This title is meant only to distinguish, in a general way, the phenomenological (Schutzian, in this case) treatment of equality from a "predicative"
(i.e., Kantian) treatment. The former, being based on experience, contextual-
izes—and thus relativizes—the conceptions and manifestations of equality
and inequality.

These aspects are clearly evidenced in Schutz's initial remarks about
inequality in his well-known 1957 essay *Equality and the Meaning Structure
of the Social World*, written at a time when the Civil Rights Movement and
the struggle to desegregate the society were gaining momentum. This was
shown in key events like the 1954 *Brown vs. Topeka Board of Education*
decision, the 1955 Montgomery (Alabama) bus boycott, the 1957 Little Rock
Nine incident in Arkansas, and the Civil Rights Act of 1957. Schutz starts
the article by pointing out that his considerations on equality are informed
by philosophical anthropology, although not in terms of a fully developed
philosophical anthropology, but instead only as a "general description" of
the activities of people in the lifeworld (1957/1964: 230). This reflects the
general tenor of his theoretical system and the latter's focus on meaning and
its genesis and development in *culturally specific* settings. Thus, it may be
said that his ideas in that essay reflect, in a more general sense, the culturalist
orientation of his phenomenology. As he himself declares it, his discussion
of equality/inequality, being detached from the latter's philosophical or theo-
logical foundations, portrays this problem as having a "relational character,"[8]
that is, as being fundamentally conditioned by the cultural system of the society. In line with this view, he says that "the common-sense aspects of equality
. . . depend upon the structure of the system of relevances [of the society],"
or on the group's "own system of typifications and relevances" (1957/1964:
226–227). Ultimately, he acknowledges the fact that for society's members,

as a rule (if not for the scientific observer), the patterns of daily life in the life-world, that is, the network of elements identified by functionalist theorists as the components of social organization (roles, statuses, role expectations, etc.), amount essentially to typifications, accepted and unquestioned by the people in general, through the natural attitude.[9] Along these lines, social actors conceive of, and relate to, the problem of equality/inequality, in every case, in conformity with "the scheme of interpretation prevailing in and accepted by the in-group without question" (1957/1964: 231). More broadly, the social world, in all its manifold aspects, is interpreted and validated by social actors on the basis of the sum-total of societally derived and sanctioned, taken-for-granted typifications. Schutz takes the society's system of relevances and typifications as a point of departure, as well as the interpretive and legitimizing frame of reference, and draws significantly on the Parsonian theory to offer an account of the functional utility of this system for the society as a whole (1957/1964: 237).

Shifting more directly to the examination of the problem of intergroup equality/inequality, Schutz relies on W.G. Sumner's conceptual dualism of ingroup/outgroup (1906/1940). Thus, the society's system of typifications ("domains of relevances") is construed as "the folkways of the ingroup" (1957/1964: 230). It is significant that this equivalence was made with the way of life of the ingroup, which is the dominant group, because it gives a clear, if indirect, indication of the power relations involved in the operation of the society's system of typifications and relevances, and the factors that sustain it.

Taking his cue from Aristotle, Schutz argues that equality and all its related aspects must be addressed within "the same domain of relevance," which means in terms of its manifestations in each sphere of social activity (e.g., inequality among musicians). To treat it otherwise, we are led to understand, amounts to trying to bring highly heterogeneous objects into the same focus of analysis, to mixing and comparing apples and oranges, so to speak. From this standpoint, Schutz sees the hierarchical ordering of the domains of relevance in society—for instance, of technicians, healers, scholars, craftsmen, and priests—as already being part of the group's relative natural conception of the world. Thus, it is part of the unquestioned, taken-for-granted social order, by members of the group. That is to say, it manifests the varying levels of privilege and power that are afforded by socially derived and approved knowledge, legitimized by a parallel hierarchy of social values

The more critical aspect here is that prevailing circumstances of intergroup inequality are unchallenged by social actors because they are part of their fund of social typifications; they are included among the things to consider, as these individuals *define their situation* "within the social cosmos" (1957/1964: 244). That being the case, when we frame this situation in the context of race and ethnic relations in societies where social life has been dichotomously split on the basis of racial status, thus creating a two-tier social order founded on racial inequality, it follows that the majority racial group (i.e., the people codified as white) and the minority racial group (i.e., the people codified as nonwhite) will orient themselves by different relevance and typification systems, This then sets the stage for significant and continuous tension and misunderstanding, when not violent clashes, between these segments, as we have pointed out. Each segment will have its own, pragmatically based conception of social equality and inequality. In current times, that is, over the last half-century or so in the United States (and quarter-century or so in South Africa), the structural assimilation of members of minority racial groups has facilitated the relatively peaceful coexistence between the hegemonic and nonhegemonic racial parts of the society. However, continuing separatism at the level of meaning has preserved the dualism and the communicative difficulties addressed above.[10]

The face-to-face relations between individuals and groups are normally brought about in terms of a dynamic interplay of subjectivities, which means that mutual perceptions, feelings, and judgments structure the exchange. Schutz explores in detail what occurs in the interaction between ingroups and outgroups, the former representing the home-group, from the standpoint of which the latter, the outside group, is evaluated. We must keep in mind, of course, that in the interaction between Group A and Group B, each group will function as both ingroup and outgroup. This relative conception of group difference has been suggested again and again in exploring the conceptual framework of Schutz's phenomenology. Thus, *under normal conditions*, and seen from this angle, individuals and/or group are *potential equals* as they enter the communicative exchange. Individuals by themselves or as members of particular groups, in entering the We-relation, are consciously aware of the objectification that awaits them—their subjectivity will come under the scrutiny of another, but, of course, the process is a reciprocal one.[11] Thus, while the appropriation of the subjectivity of the outgroup by the ingroup will always occur, the same process is reverted as the outgroup, in turn, objectifies the ingroup. In this way, group status (i.e., being an ingroup or outgroup) changes back and forth.

Also, the interaction as such, or the process of communication, between the parties involved, may be thwarted by the fact that each group relies on its own particular domain of typifications and relevances to evaluate the other group, leading to much dissonance, stereotyping, and the like. In the concrete terms of social life, the more powerful groups (the ingroups) adopt a variety of "attitudes" toward the less powerful and/or marginalized ones (the outgroups). Again, as noted above, this process is reciprocated intersubjectively, but in the concrete situation of intergroup relations, less powerful groups are generally unable to translate their mental assessments of hegemonic groups into some kind of social action that might benefit them. Ruling groups, on the other hand, are very much able to do so. Schutz adds, in this respect, that in "all of these situations, major problems of equality and equal opportunity are involved" (1964: 248), which, at the very least, reminds us of the more concrete ramifications of domination at the level of subjectivity.

These ramifications take on a special meaning when transferred to the relations between groups that are socially oppressed as a function of the society's racially binary organization. It has been discussed here how racial status in such societies is construed as an essential, hence fixed, condition, from which flows a specific set of permanent personal and group attributes. The attributes of minority racial groups will be deemed inferior, and characterized as *otherness*, by the ruling racial group. From this perspective, members of racial minorities, irrespective of the amount of change that may take place in their social situation, such as rising from hardscrabble beginnings to a very high status in some institutional sphere, remain categorized as minority persons, or permanent *others*. This will have a determining effect on the pattern of racial relations in the society.

This situation connects with the general principle in the social sciences to the effect that material change occurs more quickly and effectively achieved than nonmaterial change. The material structures of the society can be changed far more expeditiously than its ways of thinking. Its material resources—wealth, power, and so on—can change hands more easily and quickly as compared to alterations in the realm of ideas, such as ideological constructions of individuals and groups. Seen through this lens, the fact that the elimination of the structures and practices of racial domination that followed the end of the Jim Crow system did not also entail root-and-branch changes at the level of intersubjectivity can be better understood.

The foregoing discussion has led us to conclude that, in the general Schutzian framework of interpretation, inequality between social groups— special attention being focused here on the groups codified as white vs. those codified as nonwhite—revolves around the central aspect of the apprehension and construction of the subjectivity of the minority group. This has immediate repercussions for members of both the dominant and minority communities, in terms of not only identity-building but also the concrete manifestations of inequality in daily life. Thus we have a distinctive case of social domination at the level of intersubjectivity, which, in reference to the substantive problem under consideration here, involves the appropriation of the subjectivity of racial-minority persons as the mark of permanent otherness. Over the course of U.S. society's history, this process has been witnessed in institutionalized social practices, in language, in official policy, and so forth. James Baldwin captured this phenomenon well, when, in the aforementioned documentary

I Am Not Your Negro, he categorically rejected the permanent bondage of otherness—and, in so doing, echoing the same sentiment for every other American of African descent in U.S. society, like himself—by saying, "I am not a nigger, I am a man!" It is from this point of view, which underscores the affairs of consciousness as a critical driving force of social action, that we are better able to understand why in the United States, a half-century after the demolition of the Jim Crow system and its legal framework of racial oppression, the fundamental subjective construction of African-Americans (and other racial minorities as well) as permanent *Others* remains basically undisturbed, and therefore, not surprisingly, interracial tensions and hostilities still persist. Over the past few decades since the end of Jim Crow this construction of the subjectivity of the subaltern group has shifted from the rejection and contempt of the Jim Crow period to the more benign acceptance and even aggrandizement of the current time, under the politics of difference. However, at the more fundamental level, the pattern of attribution of otherness to the population segments designated as people of color has remained essentially unchanged. Persons who are formally and informally regarded as members of racial minorities are still perceived as being *the Other*. As long as this remains in effect—that is, as long as the majority population (i.e., the people defined and classified as white) continue to hold tightly to the idea that being a full-fledged, regular member of the society means being racially white—this idea will stand in the way of full societal consolidation. It will impede the effective incorporation of members of minority racial groups into national life, at the structural, cultural, biological, and psychological levels. Certainly, from a structural standpoint, racial minorities have made great strides since the end of Jim Crow in being represented in the institutional spheres of society, but this process itself has been adversely impacted by the resilience of barriers in the realm of intersubjectivity, just discussed. Moreover, structural advancement has not necessarily translated into admission to the national mainstream at the other levels of assimilation. Current generations in U.S. society, for instance, are far more open to intermarriage across the "racial lines" than even their parents, and certainly their grandparents, ever were, but cultural hurdles still remain. Subcultural differentiation continues to be accepted as a natural, race-driven phenomenon and encouraged under the operation of identity politics. Self-definition, the psychological aspect, continues to be oriented to separatism, as discussed in earlier parts of this study, and illustrated, for example, in the persisting adoption of the hyphenated identity (e.g., Korean-American). The racial dimension preserves the separation and prevents the individual's dissolution into the sea of anonymity, or universality. The implications for the issue of sociocultural integration vs. pluralism are obvious, but a careful treatment of this problem oversteps the parameters of this study.

NOTES

1. The focus placed by Schutz on the group's particular *zones of relevances* (1946/1964) as the primary map of orientation for understanding social relations, and as the main determining force of those relations, has a clear functionalist ring to it (of the Parsonian variety), inasmuch as it is essentially limited to a careful and detailed description of how various parts of social life—in particular, personal subjective experiences—operate and interconnect with the same thing in other consciousnesses, and thus produce homeostasis in the social system as a whole. In this respect, it shows a relativizing, therefore stabilizing and maintaining, tendency toward the exercise of power and control by certain social groups over other such groups.

2. This formulation is part of Schutz's discussion of objective meaning, and it throws into sharp relief that importance of the aspect of anonymity and universality, discussed earlier.

3. The idea of *deep structure* has cardinal importance in linguistics, being traced to the work of linguist Charles Hockett in the 1950s, who distinguished between *surface structure* and *deep structure.* Hockett's formulations were amplified by Noam Chomsky a few years later and became closely associated with the Chomskyan tradition of transformational generative grammar. As pertains to this presentation of race as a cultural deep structure, it would not be necessary, for the purposes of this study, to enlarge upon the matter of the 1960s dispute in the field of linguistics between the generative-grammar camp and the generative-semantics camp. Suffice it to say, in analogizing the operation of race in social life to this particular academic dispute, that this would amount to resolving the problem of whether the determining effect of race on social relations is derived from the operation of race as cultural *grammar* (i.e., a formal and independent structural grid), or of race as a *meaning-context*, which is generative in its own right, and paves the way for particular social formations (Harris, 1995). In any event, the present work leans more toward the latter interpretation, inasmuch as the case is made here for the all-important influence of meaning—specifically, the determining influence of race as an archetypal context of meaning—on every aspect of intergroup relations.

4. Some additional considerations regarding the operation of racially binary social organization and divisions are pertinent. Franklin (1997: 19) refers to this societal model, facetiously, as "that magnificent term *cultural pluralism*." In it, minority status and existence tend to persist for their own sake—that is, they become crystallized even after structural barriers to the assimilation of minority-group persons have been removed, as was the case after the dismantling of Jim Crow in the United States. One's racial status denotes *what one is*. It amounts to the reification of the condition of *particularity*, of cultural *otherness*, within which one stays indefinitely, even if it is contradicted at some point by actual changes in the person's material circumstances, professional accomplishments, and so on, within the larger society. It reflects incomplete absorption into the national mainstream, as evidenced in the fact that native-born citizens of African descent in the United States normally have the most English of last names, inasmuch as their slave ancestors inherited those last names from their masters on the Southern plantations, who happened to be overwhelmingly

Chapter 7

of old English stock—but this has had absolutely no impact on their assimilative experience—whereas immigrants from, say, Poland, *fresh off the boat*, with the most foreign-sounding and unpronounceable of names for a native English speaker, and radically different culturally, have typically been assimilated on all levels over time, because their perceived whiteness qualifies them for this experience. In the present time, all the nonwhite ethnic additions to the U.S. population are incorporated structurally, but rarely become fully absorbed into the condition of *Americanness*, even when biological assimilation (intermarriage) occurs—that is to say, the hyphenated identity will prevail. The fusion of whiteness and nonwhiteness is unworkable—the hyphen denotes a *connection*, a *side-by-side relation*, but not a fusion. The fusions that normally occur are *within* each binary racial category, but not across them. This is why a freshly arrived immigrant from, for instance, Byelorussia, may experience immediate absorption into the dominant white category and English-American dominant culture, and his or her children will identify themselves, and be identified, as simply *American*, whereas a fourth-generation Angeleno of Filipino descent will remain classified, and see himself or herself, as Filipino-American.

A final example of this assimilative model. Knute Rockne, a Norwegian-American, who became one of the most celebrated coaches of American-style football at the University of Notre Dame in the 1920s, may be cited as an exception to the rule that immigrants with very foreign-sounding names—in relation to which the case of Rockne in the dominant Anglo-American culture certainly fits—normally changed them or Anglicized them. He kept it. Yet his racial status, as well as a cultural trait that fit right in with the larger culture of the United States, namely, the love of sports, made him as much an American as any *white* person with the most English-sounding name (e.g., John Clark); in other words, he became as American as apple pie.

5. See Scheler's parallel discussion of the distribution and hierarchization of social knowledge (1980: ch. 2; also Introduction). It should also be profitable to consider Mannheim's treatment of social knowledge, his idea of "distantiation in the hierarchically organized society." He clearly suggests the idea of exclusive "ownership" (in connection with power relations), by certain social groups or classes—such as the "aristocratic *élites*"—of certain types of worldviews, who see to it that these worldviews and "systems of knowledge, shall be unshareable by the many" (1971: 311).

6. A few comments may be added regarding this issue. The experience of the Africans and their descendants on U.S. soil under slavery, as amply substantiated in the pertinent literature, decisively shaped their acculturation in the new land. Southern plantation life was marked, on the one hand, by a singularly harsh repression of aboriginal (i.e., native African) custom, and, on the other hand, by the general tendency of masters to discourage the cultural absorption of the Africans into the host culture. This meant that the slave population was left essentially with only one viable option, namely, that of forging a new subcultural lifestyle. A short period after the end of slavery, additional barriers to cultural integration were erected with the installation of the seventy-year-long Jim Crow period.

7. The harmful consequences for the larger society stemming from the problem of structured intergroup separatism should be clear. Thomas Jefferson himself, for all of his firm conviction that the emancipation of the Africans and African-Americans

from slavery, and their subsequent incorporation into the larger social fold, was an event "written in the book of destiny," expressed nevertheless his fear of the ultimate consequences of the absence of cultural integration of the country's population, when he said that "the two races will never live in a state of equal freedom under the same government, so insurmountable are the barriers which nature, habit, and opinion have established between them" (cited in Tocqueville, 1945: 3888–3889).

8. Schutz appeals to Max Weber's idea of the *relative naturliche Weltanschauung* as a theoretical frame of reference for his own treatment of equality/inequality, and his focus on the fundamental primacy of the group's cultural way of life and world-view. Weber's idea expresses the essence of the natural attitude, and Schutz finds it equivalent to Sumner's idea of "the folkways of the in-group" (1957/1964: 230).

9. The particular Schutzian treatment of equality, which relies on the Greek taxonomic system to differentiate the concept in terms of its various facets, reflects the relativistic bent of his position. The several levels of equality mentioned in the essay are to be addressed within their own respective domains of relevance, and not theorized in terms of a single, unifying principle. Thus, for example, equal respect for all, equality before the law, equal freedom of speech, equality in fortune and happiness, equal freedom of speech, equal right to vote, and equality of civil rights (1957/1964: 226–227) are all *particular* manifestations of the more fundamental condition of political equality.

10. These problems plaguing the interaction between the dominant and nondominant racial communities may be illustrated, for instance (in reference to U.S. society), with the flare-up of racial tensions and direct conflict that occurred in the city of Ferguson, Missouri, and other communities some years ago.

11. Sartre was well aware of the complex nature of intersubjective life, and more pertinently so, of its relentlessly intimidating and threatening nature owing to the continuous appropriation of subjectivity. Life in the collectivity means that we are eternally subjected to objectification by others. Our social existence is structured in this way, and we are powerfully affected by it. Sartre characterizes this situation as some kind of subjective hell from which there is no escape. "L'enfer c'est les autres," so goes the Sartrean dictum, which aptly conveys his vision of intersubjective life. Such a declaration on his part may at first be construed as misanthropic, or guided by the Hobbesian idea of the war of all against all. It is both unnecessary and impractical to try to resolve this issue within the frame of the present work. Let us just say that, fundamentally, Sartre's analysis shows sensitivity to the intersubjective complexities and challenges—the maelstrom of feeling—we all have to contend with, as we negotiate life-with-others.

Conclusion

As we conclude this journey and take stock of the ideas that formed our argument, some of these ideas or principles stand out in bold relief, above all the fact that affairs of consciousness, more precisely the aspect of meaning, play a role of first importance in the constitution of sociocultural life. This reveals Schutz's contribution to the sociological field, which is to have championed a sociology of the conscious subject, according to which "social reality is constituted in and through meaningful actions and relations" (Ferguson, 2001: 243). Modes of thinking and perceiving lie at the foundation of human action, in that they structure the way members of society create and pursue particular patterns of coexistence with others. This has been the *leitmotif* animating this entire interpretive project.

People's cultural life and their daily life in interaction with others are one and the same. Moreover, the cultural life of individuals is the basis of their identity, constantly defining who they *are*, inasmuch as, quite simply, it cannot be other than through the manifold of cultural experiences that people have—their engagements in social practices, relations with others, and so on—that they express who they are. Thus, culture-as-a-whole expresses a *social* ontology.

These premises have then been applied to the substantive area of race relations and race-based inequality. The main purpose of this interpretive project has been to address the negative effect of *race*, which is a dimension of social meaning, on intergroup relations, a task carried out here through the prism of Alfred Schutz's philosophical thought. Schutz's social phenomenology, with its emphasis on intersubjective meaning, lends itself particularly well to this type of investigation because it focuses on the constitution of the self, a process that is grounded in meaning. Cultural meanings, such as those built into the notion of race, structure the nature of the self of individuals, and, within life-in-the-collectivity, their broader interpersonal and group relations.

This study has been principally invested in the explanation of how individuals form an idea of their self in relation to because-motives, a device in Schutz's treatment of motivational contexts as the ground of human behavior. As addressed here, the constitution of the self results from a process of accountability, by means of which individuals retrieve selected experiences from the past, deemed to be relevant to their present life, and in this way account for their behavior.

This is the basic theoretical backdrop against which the dynamics of race relations, and, more importantly, given the different implications of this issue when considered in a comparative perspective, the particular experience of racial minorities in racially bipolar societies, such as the United States, have been addressed.[1] The deep structure of race and its social manifestation in the specific assignment of racial meanings to racialized persons has historically led to a distinct construction of the subjectivity of these persons, who are defined as different at the deepest (i.e., ontological) level, and thus permanently consigned to the condition of *otherness* within national life. Under these circumstances, the constitution of the self for subaltern-group members is carried out in terms of their recovery of a history of degrading racial meanings imposed on them by means of the power and activities of the society's dominant group (i.e., the people categorized as white). This in turn creates the conditions of possibility for a negative self-image, alienation from the majority way of life, and internalization of the idea of the validity and incontrovertibility of society-wide race-based separatism, whether cultural or structural, or both.

Much like the way people *do gender* in the traditional context of gender divisions and differences, that is, how they act in accordance with long-established societal definitions and expectations of gender behavior, so too in the area of race it could be said that people *do race*, meaning, traditional racial practices, definitions, and understandings are part of the broader complex of typifications of the social system. Thus, people in the natural attitude, in societies everywhere, be they multiethnic or not, abide by these social prescriptions in a nonreflective way, as a matter of course. The point that we have sought to bring to the fore here, however, is the close attachment of the society's cultural complex—its stock of knowledge, typifications, schemes of relevance, and prevalent meanings—to the interests and practices of dominant groups in the society. By implication, these cultural elements—here we have focused special attention on meaning—play a decisive role in the oppression of some groups by others. They are a pivotal aspect of social domination.

Social domination, of course, is about the harm, material and nonmaterial, brought to bear upon the lives of social minorities by particular factors, and this study aimed precisely to explain, from the standpoint of phenomenology, how this harm is manifested. Specifically, how the deep structure of race appropriates and constructs the subjectivity of the minority element, with significant negative consequences for the latter.

In general terms, the internalization of the societally sanctioned minority identity exerts a stabilizing effect on intergroup separation and differentiation, and on the subaltern status of the racialized group(s). Furthermore, when the incredibly stringent restrictions, formal and informal, imposed by racial oppression on the lives of nonwhite persons are removed (e.g., the end of Jim Crow in the United States; of *apartheid* in South Africa), a salient tendency emerges in the racialized communities, which is the fact that embracing the minority identity evolves into its glorification. This means that what is now an amnestically retrieved and assertively proclaimed is the group's identity *from within*, an identity that is *already there*—an *essential* identity. Fundamentally, as already indicated, this transformation crystallizes minority status and "foreignness," imparting to it an ontological character. This tends to neutralize and override the production of typified behavior and thinking by the individual *qua* typical member of the community. Being racialized particularizes minority persons, thus acting as an impediment to the universalization (in the Schutzian sense of anonymity) of their social existence.[2] Phrased differently, it tends to deepen the alterity of the minority community vis-à-vis the larger society, hence the former's separateness from the mainstream of national life. Regarding the question of power, it may also be said to have the latent function of preserving power asymmetry between (the people defined as) whites and nonwhites. It is not surprising therefore that, in post–Jim Crow social life in the United States, the exaltation of the ontologically grounded identity by those to whom it is assigned has met with general approbation and encouragement on the part of the majority group (a reflection of the politics of difference, addressed earlier). This is assuredly a complex issue, which has generated much, and often intense, debate.

As concerns the aspect of essentialism of this identity, it may be of service to add a note here about the inevitable intimations of (Sartrean) *bad faith*. This is in the sense of giving rise to a social ontology—inasmuch as all aspects of people's lives, including subjectivity and personhood, are socially constructed, but taken to be intrinsic to the *being* of members of social groups. This phenomenon is concretely illustrated in the affirmation of the racialized identity. In this case, the collective act of *permanently* affirming this identity locks the person into a narrower existential space, thus becoming a limiting factor. It must be kept in mind, of course, that the idea of bad faith inhabiting the adoption of the minority identity as an essential or inherent trait of the group, and the acting out of its socially sanctioned manifestations, is a problematic characterization. To begin with, it is a reflection of disadvantaged social status, a survival mechanism[3] with all the attending psychological ramifications (on this issue, see, e.g., Fanon, 1967: 49–50). Conventional sociological discourse points to its functional utility for both the affected group(s) and the society-at-large. The system gains from its stabilizing effect; minority segments derive psychological and political benefits in terms of increased self-esteem and visibility in the society's political landscape.[4]

It is true, as has been emphasized throughout, that race has an extraordinarily pervasive influence across the spectrum of social life in social systems structured on the basis of the white/nonwhite dualism. As a rule, this makes it very difficult for racialized persons to overcome this influence. That said, and without in any way detracting from the harm brought upon the process of self-constitution of racialized individuals by the systematic imposition of dehumanizing racial meanings, the effect of race is not absolutely totalizing. People in societies everywhere, under the most adverse of conditions, still construct their life conditions *as acting subjects*, and are thus able to transcend social determinations at both the existential and political levels. At the level of existence or everyday living, conscience is not stationary but moves to and fro, thus resisting social determinations (it was mentioned earlier how this phenomenon is addressed in a number of different theoretical perspectives). Therefore, at the most basic level, conscience explodes social constraints; subjectivity is fundamentally free. In the more substantively political sense, the act of embracing the societally sanctioned minority identity may be viewed as a case of group identity being used strategically toward social emancipation and political gain. In this respect, it is worth pointing here to the trenchant observation (in Chafe et al., 2001: xxiv) to the effect that, notwithstanding the common intimations of acquiescence regarding the enthusiastic adoption of the minority identity by racialized persons, this act must also be understood to contain "transcendence and purposefulness – defining a goal, reaching out to achieve it, using whatever means were available to secure the victory at hand." It represents the attempt by these persons to define themselves adaptively yet creatively, to use their collective identity as a basis for developing a certain *esprit de corps* with which to deal more effectively with the exigencies of prevailing social conditions. In the dominant/minority dialectic this is the turn society must now deal with; it must deal with what it has created.

Moreover, there is hardly any need for us to be reminded here about the innumerable cases of "minority individuals," in societies everywhere and throughout history, who, by virtue of some particular biographical circumstance and the development of their consciousness, succeeded in resounding fashion in overcoming the negative social attributions imposed on them to ensure their continuing subjugation. As we look at these cases in reference to the operation of the because-motive, we would say that these individuals, as they engaged in the process of self-building via the backward glance, effected a turn in their dialectical confrontation with the past. In recovering their history of oppression caused by negative meanings (racial-minority persons, by racist ideology; gender-minority persons, by sexist ideology), they reconstructed or transformed these meanings at a higher level of consciousness. This is the stage of enlightenment represented by what is commonly understood as political conscientization. This cognitive transformation is at once instructive and pertinent to the present work in that it foregrounds, first, the overriding importance of factors of consciousness in the constitution of social life, and secondly, the role of conscientization as a precondition for social change. In this sense, the operation of race (or, for that matter, gender) falls short of achieving a completely totalizing effect on minority persons.

After all is said and done, however, we must return to the central argument guiding this work, which devotes special attention to the generalized deleterious effect of the racialization of social life, most notably in polyethnic societies organized in a racially bipolar way, and the intractable intrasocietal divisions, tensions, and animosities that it generates. The study has looked at the dynamics of race and ethnic relations in the modern world, specifically at the operation of race as a deep structure and its formative and normative impact on social life and the harm brought by it to the lives of those perceived and codified as racial-minority persons. The investigation has been carried out by relying on meaning, as formulated in Alfred Schutz's social phenomenology, as the chief frame of reference. Thus, meaning—"the special processes of human understanding" (Grathoff, Introduction, 1989: xvii)—has been the pivotal element used toward the elucidation of a substantive problem in the social world. This procedure is congruent with Schutz's phenomenological social psychology, given the latter's amenability to the analysis of concrete social issues. In this respect, the Schutzian approach becomes an important axis of critical analysis for understanding race and ethnic relations in the social world. Its political and critical import may be evinced in the fact that it allows us to see how race *qua* system of social meanings (manifested as typifications of everyday life, such as racial terms, definitions, taxonomies, and patterns of intergroup relations) is interwoven with the workings of social power. In so doing, it amplifies the political discourse, as stated earlier, and provides an intimate portrayal of race as a system of domination within the larger practical world, or the world of everyday life.

NOTES

1. The comparative aspect may be amplified a bit further. While the process of self-constitution through the because-motive device occurs in the same basic way

everywhere, that is, it applies universally, the historical circumstances from which social actors in different societies select personal experiences that they deem relevant to the present time, and in so doing construct their self, will be different. Anthropology has provided many contrasting cases of self-identity that are immediately pertinent here, and relate to how different multiethnic social systems handle the problem of assimilation of formative groups, that is to say, whether assimilation is enforced as qualified or full-scale assimilation. The following example may be instructive. The renowned African-American writer Alice Walker, on a visit to Cuba, tried to assess the patterns of race relations of Cuban society by relying on the familiar racial definitions and categorizations of U.S. society. She soon realized the untenability of this project. The Cubans, she stated, "did not see themselves as I saw them at all. They were, like their music, well blended into their culture and did not need to separate on the basis of color, or to present any definition of themselves at all" (1983: 212). For the Cubans, then, according to Walker's analysis, the national identity was prioritized over all other identities, a phenomenon that restates the widely recognized fact in the race-and-ethnicity literature that the idea of race as such, patterns of race relations and classification, and the subjective appropriation of ethnicity all differ significantly across multiethnic/multiracial societies.

2. For a discussion of this latter effect, see, e.g., Camara (1997: 130–149). On the decentering of the self and identity, see Foucault (1976, 1994); also, Eagan (2009).

3. These considerations are also pertinent to the relations among the different minority racial segments in the society. As a rule, each one of these segments internalizes its own societally sanctioned minority identity, tailored to its own circumstances vis-à-vis those of other such communities, and indicative of the group's essential difference from other groups like it, and from the dominant racial population. This in turn gives rise to further distinctions, divisions, and power hierarchies among these groups—which is to say, within the realm of nonwhiteness itself. More precisely, groups that are located somewhat higher on this hierarchy typically seek to distinguish (and thus distance) themselves, symbolically as well as physically, from the groups considered to have lower standing in intergroup life, by seeking to emulate the ways of the society's majority racial community. This is a well-recognized phenomenon in the race-and-ethnicity literature. Bond's 1931 research on race relations in Alabama provides an excellent example. It addresses, for instance, the situation of the group that identified themselves as Creoles, who were phenotypically diverse, but sought to dissociate themselves from blacks—although, as Bond noted, they exhibited some degree of *racial hybridism* (to use Park's term; 1931: 534–551) with the black population, which in itself would have sufficed, given the enforcement of the U.S. race-classification system, to classify them with the black population as a whole. However, "no Creole person," Bond wrote (1931: 560), "would lower himself by allowing his child to go to school with [those defined as Black]." Another intermediary group reported on were the "Cajuns," who also prided themselves in not having any "Negro taint" in them, and saw themselves as the product of the Amerindian–White mixture. Interestingly enough, and consistently with the Southern enforcement of the law of hypodescent, which requires a rigid white/nonwhite dualism, these intermediary groups were barred from all social intercourse

with whites, and were despised by the latter for violating the dogma of racial purity (1931: 561–565).

4. The pivotal role of identity for members of racial groups, in the larger racial hierarchy of the society, and the maintenance of established racial arrangements, cannot be overestimated, as noted by an early twentieth-century observer (Fouillée, cited in Park, 1931: 538): "In discussions of the race problem there is one factor of supreme importance which has been so far disregarded- to wit, the opinion or *idea* which a race has of itself and the influence exerted by this idea."

References

Adams, Cecil. (2005). "The Straight Dope." *Chicago Reader* (November 21).

Adorno, Theodor. (1979). *Negative Dialectics*. New York: The Seabury Press.

Alcoff, Linda Martin. (2001). "Toward a Phenomenology of Racial Embodiment." *in* Robert Bernasconi (ed.) *Race*. Malden, MA: Blackwell Publishers.

Aldrich, Robert. (1996). *Greater France: A History of French Overseas Expansion*. New York: St. Martin's Press.

Alexander, Franz. (1937). "Psychoanalysis and Social Disorganization." *American Journal of Sociology* 42: 781–813.

Altobrando, Andrea. (2015). "The Limits of Absolute Consciousness." *Japanese Husserl Studies,* 66–86.

Almanaque Abril. (1986). Ano XII. São Paulo: Editora Abril.

Al-Saji, Alia. (2017). "Hesiter et Interrompre la vision racialisante: Bergson, Merleau-Ponty, Fanon." *Tumultes* 48: 51–70.

Appiah, K. Anthony and Amy Gutmann. (1996). *Color Conscious: The Political Morality of Race*. Princeton, NJ: Princeton University Press.

Araujo, Telmo Renato da Silva. (2016). "Raymundo Nina Rodrigues e a Questão Racial Brasileira no Século XIX." *Revista Margens Interdisciplinar* [S.l.], 1, 1, (May): 87–96. ISSN 1982-5374.

Aron, Raymond. (1970). *Main Currents in Sociological Thought*. Vol. II. New York: Basic Books.

Ashley, David and David M. Orenstein. (2001). *Sociological Theory: Classical Statements*, 5th edition. Boston, MA: Allyn and Bacon.

Baldwin, James. (1964). *The Fire Next Time*. New York: Delta Books.

Banton, Michael. (1983). *Racial and Ethnic Competition*. Cambridge: Cambridge University Press.

Baptiste, H.P., Mira L. Baptiste, and D. Gollnick. eds (1980). *Multicultural Teacher Education*. Washington, DC: American Association of Colleges for Teacher Education.

Barber, Michael. (2001). "Sartre, Phenomenology, and the Subjective Approach to Race and Ethnicity in Black Orpheus." *Philosophy and Social Criticism* 27, 3: 91–103.

———. (2018). "Alfred Schutz." *Stanford Encyclopaedia of Philosophy*. https://plato.stanford.edu/entries/schutz/.

Baldwin, James. (1964). *The Fire Next Time*. New York: Dell Publishing.

Bastide, Roger. (1971). *African Civilizations in the New World*. London: C. Hurst and Co.

Berard, T.J. (2010). "Unpacking Institutional Racism: Insights from Wittgenstein, Garfinkel, Schutz, Goffman, and Sacks." *Schutzian Research*, https://www.pdcnet.org/schutz/content/schutz_2010_0002_0109_0133.

Bergson, Henri. (1971). *Time and Free Will*. London: George Allen & Unwin.

———. (1991). *Matter and Memory*. New York: Zone Books.

Bernasconi, Robert. (2001). "The Invisibility of Racial Minorities in the Public Realm of Appearances." *in* R. Bernasconi (ed.) *Race*. Malden, MA: Blackwell Publishers.

——— and Sybol Cook. (2003a). *Race and Racism in Continental Philosophy*. Bloomington, IN: Indiana University Press.

———. (2003b). *Race and Anthropology*. Bristol: Thoemmes Press.

——— and Anika Maaza Mann. (2005) "The Contradictions of Racism: Locke, Slavery, and the Two Treatises." *in* Andrew Valls (ed.) *Race and Racism in Modern Philosophy*. Ithaca, NY: Cornell University Press.

———. (2008). "Can Race Be Thought in Terms of Facticity: A Reconsideration of Sartre's and Fanon's Existential Theories of Race." *in* Francois Raffoul and Eric Sean Nelson (eds.) *Rethinking Facticity*. Albany, NY: State University of New York Press.

———. (2012a). "Crossed Lines in the Racialization Process: Race as a Border Concept." *Research in Phenomenology* 42: 206–228.

———. (2012b). "Race, Culture, History," *in* Paul Taylor (ed.) *The Philosophy of Race*. New York: Routledge.

Binswanger, Ludwig. (1962). "Existential Analysis and Psychotherapy." *in* Hendrik M. Ruitenbeek (ed.) *Psychoanalysis and Existential Philosophy*. New York: E.P. Dutton.

———. (1968). *Being-in-the-World: Selected Papers of Ludwig Binswanger*. Jacob Needleman, ed. New York: Harper Torchbooks.

Blanc, Sébastian. (2018). "Sartre: L'Enfer C'est Les Autres." *Le Point* (January 29).

Bock, Phillip. (1988). *Rethinking Psychological Anthropology: Continuity and Change in the Study of Human Action*. New York: W.H. Freeman.

Bogardus, Emory S. (1929). "Second-Generation Mexicans." *Sociology and Social Research* XIII (January–February): 276–283.

Bond, Horace Mann. (1931). "Two Racial Islands in Alabama." *American Journal of Sociology* 36 (January): 552–567.

Bosi, Alfredo. (1992). *Dialética da Colonização*. São Paulo: Companhia das Letras.

Bouleau, Nicolas. (2011). "On Excessive Mathematization, Symptoms, Diagnosis and Philosophical Bases for Real World Knowledge." *Real World Economics*, 57: 90–105.

Bourdieu, Pierre, and Jean-Claude Passeron. (1985). *Les Héritiers*. Paris: Les Editions de Minuit.

Bradford Burns, E. (1993). *A History of Brazil*, 3rd edition. New York: Columbia University Press.

Brumm, Ursula. (1970). *American Thought and Religious Typology*. New Brunswick, NJ: Rutgers University Press.

Bryce, James. (1915). *Race Sentiment as a Factor in History*. London: The University of London Press.

Buonicore, Augusto C. (2017). "Racismo e ciência no Brasil pós-abolição (1888-1930)- Oliveira Vianna O racismo decadente." *Revista Espaço Academico*, https ://espacoacademico.wordpress.com/2017/03/04/racismo-e-ciencia-no-brasil-pos -abolicao-1888-1930-oliveira-vianna-o-racismo-decadente-2/.

Burkey, Richard M. (1978). Ethnic and Racial Groups: The Dynamics of Dominance. Menlo Park, CA: Benjamin/Cummings Press.

Burt, Alfred Leroy. (1942). *A Short History of Canada for Americans*. Minneapolis, MN: The University of Minnesota Press.

Câmara, Evandro. (1988). "Afro-American Religious Syncretism in Brazil and the United States: A Weberian Perspective." *Sociological Analysis* 48, 4 (Winter): 299–318.

———. (1997). *The Cultural One or the Racial Many: Religion, Culture, and the Interethnic Experience*. Aldershot: Ashgate Press.

———. (2003). "Dimensões Ontológicas de Raça e Cultura em Sistemas Binários. *Estudos de Sociologia*. Recife: UFPE.

———. (2013). "Puritanos Modernos: Caráter Nacional e Ideologia Religiosa na Sociedade Estadunidense." *Estudos de Sociologia* (Spring). Araraquara, UNESP.

———. (2014). "Estrutura e Significado: Implicações Fenomenológicas e Politicas do Sotaque Regional Brasileiro." *Interdisciplinary Journal of Portuguese Diaspora Studies* 3, 1: 155–176.

Campbell, Tom. (1981). *Seven Theories of Human Society*. Oxford: Clarendon Press.

Cannon, Michael. (1971). *Who's Master? Who's Man?: Australia in the Victorian Age*. Sidney: Thomas Nelson Press.

Ceaser, James. (1998). "Multiculturalism and American Liberal Democracy," *in* A. Melzer, J. Weiberger, and M. R. Zinman (eds.) *Multiculturalism and American Democracy*. Lawrence, KS: University Press of Kansas.

Chafe, William H., Raymond Gavins and Robert Korstad, eds. (2001). *Remembering Jim Crow: African-Americans Tell About Life in the Segregated South*. New York: The New Press.

Chirot, Daniel. (1986). *Social Change in the Modern Era*. Orlando, FL: Harcourt, Brace, Jovanovich.

Chua-Eoan, Howard. (2000). "Profiles in Outrage." *TIME* (September 25): 440–442.

Clark, Kenneth B. and M.P. Clark. (1950). "Emotional Factors in Racial Identification and Preference in Negro Children." *Journal of Negro Education* 19: 341–350.

———. (1957). *Prejudice and Your Child*. Boston, MA: The Beacon Press.

Codman, John. (1867). *Ten Months in Brazil*. Boston, MA: Lee and Shepard.

Coles, Robert. (1965). "The Negro American." *Daedalus: Journal of the American Academy of Arts and Sciences* 94 (Fall): 1107–1132.

Collier, J.L. (1978). *The Making of Jazz: A Comprehensive History.* Boston, MA: Houghton Mifflin.

Collingwood, R.G. (1969). *The Archaeology of Roman Britain.* London: Methuen.

Collins, Patricia Hill. (1993). "Toward a New Vision: Race, Class and Gender as Categories of Analysis and Connection." *Race, Sex & Class* 1, 1: 25–45.

Cooke, Jean, and Ann Kramer, Theodore Rowland-Entwistle. (2002). *History's Timeline.* New York: Kingfisher Publications.

Cox, O.C. (1959). *Caste, Class, and Race.* New York: Monthly Review Press.

Daniels, Roger. (1990). *Coming to America: A History of Immigration and Ethnicity in American Life. New* York: Harper Collins Publishers.

Davidson, Basil. (1966). *A History of West Africa to the Nineteenth Century.* Garden City, NJ: Doubleday& Company.

De Bary, Wm. Theodore. (1981). *Neo-Confucian Orthodoxy and the Learning of the Mind-and-Heart.* New York: Columbia University Press.

Degler, Carl N. (1971). *Neither Black Nor White: Slavery and Race Relations in Brazil and the United States.* London: MacMillan.

DeLerma, Dominique-René. (1970). *Black Music in Our Culture.* Kent, OH: Kent State University Press.

Dopp, Michael. (2002). "An Angry Young Man Grows Older." *The Chronicle of Higher Education* (August 2): B10–B11.

Dilthey, Wilhelm. (1923/1988). *Introduction to the Human Sciences: An Attempt to Lay a Foundation for the Study of Society and History.* Ramon Btanzos (trans.). Detroit, MI: Wayne State University Press.

Dollard, John. (1949). *Caste and Class in a Southern Town.* Garden City, NY: Doubleday Anchor Books.

Domingues, Heloisa Maria Bertol, and Magali Romero Sá. (2001). "The Introduction of Darwinism in Brazil." *in* Thomas Glick, Miguel Angel Puig-Samper, and Rosaura Ruiz (eds.) *The Reception of Darwinism in the Iberian World: Spain, Spanish America, and Brazil.* Dordrecht: Kluwer Academic Publishers.

Donahue, Deirdre. (1995). "A Search for Racial Identity." *USA Today* (March 9).

Dorfman, Eran. (2007). *Reapprendre a voir le monde: Merleau-Ponty face au miroir lacanien.* Dordrecht: Springer.

Dowbiggin, Ian Robert. (1997). *Keeping America Sane: Psychiatry and Eugenics in the United States and Canada, 1880-1940.* Ithaca, NY: Cornell University Press.

Dreher, Jochen. (2011). "Alfred Schutz". https://www.academia.edu/10477893/Alfred_Schutz.

Dubois, W.E.B. (1903/1990). *The Souls of Black Folk.* New York: Vintage Books.

Dumont, Louis. (2001). "Caste, Racism, and 'Stratification': Reflections of a Social Anthropologist." *in* Robert Bernasconi (ed.) *Race.* Malden, MA: Blackwell Publishers.

Eagan, Jennifer L. (2009). "The Deformation of Decentered Subjects: Foucault and Postmodern Public Administration." *International Journal of Organizational Theory and Behavior,* 12 (1): 141–162.

Eberle, Thomas. (2010). "The Phenomenological Life-World Analysis and the Methodology of the Social Sciences." *Human Studies* (33): 123–139.

———. (2014). "Methodological Implications of Phenomenological Life-World Analysis," *in* M. Staudigl and G. Berguno (eds.) *Schutzian Phenomenology and Hermeneutic Traditions*. Dordrecht: Springer.

Evans, Eric. (2011). "A British Revolution in the 19th Century?" http://www.bbc.co .uk/history/british/empire_seapower/revolution_01.shtml.

Eze, Emmanuel Chukwudi. 1997). *Race and the Enlightenment: A Reader.* Cambridge, MA: Blackwell Publishers.

Ezorsky, Gertrude. (1991). *Racism and Justice: The Case for Affirmative Action.* Ithaca, NY: Cornell University Press.

Fanon, Frantz. (1967). *Black Skin, White Masks.* New York: Grove Press.

Farley, Christopher John. (1997). "Kids and Race." *Time* (November 24): 88–91.

Feagin, Joe R. and Clairece Booher Feagin. (1993). *Race and Ethnic Relations.* Englewood Cliffs, NJ: Prentice-Hall.

Ferguson, Harvie. (2001). "Phenomenology and Social Theory." *in* George Ritzer and Barry Smart (eds.) *Handbook of Social Theory*. London: SAGE Publications.

——— . (2006). *Phenomenological Sociology: Experience and Insight in Modern Society.* London: SAGE Publications.

Ferry, Jules. (1897). "Speech Before the French Chamber of Deputies, March 28, 1884." *in* Paul Robiquet, (ed.) *Discours et Opinions de Jules Ferry.* Paris: Armand Colin & Cie.

Foucault, Michel. (1976). "Two Lectures." *in* Colin Gordon (ed.) *Power/Knowledge: Selected Interviews and Other Writings, 1972-1977*, 78–108. New York: Pantheon Books.

———. (1994). "Self-Writing." *in* P. Rabinow (ed.) *Ethics: Essential Works of Foucault, 1954-1984*, vol. I, 303–319. New York: New Press Publishers.

Franco, Sérgio de Gouvêa. (2012). "Dilthey: Compreensão e Explicação, e Possíveis Implicações Para o Metodo Clínico." *Revista LatinoAmericana de Psicopatologia Fundamental* 15, 1 (March).

Franklin, John Hope. (1969). *From Slavery to Freedom*, 3rd edition. New York: Vintage Books.

———. (1997). "Ethnicity in American Life: The Historical Perspective," *in* Virginia Cyrus (org.) *Experiencing Race, Class, and Gender in the United States*. Mayfield Press.

Frazier, E. Franklin. (1957). *Race and Culture Contacts in the New World*. Boston, MA: Beacon Press.

Freyre, Gilberto. (1933). *Casa Grande e Senzala: Formação da Familia Brasileira Sob o Regime da Economia Patriarcal.* Rio de Janeiro: Maia & Schmidt Ltda.

———. (1951). *Sobrados e Mocambos: Decadencia do Patriarcado Rural e Desenvolvimento do Urbano.* Rio de Janeiro: Livraria José Olympio Editôra.

———. (1956). *The Masters and the Slaves: A Study in the Development of Brazilian Civilization.* New York: Alfred Knopf.

———. (1990). *Ordem e Progresso.* Rio de Janeiro: Editôra Record.

Gajewski, Ryan. (2015). *"Hunger Games* Star Criticizes Taylor Swift, Madonna, for 'Rampant' Appropriation of Black Culture." https://www.hollywoodreporter.com/news/hunger-games-star-criticizes-taylor-789199.

Galton, Francis. (1904). "Eugenics: Its Definition, Scope, and Aims." *The American Journal of Sociology.* Chicago, IL: The University of Chicago Press.

Genovese, Eugene. (1976). *Roll, Jordan, Roll.* New York: Vintage Books.

Gibbons, Alison. (2017). "Postmodernism is Dead. What Comes Next?." *Times Literary Supplement.* https://www.the-tls.co.uk/articles/public/postmodernism-dead-comes-next/.

Giddens, Anthony. (1984). *The Constitution of Society: Outline of the Theory of Structuration.* Cambridge: Polity Press.

———. (1992). *The Transformation of Intimacy: Sexuality, Love, and Eroticism in Modern Societies.* Stanford, CA: Stanford University Press.

Gregory, Sophronia Scott. (1992). "The Hidden Hurdle." *TIME* (March 16): 44–46.

Grossberg, Lawrence, Cary Nelson, Paula Treichler, eds. (1992). *Cultural Studies.* New York: Routledge.

Guimarães, Antonio Sergio Alfredo. (1999). *Racismo e Anti-Racismo no Brasil.* São Paulo: Editora 34 Ltda.

Gurwitsch, Aron. (1962). "The Common-Sense World as Social Reality." *Social Research* 29, 1 (Spring): 50–72.

Gillborn, David. (1995). "Racism, Identity and Modernity: Pluralism, Moral Antiracism and Plastic Ethnicity." *International Studies in Sociology of Education* 5 (1): 3–23.

Gilman, Charlotte Perkins. (1908). "A Suggestion on the Negro Problem." *American Journal of Sociology* 14: 78–85.

Glaude, Eddie S. (2016). *Democracy in Black: How Race Still Enslaves the American Soul.* New York: Broadway Books.

Goodell, William. (1853). *The American Slave Code.* New York: American and Foreign Anti-Slavery Society.

Gordon, Lewis. (2002). "Sartrean Bad Faith and Antiblack Racism." In Julie Ward and Tommy Lott (eds.) *Philosophers on Race: Critical Essays.* Oxford: Blackwell Publishers.

Gordon, Milton M. (1961). "Assimilation in America: Theory and Reality." *Daedalus, Journal of the American Academy of Arts and Sciences* 90 (Spring): 263–285.

———. (1964). *Assimilation in American Life.* New York: Oxford University Press.

Gossett, Thomas. (1969). *Race: The History of an Idea in America.* New York: Schocken Books.

Grant, Madison. (1916). *The Passing of the Great Race, or the Racial Basis of European History.* New York: Charles Scribner's Sons.

Grathoff, Richard. (1989). *The Correspondence of Alfred Schutz and Aaron Gurwitsch. R.*

Grathoff, ed. Bloomington, IN: Indiana University Press.

Habermas, Jurgen. (1989). *On the Logic of the Social Sciences.* Cambridge, MA: The MIT Press.

Hackett, Stuart C. (1979). *Oriental Philosophy.* Madison, WI: University of Wisconsin Press.

Halbwachs, Maurice. (1939). "Individual Consciousness and Collective Mind." *American Journal of Sociology* 44: 812–822.

Hall, Stuart. (1992). "Cultural Studies and Its Theoretical Legacies." *in* L. Grossberg, C. Nelson, and P. Treichler (eds.) *Cultural Studies*, 277–294. New York: Routledge.

Handlin, Oscar. (1957). *Race and Nationality in American Life*, 4th edition. New York: Doubleday.

Harris, Marvin. (1974). *Patterns of Race Relations in the Americas.* New York: W.W. Norton.

———. (1997). *Culture, People, Nature: An Introduction to General Anthropology.* New York: Longman.

Harris, Randy Allen. (1995). *The Linguistic Wars.* New York: Oxford University Press.

Heidegger, Martin. (1965). *Being and Time.* London: SCM Press Ltd.

Herskovits, Melville. (1972). *The Myth of the Negro Past.* Boston, MA: Beacon Press.

Hill, Howard C. (1919). "The Americanization Movement." *The American Journal of Sociology* 24 (May): 609–642.

Hitzler, Ronald and Thomas S. Eberle. (2004). "Phenomenological Life-World Analysis." *in* Uwe Flick, Ernst von Kardoff, and Ines Steinke (eds.) *A Companion to Qualitative Research.* 67–71. London: SAGE Publications.

Hofstadter, Richard. (1960). *Social Darwinism in American Thought.* Boston, MA: The Beacon Press.

Horn, Heather. (2015). "Is Eastern Europe Any More Xenophobic Than Western Europe?" https: //www.theatlantic.com/international/archive/2015/10/xenophobia -eastern-europe-refugees/410800/.

Horsman, Reginald. (1981). *Race and Manifest Destiny: The Origins of American Racial Anglo-Saxonism.* Cambridge, MA: Harvard University Press.

Hsu, Hua. (2017). "Stuart Hall and the Rise of Cultural Studies." *The New Yorker* (July 17). https://www.newyorker.com/books/page-turner/stuart-hall-and-the-rise -of-cultural-studies.

Hudson, Winthrop S. (1965). *Religion in America.* New York: Charles Scribner's Sons.

Hughes, Everett Cherrington. (1945). "Dilemmas and Contradictions of Status." *American Journal of Sociology* 50 (5): 353–359.

——— and Helen MacGill Hughes. (1952). *Where Peoples Meet: Racial And Ethnic Frontiers.* Glencoe, IL: The Free Press.

Hughes, H. Stuart. (1977). Consciousness and Society: The Reorientation of European Social *Thought, 1890-1930.* New York: Vintage Books.

Isaacs, Harold R. (1963). *The New World of Negro Americans.* New York: The John Day Company.

Jonas, Hans. (1959). "Alfred Schutz, 1899-1959." *Social Research* 26: 471–474.

Kenaga, Heidi. (1999). "'America is Developing a Distinct Type of Man': Stark Love, Eugenics, and Nativist Discourses of the 1920s." *in* Reynolds Scott-Childress (ed.)

Race and the Production of Modern American Nationalism. New York: Garland Publishing.

Knox, Robert. (1850). *The Races of Men: A Fragment*. Philadelphia, PA: Lea & Blanchard.

Kojève, Alexandre. (1980). *Introduction to the Reading of Hegel*. Ithaca, NY: Cornell University Press.

Kottak, Conrad P. (2004). *Cultural Anthropology*, 10th edition. New York: McGraw-Hill.

Lacayo, Richard. (1989). "Between Two Worlds." *Time* (March 13): 58–68.

Laing, R.D. (1962). "Ontological Insecurity." *in* Hendrik M. Ruitenbeek (ed.) *Psychoanalysis and Existential Philosophy*. New York: E.P. Dutton.

Landgrebe, Ludwig. (1940). "The World as a Phenomenological Problem." *Philosophy and Phenomenological Research* 1: 35–58.

Lapoujade, David. (2005). "The Normal and the Pathological in Bergson." *Modern Language Notes* 120, 5 (December): 1146–1155.

Lengermann, Patricia and Jill Niebrugge. (1995). "Intersubjectivity and Domination: A Feminist Investigation of the Sociology of Alfred Schutz." *Sociological Theory* 13, 1 (March): 25–36.

Leonard, Neil. (1970). *Jazz and the White Americans*. Chicago, IL: The University of Chicago Press.

Lornor, Max. (1987). *America as a Civilization*. New York: Henry Hold and Company.

Little, Daniel. (2009). "The German Debate Over Method." *Understanding Society* (December 4).

Littleton, C. Scott. (1996). *Eastern Wisdom*. New York: Henry Holt and Company.

Long, Elizabeth. (1997). *From Sociology to Cultural Studies: New Perspectives*. Oxford: Blackwell Publishers.

Lyotard, Jean-François. (1984). *The Postmodern Condition: A Report on Knowledge*. Manchester: Manchester University Press.

Macey, David. (1999). "Fanon, Phenomenology, Race." *Radical Philosophy* (May/June): 8–14.

Maddison, Angus. (2001). *The World Economy: A Millennial Perspective*. Development Centre of the Organisation for Economic Cooperation and Development.

Mannheim, Karl. (1971). *From Karl Mannheim*. Kurt H. Wolff (ed. and Introduction). New York: Oxford University Press.

Marger, Martin. (1991). *Race and Ethnic Relations: American and Global Perspectives*. Belmont, CA: Wadsworth Publishing Company.

Martindale, Don. (1981). *The Nature and Types of Sociological Theory*, 2nd edition. Prospect Heights, IL: Waveland Press.

Martí, José. (1975). *Inside the Monster: Writings on the United States and American Imperialism*. New York: Monthly Review Press.

Marx, Karl. (1994). "Theses on Feuerbach." *in* Lawrence Simon (ed.) *Karl Marx, Selected Writings*. New York: Hackett Publishing Company.

May, Rollo, Ernest Angel, and Henri F. Ellenberger. (1958). *Existence: A New Dimension in Psychiatry and Psychology*. New York: Basic Books.

McCall, Raymond. (1983). *Phenomenological Psychology: An Introduction*. Madison, WI: The University of Wisconsin Press.

McIntyre, Alasdair. (1984). *After Virtue: A Study in Moral Theory*. Notre Dame, IN: University of Notre Dame Press.

McKay, J.P. et al. (2011). *A History of Western Society*, 10th edition. Boston, MA: Bedford / St. Martin's Press.

Mead, George Herbert. (1930). "Cooley's Contribution to American Social Thought." *American Journal of Sociology*, 35 (5): 693–706.

———. 1962). *Mind, Self, & Society, from the Standpoint of a Social Behaviorist*. Chicago, IL: The University of Chicago Press.

Merk, Frederick. (1966). *Manifest Destiny and Mission in American History*. New York: Vintage Books.

Meyerhoff, Hans. (1955). *Time in Literature*. Berkeley and Los Angeles, CA: University of California Press.

Miller, Jean Baker. (1976). *Toward a New Psychology of Women*. Boston, MA: Beacon Press.

Mills, Charles. (1997). *The Racial Contract*. New York: Cornell University Press.

———. 1998). *Blackness Visible: Essays on Philosophy and Race*. Ithaca, NY: Cornell University Press.

Minkowski, Eugene. (1958). "Findings in a Case of Schizophrenic Depression." *in* Rollo May et al. (eds.) *Existence: A New Dimension in Psychiatry and Psychology*. New York: Basic Books.

Monserrat, Marcelo. (2001). "The Evolutionist Mentality in Argentina: An Ideology of Progress." *in* Thomas Glick, Miguel Angel Puig-Samper, and Rosaura Ruiz (eds.) *The Reception of Darwinism in the Iberian World: Spain, Spanish America, and Brazil*. Dordrecht: Kluwer Academic Publishers.

Moody, Anne. (1968). *Coming of Age in Mississippi*. New York: Laurel Books.

Münch, Richard. (1994). *Sociological Theory: From the 1920s to the 1960s*, vol. II. Chicago, IL: Nelson-Hall Publishers.

Muzzetto, Luigi. (2006). "Time and Meaning in Alfred Schutz." *Time and Society* 15 (1): 5–31.

Myers, Linda James. (1987). "The Deep Structure of Culture: Relevance of Traditional African Culture in Contemporary Life." *Journal of Black Studies* 18 (1): 72–85.

Myrdal, Gunnar. (1962). *An American Dilemma: The Negro Problem and Modern Democracy*, vols I and II. New York: Harper Torchbooks.

Natanson, Maurice. (1968). "Alfred Schutz on Social Reality and Social Science." *Social Research* 35 (Summer): 217–244.

———. (1973). *Phenomenology and the Social Sciences*. Evanston, IL: Northwestern University Press. Press.

———. (1977). "Alfred Schutz Symposium: The Pregiveness of Sociality." *in* Don Ihde and Richard Zaner (eds.) *Interdisciplinary Phenomenology*. Martinus Nijhoff. The Hague.

———. (1986). *Anonymity: A Study in the Philosophy of Alfred Schutz*. Bloomington, IN: Indiana University Press.

Nina Rodrigues, Raymundo. (1977). *Os Africanos no Brasil*, 5th edition. São Paulo: Companhia Editôra Nacional.

Nogueira, Oracy. (1955). "Preconceito Racial de Marca e Preconceito Racial de Origem." *Anais do XXXI Congresso Internacional de Americanistas*. São Paulo, SP.

Novak, Michael. (1971). "White Ethnic." *Harper's Magazine* (September): 44–50.

Omi, Michael and Howard Winant. (1994). *Racial Formations in the United States from the 1960s to the 1990s*, 2nd edition. New York: Routledge.

Ortega, Mariana. (2016). *In-Between: Latina Feminist Phenomenology, Multiplicity, and the Self*. Albany, NY: SUNY Press.

Oxford Wright, Richard. (1966). *Black Boy*. New York: Harper Perennial.

Park, Robert E. (1931). "Mentality of Racial Hybrids." *American Journal of Sociology* 36 (January): 534–551.

———. (1964). *Race and Culture: Essays in the Sociology of Contemporary Man*. Glencoe, IL: The Free Press.

Parry, Hannah. (2015). "Refugees from War-Torn Syria Claim Racism Is so Extreme in Germany

Parsons, Talcott. (1954). "A Revised Analytical Approach to the Theory of Social Stratification." *in Essays in Sociological Theory*. Glencoe, IL: The Free Press.

———. (1966). *The Structure of Social Action*, 4th edition. New York: The Free Press.

Peretti, Bruce William. (1997). *Jazz in American Culture*. Chicago, IL: Ivan R. Dee Publishing.

Pinkney, Alphonso. (2000). *Black Americans*, 5th edition. Prentice-Hall.

Poppino, Rollie E. (1973). *Brazil: The Land and the People*, 2nd edition. New York: Oxford University Press.

Power, Jr., Thomas F. (1966). *Jules Ferry and the Renaissance of French Imperialism*. New York: Octagon Books.

Prado, Paulo. (1962). *Retrato do Brasil: Ensaio sobre a Tristeza Brasileira*. Rio de Janeiro: Livraria José Olympio Editôra.

Proust, Marcel.. (1913/1988). *A La Recherche du Temps Perdu, vol. I. Du Côté de Chez Swann*. Paris: Éditions Gallimard.

Psathas, George. (1973). *Phenomenological Sociology: Issues and Applications*. New York: John Wiley and Sons.

Public Health, and Latin America's Only Sterilization Law." *The Hispanic American Historical Review* 91 (3): 431–443.

Quarles, Benjamin. (1976). *The Negro in the Making of America*. New York: MacMillan.

Ramos, Arthur. (1933). *Freud, Adler, e Jung: Ensaios de Psychanalyse Orthodoxa e Heretica*. Rio de Janeiro: Editôra Guanabara.

Rex, John. (1983). *Race Relations in Sociological Theory*, 2nd edition. New York: Schocken Books.

Rodriguez, Richard. (1983). *Hunger of Memory: The Education of Richard Rodriguez*. New York: Bantam Books.

———. (2003). "'Blaxicans' and Other Reinvented Americans." *The Chronicle of Higher Education* (September 12): B10–B11.

Rogers, Jazmine. (2015). "Activist Slams Kendrick Lamar Over Light-Skinned Fiancee: 'I Will Never Support Him.'" https://madamenoire.com/523797/activist-slams-kendrick-lamar-over- light-skinned-fiancee-i-will-never-support-him/.

Romo, Ricardo. (1996). "Mexican-Americans: Their Civic and Political Incorporation." *in* Silvia Pedraza and Ruben G. Rumbaut (eds.) *Origins and Destinies: Immigration, Race, and Ethnicities in America.* Belmont, CA: Wadsworth Publishing Company.

Roosevelt, Theodore. (1899/ 2009). *The Strenuous Life: Essays and Addresses.* Mineola, NY: Dover Publications.

Ross, Edward A. (1914). *The Old World in the New.* New York: Century Co.

Rothman, Lily. (2018). "A Witness to Slavery Is Finally Heard." *Time* (May 21): 50–51.

Salamon, Gayle. (2018). "What Is Critical about Critical Phenomenology?" *Puncta* 1: 8–17.

Sandburg, Carl. (1919/2013). *The Chicago Race Riots: July 1919.* Mineola, NY: Dover Publications.

Sartre, Jean-Paul. (1948/1965). "Black Orpheus." *The Massachusetts Review* 6, n. 1 (Autumn 1964–Winter 1965): 13–52.

Sawer, Patrick. (2015). "Revealed: How Britons Welcomed Black Soldiers During World War II, And Fought Alongside Them Against Racist G.I.'s." https://www.tel egraph.co.uk/history/world-war-two/12035018/Revealed-How Britons- welcomed -black-soldiers-during-WWII-and-fought-alongside-them-against-racist-GIs.html.

Schaefer, Richard T. (1996). *Racial and Ethnic Groups*, 6th edition. New York: Harper Collins.

Scheler, Max. (1980). *Problems of a Sociology of Knowledge.* Kenneth W. Stikkers (ed. and Introduction). Manfred S. Frings (transl). London: Routledge and Kegan Paul.

Schutz, Alfred. (1944). "The Stranger: An Essay in Social Psychology." *American Journal of Sociology* 49 (May): 499–507.

———. (1945a). "Some Leading Concepts of Phenomenology." *Social Research* 12 (1): 78–97.

———. (1945b). "On Multiple Realities." *Philosophy and Phenomenological Research* 5 (June): 533–576.

———. (1945c). "The Homecomer." *The American Journal of Sociology* 50 (March): 369–376.

———. (1946/1964). "The Well-Informed Citizen: An Essay on the Social Distribution of Knowledge." *in* Arvid Brodersen (ed.) *Collected Papers II.* The Hague: Martinus Nijhoff.

———. (1957/1964). "Equality and the Meaning-Structure of the Social World." *in* Arvid Brodersen (ed.) *Collected Papers* II. The Hague: Martinus Nijhoff.

———. (1967). "Phenomenology of the We-Experience, and the Structure of the Interpersonal World." *in* Kelly, W. and Tallon, A. (eds.) *Readings in the Philosophy of Man.* New York: McGraw-Hill.

———. (1970a). "Concept and Theory Formation in the Social Sciences." *in* Dorothy Emmet and Alasdair MacIntyre (eds.) *Sociological Theory and Philosophical Analysis.* New York: The MacMillan Company.

————. (1970b). "The Problem of Rationality in the Social World." *in* Dorothy Emmet and Alasdair MacIntyre (eds.) *Sociological Theory and Philosophical Analysis*. New York: The MacMillan Company.

————. (1970c). *Reflections on the Problem of Relevance*. Richard M. Zaner, ed. New Haven, CT: Yale University Press.

————. and Thomas Luckmann. (1973). *The Structures of the Life-World*. Richard M. Zaner and H. Tristam Engelhardt Jr. (transl.), vol. I. Evanston, IL: Northwestern University Press.

————. (1978). "Parsons' Theory of Social Action: A Critical Review." *in* Richard Grathoff (ed.) *The Theory of Social Action: The Correspondence of Alfred Schutz and Talcott Parsons*. Bloomington, IN: Indiana University Press.

————. and Thomas Luckmann. (1989). *The Structures of the Life-World*, vol. II. Evanston, IL: Northwestern University Press.

————. (1997). *The Phenomenology of the Social World*. George Walsh and Frederick Lehnert (transl.) Evanston, IL: Northwestern University Press.

Scott-Childress, Reynolds J., ed. (1999). *Race and the Production of Modern American Nationalism*. New York: Garland Publishing.

Shea, Christopher. (1993). "Does Student Housing Encourage Racial Separatism on Campus?" *The Chronicle of Higher Education* (July 14): A26–A27.

Sheth, Falguni A. (2009). *Toward a Political Philosophy of Race*, Albany, NY: SUNY Press.

Shillington, Kevin. (1989). *History of Africa*. New York: St. Martin's Press.

Simpson, G.E. and J.M. Yinger. (1965). *Racial and Cultural Minorities*. New York: Harper and Row.

Skarda, Christine. (1979). "Alfred Schutz's Phenomenology of Music." *Journal of Musicological Research* (3): 75–132.

Small, Albion W. (1915). "The Bonds of Nationality." *American Journal of Sociology* 20 (March): 629–683.

Smith, M.G. (1965). *The Plural Society in the British West Indies*. Berkeley, CA: The University of California Press.

Snyder, Louis L., ed. (1962). *The Imperialism Reader: Documents and Readings on Modern Expansionism*. Princeton: D. Van Nostrand Company, Inc.

Souza, Ricardo Luiz de. (2007). "Método, Raça, e Identidade Nacional em Silvio Romero." *Revista de Historia Regional* 9 (1).

Srubar, Ilja. (1999). "The Origin of the Political." *in* Lester Embree (ed.) *Schutzian Social Science*, 23–45. Dordrecht: Kluwer Academic Publishers.

Stampp, Kenneth M. (1956). *The Peculiar Institution: Slavery in the Antebellum South*. New York: Vintage Books.

Staudigl, Michael. (2012). "Racism: On the Phenomenology of Embodied Desocialization." *Continental Philosophy Review* 45: 23–39.

Stepan, Nancy Leys. (1992). "Race, Gender, and Nation in Argentina: The Influence of Italian Eugenics." *History of European Ideas* 15 (4–6): 749–756.

Stern, Alexandra Minna. (2011). "'The Hour of Eugenics' in Veracruz, Mexico: Radical Politics,

Stonequist, Everett V. (1935). "The Problem of the Marginal Man." *American Journal of Sociology* 41: 1–12.

Suarez y Lopez-Guazo, Laura. (2001). *in* Thomas Glick, Miguel Angel Puig-Samper, and Rosaura Ruiz (eds.) *The Reception of Darwinism in the Iberian World: Spain, Spanish America, and Brazil.* Dordrecht: Kluwer Academic Publishers.

Sumner, William Graham. (1906/1940). *Folkways.* New York: Mentor Books.

Swingewood, Alan. (1993). *A Short History of Sociological Thought,* 2nd edition. New York: St. Martin's Press.

Taagepera, Rein. (1997). "Expansion and Contraction Patterns of Large Polities: Context for Russia. *International Studies Quarterly* 41 (3): 475–504.

Tannenbaum, Frank. (1946). *Slave and Citizen: The Negro in the Americas.* New York: Vintage Books.

———. (1969). *The Balance of Power in Society.* New York: The MacMillan Company.

They Want to Go Home as Growing Unrest and Anti-Muslim Feeling Sees Attacks On Foreigners Soar." *Daily Mail.com* (July 30). https://www.dailymail.co.uk/news/article-3179916/Refugees-war-torn-Syria-claim-racism-Germany-extreme-want-HOME-growing-unrest-anti-Muslim-feeling-sees-attacks-foreigners-soar.html.

Thomas, W.I. (1912). "Race Psychology: Standpoint and Questionnaire, With Particular Reference to the Immigrant and the Negro." *American Journal of Sociology* 17: 725–775.

———. with Dorothy Swaine Thomas. (1928). *The Child in America: Behavior Problems and Programs.* New York: Alfred A. Knopf.

Tocqueville, Alexis de. (1945). *Democracy in America,* 2 vols. New York: Vintage Books.

Tymieniecka, Anna-Teresa. (1962). *Phenomenology and Science in Contemporary European Thought.* New York: The Noonday Press.

Van den Berghe, Pierre L. (1970). *Race and Ethnicity: Essays in Comparative Sociology.* New York: Basic Books.

———. (1978). *Race and Racism in Comparative Perspective.* New York: John Wiley & Sons.

———. (1995). "Does Race Matter?" *Nations and Nationalism* 1 (3): 357–368.

Velho, Gilberto and Howard Becker. (1992). "Project, Emotion, and Orientation in Complex Societies." *Sociological Theory,* 10 (1) (Spring): 6–20.

Vijay, Devesh. (2016). "The Rise of Liberal Democracy in Britain: 1780-1918." http://slideplayer.com/slide/10173795/.

Visweswaran, Kamala. (2001). "Is There a Structuralist Analysis of Racism? On Louis Dumont's Philosophy of Hierarchy." *in* Robert Bernasconi (ed.) *Race.* Malden, MA: Blackwell Publishers.

Wagley, Charles and Marvin Harris. (1958). *Minorities in the New World.* New York: Columbia University Press.

Wagner, Helmut. (1973). "The Scope of Phenomenological Sociology: Considerations and Suggestions." *in* George Psathas (ed.) *Phenomenological Sociology: Issues and Applications.* Hoboken, NJ: John Wiley & Sons.

Walker, Alice. (1983). *In Search of Our Mothers' Gardens.* New York: Harcourt Brace Jovanovich.

Ward, Julie K. and Tommy L. Lott, eds. (2002). *Philosophers on Race: Critical Essays.* Malden, MA: Blackwell Publishers.

Warner, W. Lloyd. (1936). "American Caste and Class." *American Journal of Sociology,* XLII (September): 234–237.

Waters, Mary C. (1996). "Optional Ethnicities: For Whites Only?." *in* Silvia Pedraza and Ruben G. Rumbaut (eds.) *Origins and Destinies: Immigrations, Race, and Ethnicity in America.* Belmont, CA: Wadsworth Press.

Weate, Jeremy. (2001). "Fanon, Merleau-Ponty and the Difference of Phenomenology." *in* Robert Bernasconi (ed.) *Race.* Malden, MA: Blackwell Publishers.

Weinberg, Albert K. (1935). *Manifest Destiny: A Study of Nationalist Expansionism in American History.* Baltimore, MD: The Johns Hopkins University Press.

Wilkins, David B. (1996). "Introduction: The Context of Race." *in* K. Anthony Appiah and Amy Gutmann (eds.) *Color Conscious: The Political Morality of Race.* Princeton, NJ: Princeton University Press.

Willems, Emilio. (1980). *A Aculturação dos Alemães no Brasil.* São Paulo: Companhia Editôra Nacional.

Williams, Raymond. (1958). *Culture and Society: 1780-1950.* New York: Harper and Row.

Williams, Patricia J. (1991). *The Alchemy of Race and Rights.* Cambridge, MA: Harvard University Press.

Wolff, Kurt. (1971). Introduction to *From Karl Mannheim.* Kurt H. Wolff, ed. New York: Oxford University Press.

———. (2008). *The Outsider.* New York: Harper Perennial.

Yetman, Norman R. and C. Hoy Steele. (1975). *Majority and Minority: The Dynamics of Racial and Ethnic Relations.* Boston, MA: Allyn and Bacon.

Yinger, J. Milton. (1961). "Social Forces Involved in Group Identification and Withdrawal." *Daedalus: Journal of the American Academy of Arts and Sciences* 90 (Spring): 247–262.

Zaner, Richard. (1961). "Theory of Intersubjectivity: Alfred Schutz." *Social Research* 28: 71–93.

———. (1973). "Solitude and Sociality: The Critical Foundations of the Social Sciences." *in* George Psathas (ed.) *Phenomenological Sociology: Issues and Applications.* New York: John Wiley and Sons.

Zeynep, Direk. (2017). "Critical Philosophy of Race as Political Phenomenology." *Comparative and Continental Philosophy* 9 (2): 130–139.

Zimmermann, Eduardo A. (1992). "Racial Ideas and Social Reform: Argentina, 1890-1916." *The Hispanic-American Historical Review* 72 (1): 23–46.

Zucchino, David. (2016). "'I've Become a Racist': Migrant Wave Unleashes Danish Tensions Over Identity." *The New York Times,* 1–7 (September 5). https://www.nytimes.com/2016/09/06/world/europe/denmark-migrants-refugees-racism.html.

Index

Age of Discovery, 6–7; slavery and, 6–7; and the spice trade, 6
Americanization movement its dual nature, 20–22
assimilation of the Africans under U.S. slavery, 56, 222; and the dominant social consciousness, 162–65; dualism in the U.S. pattern, 35, 189–90, 193–95; and the idea of cultural appropriation, 36; and intrasocietal structural separatism, 144–46; and the physical freedom of the slaves, 31; and stratification across U.S. nonwhite groups, 230; and syncretism, 193–95

colonialism by the French in Brasil, 34; internal, 34–35; and *Manifest Destiny*, 15–17, 34; and race consciousness, 18; and Social Darwinism, 14–15; by the United States, 13–14; and *the white man's burden*, 14–15
Compact Set-up for Post-Racial South, 1
cross-referencing, 86–87
cultural appropriation and racial essentialism, 36
culture as social ontology, 160–62

Daseinanalyse and socialization, 104
decolonization its evolution in the twentieth century, 23; and race consciousness, 23–25
doing race, 226

the ethnic enclave its dual nature in the U.S., 35

the *Great Migration to the North*, 22–23

hermeneutics and social explanation, 68–69
the *home-world vs.* the *alien-world*, 142–46

idealism: in Cooley, 121
the idea of *négritude*; in Fanon, 49–51; in Sartre, 51–52
immigration in Australia, 19–20; in Brasil, 34; in the 1700s–1900s, 18–23; and racialist doctrines, 21–23

Mead's notion of *self-interaction*, 120–21
meaning: and *attention à la vie*, 97, 103, 118; and the *durée*, 98–100, 116; social effect on behavior, 116–17, 119

247

About the Author

Evandro Camara is professor of sociology at Emporia State University. He is the author of *The Cultural One or the Racial Many: Religion, Culture, and the Interethnic Experience.* His doctorate is from the University of Notre Dame, and his areas of research interest are sociological theory, cultural sociology, race and ethnicity, and religion.